Another Potful

of Recipes

Another Potful

of Recipes

A HEALTHY EXCHANGES® COOKBOOK

JoAnna M. Lund
with Barbara Alpert

A Perigee Book

Before using the recipes and advice in this book, consult your physician or health-care provider to be sure they are appropriate for you. The information in this book is not intended to take the place of any medical advice. It reflects the author's experiences, studies, research, and opinions regarding a healthy lifestyle. All material included in this publication is believed to be accurate. The publisher assumes no responsibility for any health, welfare, or subsequent damage that might be incurred from the use of these materials.

A Perigee Book
Published by The Berkley Publishing Group
A division of Penguin Group (USA) Inc.
375 Hudson Street
New York, New York 10014

For more information about Healthy Exchanges products, contact:
Healthy Exchanges, Inc.
P.O. Box 80
DeWitt, Iowa 52742-0080
(563) 659-8324
Fax: (563) 659-2126
www.HealthyExchanges.com
HealthyJo@aol.com

First edition: October 2003

Library of Congress Cataloging-in-Publication Data

Lund, JoAnna M.
    Another potful of recipes : a healthy exchanges cookbook / JoAnna M. Lund with Barbara Alpert.— 1st ed.
        p.cm.
    Includes index.
    ISBN 0-399-52929-2
    1. Electric cookery, Slow. I. Alpert, Barbara. II. Title.

TX827L858 2003
641.5'884—dc21

                                                                    2003051718

Printed in the United States of America
10 9 8 7 6 5 4 3 2 1

This book is dedicated in loving memory to my parents, Jerome and Agnes McAndrews. Mom was considered one of the "best cooks" in Lost Nation, Iowa, and was Daddy ever proud of her accomplishments! If the PTA was holding a bake sale, the first words from the committee would be, "Let's see what Agnes is bringing." For just about every church supper, she was in charge of something—usually dessert. And when neighbors or friends suffered illness or hardship in the family, Mom was usually the first one there with food and comfort.

She especially loved stirring up casseroles and desserts, and you'll find this collection has an abundance of both. I've simply taken many of her specialties and made them healthier, easier to fix, and all prepared in the slow cooker!

In addition to sharing food, Mom dearly loved sharing her poems. This is just one of the hundreds she wrote in her lifetime. May you enjoy Mom's words and my recipes as you stir up memories to be savored by your loved ones for years to come!

Wild Grapes

The wild grapes still grow along the fence
where a farmhouse used to stand.
Nothing else remains except its frame
on the weed infested land.
I wonder what the folks were like
who lived here so long ago.
Did they share many of the problems
and joys that we of today know?
I try to imagine how many tots
ran in and out the door.

Or, if there were any soldiers
who didn't return from war.
If those homesteads and houses could talk
what great stories we would hear.
Like the tales of the early settlers
and the dangers they had to fear.
It makes me sad to see old buildings
abandoned . . . deserted and forlorn.
They remind me of forgotten souls
who have no one left to mourn.
It's time for me to leave this silent place.
My basket is full at last.
The choice grape preserves I plan to make
will be a memorial to the past.

—Agnes Carrington McAndrews

Contents

Acknowledgments

Wow! We did it! What did we do? With the help of some very special people, we managed to get this book from idea to reality in a matter of just a few months. For helping me "put a book together" so fast, I want to thank:

Shirley Morrow, Rita Ahlers, Phyllis Bickford, Connie Schultz, Gina Griep, and Jean Martens. Each one helped me by typing or testing or tasting all 200 recipes in this collection.

Cliff Lund. When he saw that time was ticking away, he did everything he could do to lighten my load in other ways so I could devote my energies to finishing this project.

Barbara Alpert. Even though she was busy herself with graduate school and teaching youngsters, she just rolled up her sleeves to help me get my manuscript done on time.

Coleen O'Shea. When I told her that I wanted to write another slow cooker cookbook because I had so many new recipes I wanted to share, she helped me "make it happen . . ." fast.

John Duff, Barbara O'Shea, and everyone on my team at Putnam. I'm thankful that they continue to want me to create my "common folk" healthy recipes and help me share them in my books.

God. I prayed for help—not only in writing a quality book on a tight time line—but also in living my life in a way that would be pleasing to Him while doing it—and both the recipes and words just seem to flow.

Slowing Down—
and Picking Up
the Pace of Living

When I created my first collection of recipes for the slow cooker, I wrote about slowing down the way I live my life and how getting out of the fast lane could have very positive results for anyone brave enough to make that kind of lifestyle change. I heard from many readers of my books and newsletter that what I said made real sense to them at the time.

Now I'd like to update that philosophy a little bit, in part because events of the past several years have made me feel even more that every day is precious and that life is meant to be lived as fully as possible. Streamlining your food preparation so that "slow and steady wins the race" is only the first step. Now I want to encourage you to take that freed-up time and decide not to waste another minute in making every part of your life reflect your truest desires and deepest longings.

Health

Have you been putting off a visit to your doctor because you've always told yourself that regular checkups are just "looking for trouble"? Have you made a practice of having the recommended tests for people your age, or have you based your self-care philosophy on an uneventful personal and family medical history? Have you been meaning to make time for heart-healthy physical activity but haven't ever decided what to do or when to do it?

You're not alone.

Many, many people delay visiting their physicians because they feel generally okay. Many others take note of symptoms but talk themselves out of getting them checked. And still others put off medical tests because getting them is inconvenient, costly, or just too scary to contemplate. The problem with doing any of those things is that something may be wrong—and the sooner you find out about it, the better chance you have to treat it and ensure that you can live healthy for many years to come. A friend's mother recently had her usual checkup, which included a chest X ray. Only because her cardiologist didn't like the look of something did she get referred for further testing. The result—a diagnosis of early-stage lung cancer. She was lucky, though. The surgeon removed it, and her prognosis is excellent. If she'd waited for symptoms to develop, her doctors told her, the situation would have been much less hopeful.

Time is precious. I don't mean that just the usual way, either. Yes, spending time with those we love is important. But even a delay of weeks can mean the difference between living a healthy life and struggling to cope with serious illness. So to quote the old song, take good care of yourself, because you belong to all those who love you!

Now what about that commitment to exercise, to get your heart pumping a little faster at least a few days every week? You've been meaning to do it, but little things and big things keep getting in the way. Well, now that your dinner is bubbling away in the slow cooker, take a walk. Dance to some big-band music with your husband or your kids. Ride a bike to the post office. *Do something.* Do it today!

Family

Does your house or apartment resemble a bus station, with people running in and running out, greeting each other in passing but spending little or no time together on a regular basis? We're all so busy, so overscheduled, that we've let our families slip away from us.

Ask yourself this: When was the last time you sat down with your spouse, kids, or adult siblings and just talked about something substantial—good memories, hopes and dreams, plans for the future?

If the answer is "Not for a long time," or even "Never," I want to suggest an immediate change. Instead of saying, "Yes, well, I'm going to have to do that one of these days," grab your calendar right now. Right now, please! Now dial the phone or sit down with your family member and make a date. Write it on the calendar, circle it in red, and promise yourself not to cancel when life gets busy.

The time we spend talking and listening to the people we care about is the "good stuff." If we don't take time to know the people closest to us, we're much more likely to feel isolated, lonely, and depressed, especially as we grow older. By strengthening the bonds between us, we're building precious bridges to a future made immeasurably richer because of our improved relationships.

Friends

Now that you've made time for your family members, take a few minutes to reflect on the state of your friendships. Have you let people dear to you slip away because life is so busy or because they've moved away? Have you spent less time in recent months in activities you used to enjoy, like singing in the church choir or volunteering at your child's school?

It sounds like time for a change. Yes, right now. Why don't you put down this book and pick up the phone or the most recent church bulletin? Choose just one thing to add to your schedule. This is not about stressing yourself out by overextending yourself, but it could definitely be time to renew a connection that can make you feel good.

But what if your old friends are unavailable, your voice isn't what it once was, and your kids are out of school and living their own lives? I'm glad you asked! I meet so many wonderful people who have had the courage to reach out to new people even in their later years. If you discover that your circle of friends is too small, why not enlarge it through some action of your own? It could mean taking an adult-education class or visiting a local hospital's pediatric ward to read to the kids.

The world is full of people who need people, as the famous Barbra Streisand song says. You could make a decision today to be one of those people and fill someone's need. By reaching out to others, we also help ourselves. And by daring to do something new, we give our spirits a little kick in the pants, refreshing our souls in more ways than we know.

Work

Are you surprised that I'm including work in this section? You may already be working harder than you'd like, or perhaps you don't love what you're doing the way you used to. Well, in my "slow down, pick up the pace" philosophy, I want to suggest that you think about what you want your work to be. Are you headed where you want to be going, and is your work goal somewhere in sight?

It's awfully easy to get in a work rut, to keep doing what we've been doing for longer than we can remember. But by doing that, we often lose sight of where work can take us, if our work is truly a vocation, a calling. I'm not suggesting that you quit a job you don't love, not in this economy. But I do think it makes good emotional sense to take stock regularly, to ask yourself about what you want to accomplish in this part of your life. Are you satisfied with your work, or do you need new challenges? Are you working with numbers and would rather be working with people? Are you working at home but feel stifled by the isolation?

My writing partner, Barbara, asked herself those questions a couple of years ago. After some serious reflection, she decided to train for a new career and become a teacher. "Even though most of my colleagues are 10 or 20 years younger, I feel as if I'm doing the right thing for me," she told me. "Working with children is very intense, very hard sometimes, but it's satisfying in a way that my other jobs haven't been."

Even if you decide you're exactly where you should be job-wise, it's good to think about your job description—and what, if anything, you want to do to expand or change it. Are you up to date in terms of computer skills? Will your company send you to a professional conference or for additional training? How can you *grow* in your job?

Big questions, I know, but worth asking. So I hope you'll take the time to reflect and see where your thoughts take you. We spend so many hours of our days working, it's important that we do what we can to make our work fulfilling in whatever ways we can.

Home

Have you been putting off making changes to your environment at home because of money, time, or a lack of inspiration about what to change if you could? Whatever the reason may be, why not take a fresh look at your home and see what little and bigger changes you can make to add to your comfort, increase your calm, even improve your social life?

For example, is your dining room table covered with work, old newspapers, or your sewing machine? That makes it hard to invite anyone over for lunch or dinner, doesn't it? Maybe if you decided just to clear off the table this weekend, finding somewhere to store all those items, you could invite someone over for an easy, tasty slow cooker meal.

Sometimes the smallest changes can make a surprising difference. If you find a sale at your favorite home store, you might be amazed at how much it will perk you up to add a couple of new towels in a contrasting color to those you already have. (One friend treats herself to a new bathsheet every few months, which she says turns her everyday shower into a spa visit!)

Ask yourself: Is your current setup working for you? If your CDs are racked in such a dark corner that you never listen to them, see if there's somewhere brighter they could be stored. A little more music can boost anyone's joy in life!

Changes to your home can be inexpensive but provide a lot of pleasure. Instead of saying, "I should do that sometime soon," do it today, or tomorrow, for sure!

Dreams

Too tired to dream? Too exhausted or overwhelmed by coping with everyday problems to muse about travel, going back to school, or doing something else you've always dreamed about? Let me suggest that perhaps it's because you're so drained that you NEED to dream a little, and right away!

It's our dreams that energize us, propel us into exciting new places or activities, and give us a really good reason to keep going. So the next time you turn on your slow cooker, turn on the part of your brain and heart that will help you figure out what would make you happier than you are at this moment. If it's a new relationship, promise yourself to do one thing to make it more likely to happen, whether it's trying out an online dating site or getting up the courage to talk to a fellow cheerleader at your son's soccer game. If it's a new or different job, decide to do one thing to find out more about what opportunities might be possible. If it's a new look, start by cutting out pictures from magazines that will help you choose a fresh style just right for the new you.

I believe that if you take the time to dream, you will begin to shape the future in which you want to live. Start today by doing just a little something to make your life the best it can be—for you. By choosing to stop procrastinating about these kinds of changes, you'll discover a world of difference: the world you make!

Food Exchanges

and Weight Loss

Choices™

I f you've ever been on one of the national weight-loss programs like Weight Watchers or Diet Center, you've already been introduced to the concept of measured portions of different food groups that make up your daily food plan. If you are not familiar with such a system of weight-loss choices or exchanges, here's a brief explanation. (If you want or need more detailed information, you can write to the American Dietetic Association or the American Diabetes Association for comprehensive explanations.)

The idea of food exchanges is to divide foods into basic food groups. The foods in each group are measured in servings that have comparable values. These groups include Proteins/Meats, Breads/Starches, Vegetables, Fats, Fruits, Fat-Free Milk, Free Foods, and Optional Calories.

Each choice or exchange included in a particular group has about the same number of calories and a similar carbohydrate, protein, and fat content as the other foods in that group. Because any food on a particular list can be "exchanged" for any other food in that group, it makes sense to call the food groups *exchanges* or *choices*.

I like to think we are also "exchanging" bad habits and food choices for good ones!

By using Weight Loss Choices or exchanges, you can choose from a variety of foods without having to calculate the nutrient value of each one. This makes it easier to include a wide variety of foods in your daily menus and gives you the opportunity to tailor your choices to your unique appetite.

If you want to lose weight, you should consult your physician or other weight-control expert regarding the number of servings that would be best for you from each food group. Since men generally require more calories than women, and since the requirements for growing children and teenagers differ from those of adults, the right number of exchanges for any one person is a personal decision.

I have included a suggested plan of weight-loss choices in the pages following the exchange lists. It's a program I used to lose 130 pounds, and it's the one I still follow today.

(If you are a diabetic or have been diagnosed with heart problems, it is best to meet with your physician before using this or any other food program or recipe collection.)

Food Group Weight Loss Choices/Exchanges

Not all food group exchanges are alike. The ones that follow are for anyone who's interested in weight loss or maintenance. If you are a diabetic, you should check with your health-care provider or dietitian to get the information you need to help you plan your diet. Diabetic exchanges are calculated by the American Diabetic Association, and information about them is provided in *The Diabetic's Healthy Exchanges Cookbook* (Perigee Books).

Every Healthy Exchanges recipe provides calculations in three ways:

- Weight Loss Choices/Exchanges

- Calories, Fat, Protein, Carbohydrates, and Fiber in grams, and Sodium and Calcium in milligrams

- Diabetic Exchanges calculated by a registered dietitian

Healthy Exchanges recipes can help you eat well and recover your health, whatever your health concerns may be. Please take a few minutes to review the exchange lists and the suggestions that follow on how to count them. You have lots of great eating in store for you!

Proteins

Meat, poultry, seafood, eggs, cheese, and legumes. One exchange of Protein is approximately 60 calories. Examples of one Protein choice or exchange:

1 ounce cooked weight of lean meat, poultry, or seafood
2 ounces white fish
1½ ounces 97% fat-free ham
1 egg (limit to no more than 4 per week)
¼ cup egg substitute
3 egg whites
¾ ounce reduced-fat cheese
½ cup fat-free cottage cheese
2 ounces cooked or ¾ ounces uncooked dry beans
1 tablespoon peanut butter (also count 1 fat exchange)

Breads

Breads, crackers, cereals, grains, and starchy vegetables. One exchange of Bread is approximately 80 calories. Examples of one Bread choice or exchange:

1 slice bread or 2 slices reduced-calorie bread (40 calories or less)
1 roll, any type (1 ounce)
½ cup cooked pasta or ¾ ounce uncooked (scant ½ cup)
½ cup cooked rice or 1 ounce uncooked (⅓ cup)
3 tablespoons flour
¾ ounce cold cereal
½ cup cooked hot cereal or ¾ ounce uncooked (2 tablespoons)
½ cup corn (kernels or cream-style) or peas
4 ounces white potato, cooked, or 5 ounces uncooked
3 ounces sweet potato, cooked, or 4 ounces uncooked
3 cups air-popped popcorn

7 fat-free crackers (¾ ounce)
3 (2½-inch squares) graham crackers
2 (¾-ounce) rice cakes or 6 mini
1 tortilla, any type (6-inch diameter)

Fruits

All fruits and fruit juices. One exchange of Fruit is approximately 60 calories. Examples of one Fruit choice or exchange:

1 small apple or ½ cup slices
1 small orange
½ medium banana
¾ cup berries (except strawberries and cranberries)
1 cup strawberries or cranberries
½ cup canned fruit, packed in fruit juice or rinsed well
2 tablespoons raisins
1 tablespoon spreadable fruit spread
½ cup apple juice (4 fluid ounces)
½ cup orange juice (4 fluid ounces)
½ cup applesauce

Fat-Free Milk

Milk, buttermilk, and yogurt. One exchange of Fat-Free Milk is approximately 90 calories. Examples of one Fat-Free Milk choice or exchange:

1 cup fat-free milk
½ cup evaporated fat-free milk
1 cup low-fat buttermilk
¾ cup plain fat-free yogurt
⅓ cup nonfat dry milk powder

Vegetables

All fresh, canned, or frozen vegetables other than the starchy vegetables. One exchange of Vegetable is approximately 30 calories. Examples of one Vegetable choice or exchange:

½ cup vegetable
¼ cup tomato sauce
1 medium fresh tomato
½ cup vegetable juice
1 cup shredded lettuce or cabbage

Fats

Margarine, mayonnaise, vegetable oils, salad dressings, olives, and nuts. One exchange of Fat is approximately 40 calories. Examples of one Fat choice or exchange:

1 teaspoon margarine or 2 teaspoons reduced-calorie margarine
1 teaspoon butter
1 teaspoon vegetable oil
1 teaspoon mayonnaise or 2 teaspoons reduced-calorie
    mayonnaise
1 teaspoon peanut butter
1 ounce olives
¼ ounce pecans or walnuts

Free Foods

Foods that do not provide nutritional value but are used to enhance the taste of foods are included in the Free Foods group. Examples of these are spices, herbs, extracts, vinegar, lemon juice, mustard, Worcestershire sauce, and soy sauce. Cooking sprays and artificial sweeteners used in moderation are also included in this group. However, you'll see that I include the caloric value of artificial sweeteners in the Optional Calories of the recipes.

You may occasionally see a recipe that lists "free food" as part of the portion. According to the published exchange lists, a free food contains fewer than 20 calories per serving. Two or three servings per day of free foods/drinks are usually allowed in a meal plan.

Optional Calories

Foods that do not fit into any other group but are used in moderation in recipes are included in Optional Calories. Foods that are counted in this way include sugar-free gelatin and puddings, fat-free mayonnaise and dressings, reduced-calorie whipped toppings, reduced-calorie syrups and jams, chocolate chips, coconut, and canned broth.

Sliders ™

These are 80 Optional Calorie increments that do not fit into any particular category. You can choose which food group to *slide* these into. It is wise to limit this selection to approximately three to four per day to ensure the best possible nutrition for your body while still enjoying an occasional treat.

Sliders may be used in either of the following ways:

1. If you have consumed all your Protein, Bread, Fruit, or Fat-Free Milk Weight Loss Choices for the day and you want to eat additional foods from those food groups, you simply use a Slider. It's what I call "healthy horse trading." Remember that Sliders may not be traded for choices in the Vegetables or Fats food groups.

2. Sliders may also be deducted from your Optional Calories for the day or week. One-quarter Slider equals 20 Optional Calories; ½ Slider equals 40 Optional Calories; ¾ Slider equals 60 Optional Calories; and 1 Slider equals 80 Optional Calories.

Healthy Exchanges Weight Loss Choices

My original Healthy Exchanges program of Weight Loss Choices was based on an average daily total of 1,400 to 1,600 calories per day. That was what I determined was right for my needs, and for those of most women. Because men require additional calories (about 1,600 to 1,900), here are my suggested plans for women and men. (*If you require more or fewer calories, please revise this plan to meet your individual needs.*)

Each day, women should plan to eat:

2 Fat-Free Milk choices, 90 calories each
2 Fat choices, 40 calories each
3 Fruit choices, 60 calories each
4 Vegetable choices or more, 30 calories each
5 Protein choices, 60 calories each
5 Bread choices, 80 calories each

Each day, men should plan to eat:

2 Fat-Free Milk choices, 90 calories each
4 Fat choices, 40 calories each
3 Fruit choices, 60 calories each
4 Vegetable choices or more, 30 calories each
6 Protein choices, 60 calories each
7 Bread choices, 80 calories each

Young people should follow the program for men but add 1 Fat-Free Milk choice for a total of 3 servings.

You may also choose to add up to 100 Optional Calories per day, and up to 21 to 28 Sliders per week at 80 calories each. If you choose to include more Sliders in your daily or weekly totals, deduct those 80 calories from your Optional Calorie "bank."

A word about Sliders: These are to be counted toward your totals after you have used your allotment of choices of Fat-Free

Milk, Protein, Bread, and Fruit for the day. By "sliding" an additional choice into one of these groups, you can meet your individual needs for that day. Sliders are especially helpful when traveling, stressed-out, eating out, or for special events. I often use mine so I can enjoy my favorite Healthy Exchanges desserts. Vegetables are not to be counted as Sliders. Enjoy as many Vegetable choices as you need to feel satisfied. Because we want to limit our fat intake to moderate amounts, additional Fat choices should not be counted as Sliders. If you choose to include more fat on an *occasional* basis, count the extra choices as Optional Calories.

Keep a daily food diary of your Weight Loss Choices, checking off what you eat as you go. If, at the end of the day, your required selections are not 100 percent accounted for, but you have done the best you can, go to bed with a clear conscience. There will be days when you have ¼ Fruit or ½ Bread left over. What are you going to do—eat two slices of an orange or half a slice of bread and throw the rest out? I always say, "Nothing in life comes out exact." Just do the best you can . . . *the best you can.*

Try to drink at least eight 8-ounce glasses of water a day. Water truly is the "nectar" of good health.

As a little added insurance, I take a multivitamin each day. It's not essential, but if my day's worth of well-planned meals "bites the dust" when unexpected events intrude on my regular routine, my body still gets its vital nutrients.

The calories listed in each group of choices are averages. Some choices within each group may be higher or lower, so it's important to select a variety of different foods instead of eating the same three or four all the time.

Use your Optional Calories! They are what I call "life's little extras." They make all the difference in how you enjoy your food and appreciate the variety available to you. Yes, we can get by without them, but do you really want to? Keep in mind that you should be using all your daily Weight Loss Choices first to ensure you are getting the basics of good nutrition. But I guarantee that Optional Calories will keep you from feeling deprived—and help you reach your weight-loss goals.

JoAnna's Ten Commandments of Successful Cooking

A very important part of any journey is knowing where you are going and the best way to get there. If you plan and prepare before you start to cook, you should reach mealtime with foods to write home about!

1. **Read the entire recipe from start to finish** and be sure you understand the process involved. Check that you have all the equipment you will need *before* you begin.

2. **Check the ingredient list** and be sure you have *everything* and in the amounts required. Keep cooking sprays handy—while they're not listed as ingredients, I use them all the time (just a quick squirt!).

3. **Set out *all* the ingredients and equipment needed** to prepare the recipe on the counter near you *before* you start. Remember that old saying *A stitch in time saves nine?* It applies in the kitchen, too.

4. **Do as much advance preparation as possible** before actually cooking. Chop, cut, grate, or do whatever is needed to prepare the ingredients and have them ready before you start to mix. Turn the oven on at least ten minutes before putting food in to bake, to allow the oven to preheat to the proper temperature.

5. **Use a kitchen timer** to tell you when the cooking or baking time is up. Because stove temperatures vary slightly by manufacturer, you may want to set your timer for five minutes less than the suggested time just to prevent overcooking. Check the progress of your dish at that time, then decide if you need the additional minutes or not.

6. **Measure carefully.** Use glass measures for liquids and metal or plastic cups for dry ingredients. My recipes are based on standard measurements. Unless I tell you it's a scant or full cup, measure the cup level.

7. **For best results, follow the recipe instructions exactly.** Feel free to substitute ingredients that *don't tamper* with the basic chemistry of the recipe, but be sure to leave key ingredients alone. For example, you could substitute sugar-free instant chocolate pudding for sugar-free instant butterscotch pudding, but if you used a six-serving package when a four-serving package was listed in the ingredients, or you used instant when cook-and-serve is required, you won't get the right result.

8. **Clean up as you go.** It is much easier to wash a few items at a time than to face a whole counter of dirty dishes later. The same is true for spills on the counter or floor.

9. **Be careful about doubling or halving a recipe.** Though many recipes can be altered successfully to serve more or fewer people, *many cannot.* This is especially true when it comes to spices and liquids. If you try to double a recipe that calls for 1 teaspoon pumpkin-pie spice, for example, and you double the spice, you may end up with a too-spicy taste. I usually suggest increasing spices or liquid by 1½ times when doubling a recipe. If it tastes a little bland to you, you can increase the spice to 1¾ times the original amount the next time you prepare the dish. *Remember:* You can always add more, but you can't take it out after it's stirred in.

   The same is true with liquid ingredients. If you wanted to **triple** a main dish recipe because you were planning to serve a crowd, you might think you should use three times as much of every ingredient. Don't, or you could end up with soup instead! If the original recipe calls for 1¾ cup tomato sauce, I'd suggest using 3½ cups when you **triple** the recipe (or 2¾ cups if you **double** it). You'll still have a good-tasting dish that won't run all over the plate.

10. **Write your reactions next to each recipe once you've served it.** Yes, that's right, I'm giving you permission to write in this book. It's yours, after all. Ask yourself: Did everyone like it? Did you have to add another half teaspoon chili seasoning to please your family, who like to live on the spicier side of the street? You may even want to rate the recipe on a scale of 1☆ to 4☆, depending on what you thought of it. (Four stars would be the top rating—and I hope you'll feel that way about many of my recipes.) Jotting down your comments while they are fresh in your mind will help you personalize the recipe to your own taste the next time you prepare it.

Secrets for Slow Cooker Success: What I've Learned Along the Way

Creating and testing recipes is a terrific time to discover what works for the home cook—and what definitely doesn't! Because each dish is tested and retested to get it just right, I learn firsthand about possible pitfalls; and because I'm preparing so many different recipes over the course of several months, I find the best and easiest methods to streamline healthy food preparation so I can pass them along to you.

All of my cookbooks to date and most of the recipes I've shared in my newsletter emphasize stovetop, microwave, and oven cooking, for which very little "equipment" instruction is required. But each slow cooker may be slightly different from others on the market, so I encourage you to begin your new adventure into slow cooking by carefully reading all the materials that came with your particular model. The manufacturers use their appliances in test kitchens before offering them to consumers, and they may have some good ideas that will help you get the most out of the one you purchase.

(If your slow cooker is ten years old or older, treat yourself to a new one, and make sure that it has a removable liner. While we were testing the recipes for this book, we tried using some older cookers from the 1970s and 1980s that we borrowed from friends and found that the results weren't as reliable. The older appliances didn't keep an even temperature, and some never even got warm enough to cook the food thoroughly. If you believe in the possibilities and convenience of slow cooking enough to invest in this cookbook, then I hope you will spend a few dollars more and get a new cooker, too!)

Some Great Reasons to Use a Slow Cooker

Slow cooker recipes work *with* your schedule, not the other way around. If you like, you can prepare your meal in advance, store the liner container in your refrigerator and then put it on to cook all the way while you are out for the day. What could be more perfect for today's busy lifestyles? Depending on your schedule, you can prepare the recipe the night before or first thing in the morning, turn the cooker on before you leave the house for work or play, and your meal will be waiting for you when you return home hours later.

More **nutrients are retained** in the food you prepare in a slow cooker because of the lower temperature used. Extra-lean meats cook tender because of the slow and long cooking, so you get both good taste and the health benefits of eating food lower in fat. And slow cooker meals **cut way down on clean-up**—you're only using one pot!

Did you know that **slow cookers are excellent energy savers?** When you cook on LOW, you use less energy than you would with a 100-watt light bulb.

Even so, **slow cookers still provide a safe cooking environment for foods.** According to the USDA, bacteria in foods is killed at a temperature of 165 degrees Fahrenheit if maintained for 2 hours or more. Because the LOW setting on slow cookers cooks at 185 to 200 degrees, it is well above the safety limit.

Less counter space is needed for cooking, so slow cookers are ideal for RV cooking as well as on boats, in cabins, and in efficiency kitchens.

When cooking on LOW, **you can leave your home** without any worries about having to "watch the pot boil." Low heat will not dry out or burn foods.

Slow cookers don't heat up the kitchen, so they are perfect for summer cooking.

Exact cooking times are not critical, so if you are delayed and don't get home exactly when you planned, your food won't be too overdone.

Slow cookers are **great for buffets and informal dining** because you can serve directly from the pot. You can actually use your slow cooker as a chafing dish to keep the food warm.

The Basics

All of my recipes were created and cooked in either 3½-, 4-, or 5-quart slow cookers, and **most of the recipes were designed to serve 4 to 6 people.** If that's the right number for your family or household, your main meal is covered; for smaller families, you've got planned leftovers for the coming week's work lunches.

Most **vegetables cook better when cut into small pieces or quartered.** Also, I recommend placing vegetables on the sides or bottom of the container. Root vegetables, such as carrots, potatoes, turnips, and parsnips, will take longer to cook than other vegetables and will cook best when covered by liquid.

(Some vegetables, such as **onions or carrots,** can also develop a more intense flavor during the slow cooking process, so you may want to decrease the amount called for. In my recipes, try it my way first and note if the finished dish is too strongly flavored for you. I just wanted you to be aware of this possibility.)

Meats usually cook faster than vegetables.

I suggest **browning ground meats for better flavor and texture** in the finished dish. Except for ground meats, however, you *don't* need to brown your meat before adding it to the recipes. Even though I ask you to use extra-lean cuts of meat, the slow cooker will tenderize it nicely during the long cooking process.

Whole herbs and spices are usually more intense when cooked in a slow cooker, so a little generally goes a long way. But very fine ground spices can lose some flavor as the hours pass. I've adjusted for this in my recipes, but if you are planning to use your slow cooker for other dishes, keep this in mind—and remember that it's probably best to do most of your seasoning shortly before serving.

Pasta has a tendency to fall apart or become gummy in the slow cooker if cooked too long, but only if it starts out *uncooked*. Cooked pasta, added to the pot from the beginning, manages to hold its shape even if the recipe is simmering away for 6 to 8 hours. So, **if you are using pasta in a recipe that calls for longer cooking times, it's better to add it only in the last 2 or 3 hours.** Or, you could cook it conventionally on the top of the stove and stir it in just before serving.

Skim milk has a tendency to curdle, and **natural cheese** will break down during extended cooking. Evaporated skim milk, condensed soups, processed cheeses, and nonfat dry milk powder work much better.

For **best results**, fill the pot at least half full of ingredients.

Since the **liquid content** of meats and vegetables will vary, sometimes a recipe will have more liquid than desired. The extra can be drained off or reduced by taking the cover off and cooking on HIGH for 30 to 45 minutes. Most if not all recipes cooked on LOW will be juicier, since the lower heat keeps the liquid from boiling away. That's the main reason you need to begin with less liquid when cooking on LOW than you would need if simmering in a pot on the stove.

If you use frozen foods, you will need to add an extra 2 to 3 hours cooking time. That's why I suggest throughout this book that you "thaw" frozen veggies by placing them in a colander and running hot water over them for a couple of minutes, then draining them carefully. By spending a few extra minutes at the start, you'll save hours later on!

All ingredients in most recipes can be added at the same time. Try, though, to add liquids and sauces last. Be sure to mix well before closing the lid and then again when lifting the lid off the finished product.

For **easier clean-up,** spray the inside of your pot with a nonstick cooking spray before using it each time.

To **protect the slow cooker liner,** try not to subject it to sudden temperature changes. For example, don't preheat the cooker and then add food.

Cooking Temperatures

Remember that the **cooking temperature in a slow cooker** is about 200 degrees (or just below boiling) when it's set on LOW and about 300 degrees when it's set on HIGH. Slow cooking is what gives the dish such a moist and tender taste. One hour on HIGH is usually equal to two hours on LOW. LOW is the best choice most of the time, but read the instructions carefully. Some dishes do better when cooked on HIGH. Consider what I've chosen for my recipes and evaluate your results, so you can start to experiment with your own family favorites. One important note: *Never* leave the slow cooker unattended if you are cooking on HIGH, as occasional stirring may be necessary.

When **cooking on the LOW setting**, don't be tempted to "lift the lid" just to stir or check on the progress of your meal. By doing that, you release the all-important heat and steam that are necessary for success, and so you will likely have to add to the cooking time called for in the recipe. Your best bet is only to take the lid off your slow cooker close to the first suggested cooking time, to test for doneness (for example, at 6 hours if the recipe suggests 6 to 8 hours), OR if the recipe explicitly tells you to!

However, when **cooking on HIGH** for short periods, an occasional stirring of the pot helps to distribute the flavors and generally doesn't affect the called-for cooking time.

Trouble-Shooting— What If the Dish Isn't Done?

If a recipe isn't done after the 6 to 8 hours suggested, one of the following reasons could be causing the problem:

1. **House voltage variations.** This is more commonplace than you might expect. The slight fluctuations in power do not have a noticeable effect on most appliances, but due to the extended cooking times a slow cooker demands, these

variations in power can require longer cooking times for some ingredients.

2. **Higher altitudes.** If you live at an altitude above 3,500 feet, you may need to add 1 to 2 hours to the suggested cooking times. Not every recipe may need more time, so you'll have to experiment and decide what works best for you.

3. **Extreme humidity.** It may surprise you to learn that very high humidity can cause ingredients to cook more slowly than expected. If you are using a new slow cooker with a reliable temperature, it's almost impossible to "overcook" most dishes. If you suspect your environment may require additional cooking time, allow for it the first few times out. You'll soon learn through experience what works best for your cooker, your kitchen, and you.

Preparing Just About Anything in Your Slow Cooker

Here's a quick guideline to **convert your own favorite recipes to the slow cooker method:** A recipe that bakes for one hour at 350 degrees should be cooked on LOW for 6 to 8 hours; a recipe that bakes for 30 minutes at 325 degrees should be cooked on LOW for 3 to 4 hours. Remember to cut the liquid considerably when converting a non–slow cooker recipe—about half of what's originally called for is a good place to start. The only exception to this rule are soups and any recipes that contain long-grain converted rice.

Now, let me end as I started—no matter which model of slow cooker you buy, **be sure to read the manufacturer's specific instructions** for proper settings, safety, and cleaning of your particular brand.

Let the cooking—and your liberation from the kitchen—begin!

Help Me Cook Healthy: My Best Healthy Exchanges Cooking Tips

The word *moderation* best describes **my use of fats, sugar substitutes, and sodium** in these recipes. Wherever possible, I've used cooking spray for sautéing and for browning meats and vegetables. I also use reduced-calorie margarine and fat-free mayonnaise and salad dressings. Lean ground turkey or ground beef can be used in the recipes. Just be sure whatever you choose is at least *90 percent lean.*

Sugar Substitutes

I've also included **small amounts of sugar substitutes as the sweetening agent** in many of the recipes. I don't drink a hundred cans of soda a day or eat enough artificially sweetened foods in a 24-hour time period to be troubled by sugar substitutes. But if this is a concern of yours and you *do not* need to watch your sugar intake, you can always replace the sugar substitutes with processed sugar and the sugar-free products with regular ones.

I created my recipes knowing they would also be used by hypoglycemics, diabetics, and those concerned about triglycerides.

If you choose to use sugar instead, be sure to count the additional calories.

A word of caution when cooking with **sugar substitutes**: Use **sucralose-** or **saccharin-**based sweeteners when **heating or baking**. In recipes that **don't require heat, aspartame** (known as NutraSweet) works well in uncooked dishes but leaves an aftertaste in baked products.

Splenda and **Sugar Twin** are my best choices for sugar substitutes. They measure like sugar, you can cook and bake with them, they're inexpensive, and they are easily poured from their boxes. (If you can't find **Splenda** in your store yet, try their website: http://www.splenda.com, to order directly.)

Many of my recipes for quick breads, muffins, and cakes include a package of sugar-free instant pudding mix, which is sweetened with NutraSweet. Yet I've been told that NutraSweet breaks down under heat. I've tested my recipes again and again, and here's what I've found: Baking with a NutraSweet product sold for home sweetening doesn't work, but baking with NutraSweet-sweetened instant pudding mixes turns out great. I choose not to question why this is, but continue to use these products in creating my Healthy Exchanges recipes.

How much sweetener is the right amount? I use pourable Splenda, Sugar Twin, Brown Sugar Twin, and Sprinkle Sweet in my recipes because they measure just like sugar. What could be easier? I also use them because they work wonderfully in cooked and baked products.

If you are using a brand other than these, you need to check the package to figure out how much of your sweetener will equal what's called for in the recipe.

If you choose to use real sugar or brown sugar, then you would use the same amount the recipe lists for pourable Splenda, Sugar Twin, or Brown Sugar Twin.

You'll see that I list only the specific brands when the recipe preparation involves heat. In a salad or other recipe that doesn't require cooking, I will list the ingredient as "sugar substitute to equal 2 tablespoons sugar." You can then use any sweetener you choose—Equal, Sweet 'n Low, Sweet Ten, or any other aspartame-based sugar substitute. Just check the label so you'll be using the right amount to equal those 2 tablespoons of sugar. Or, if you choose, you can use regular sugar.

With Healthy Exchanges recipes, the "sweet life" is the only life for me!

Pan Sizes

I'm often asked why I use an **8-by-8-inch baking dish** in my recipes. It's for portion control. If the recipe says it serves 4, just cut down the center, turn the dish, and cut again. Like magic, there's your serving. Also, if this is the only recipe you are preparing requiring an oven, the square dish fits into a tabletop toaster oven easily and energy can be conserved.

While many of my recipes call for an 8-by-8-inch baking dish, others ask for a 9-by-9-inch cake pan. If you don't have a 9-inch-square pan, is it alright to use your 8-inch dish instead? In most cases, the small difference in the size of these two pans won't significantly affect the finished product, so until you can get your hands on the right size pan, go ahead and use your baking dish.

However, since the 8-inch dish is usually made of glass and the 9-inch cake pan is made of metal, you will want to adjust the baking temperature. If you're using a glass baking dish in a recipe that calls for a 9-inch pan, be sure to lower your baking temperature by 15 degrees *or* check your finished product at least 6 to 8 minutes before the specified baking time is over.

But it really is worthwhile to add a 9-by-9-inch pan to your collection, and if you're going to be baking lots of my Healthy Exchanges cakes, you'll definitely use it frequently. A cake baked in this pan will have a better texture, and the servings will be a little larger. Just think of it—an 8-by-8-inch pan produces 64 square inches of dessert, while a 9-by-9-inch pan delivers 81 square inches. Those 17 extra inches are too tasty to lose!

To make life even easier, **whenever a recipe calls for ounce measurements** (other than raw meats), I've included the closest cup equivalent. I need to use my scale daily when creating recipes, so I've measured for you at the same time.

Freezing Leftovers

Most of the recipes are for **4 to 8 servings.** If you don't have that many to feed, do what I do: Freeze individual portions. Then all you have to do is choose something from the freezer and take it to work for lunch or have your evening meals prepared in advance for the week. In this way, I always have something on hand that is both good to eat and good for me.

Unless a recipe includes hard-boiled eggs, cream cheese, mayonnaise, or a raw vegetable or fruit, **the leftovers should freeze well**. (I've marked recipes that freeze well with the symbol of a **snowflake** ❋.) This includes most of the cream pies. Divide any recipe into individual servings and freeze for your own "TV" dinners.

Another good idea is **cutting leftover pie into individual pieces and freezing each one separately** in a small Ziploc freezer bag. Once you've cut the pie into portions, place them on a cookie sheet and put it in the freezer for 15 minutes. That way, the creamy topping won't get smashed and your pie will keep its shape.

When you want to thaw a piece of pie for yourself, you don't have to thaw the whole pie. You can practice portion control at the same time, and it works really well for brown-bag lunches. Just pull a piece out of the freezer on your way to work, and by lunchtime you will have a wonderful dessert waiting for you.

Why do I so often recommend freezing leftover desserts? One reason is that if you leave baked goods made with sugar substitute out on the counter for more than a day or two, they get moldy. Sugar is a preservative and retards the molding process. It's actually what's called an antimicrobial agent, meaning it works against microbes such as molds, bacteria, fungi, and yeasts that grow in foods and can cause food poisoning. Both sugar and salt work as antimicrobial agents to withdraw water from food. Since microbes can't grow without water, food protected in this way doesn't spoil.

So what do we do if we don't want our muffins to turn moldy, but we also don't want to use sugar because of the excess carbohydrates and calories? Freeze them! Just place each muffin or individually sliced bread serving into a Ziploc sandwich bag, seal, and toss into your freezer. Then, whenever you want one for a snack or a meal, you can choose to let it thaw naturally or "zap" it in the microwave. If you know that baked goods will be eaten within a day or two, packaging them in a sealed plastic container and storing in the refrigerator will do the trick.

Unless I specify "covered" for simmering or baking, prepare my recipes **uncovered.** Occasionally you will read a recipe that asks you to cover a dish for a time, then to uncover, so read the directions carefully to avoid confusion—and to get the best results.

Cooking Spray

Low-fat cooking spray is another blessing in a Healthy Exchanges kitchen. It's currently available in three flavors:

- **OLIVE OIL or GARLIC FLAVORED** when cooking Mexican, Italian, or Greek dishes

- **BUTTER or LEMON FLAVORED** when a hint of butter or lemon is desired

- **REGULAR** for everything else.

A quick spray of butter flavored makes air-popped popcorn a low-fat taste treat, or try it as a butter substitute on steaming hot corn on the cob. One light spray of the skillet when browning meat will convince you that you're using "old-fashioned fat," and a quick coating of the casserole dish before you add the ingredients will make serving easier and clean-up quicker.

Baking Times

Sometimes I give you a range as a **baking time,** such as 22 to 28 minutes. Why? Because every kitchen, every stove, and every chef's cooking technique is slightly different. On a hot and humid day in Iowa, the optimum cooking time won't be the same as on a cold, dry day. Some stoves bake hotter than the temperature setting indicates; other stoves bake cooler. Electric ovens usually are more temperamental than gas ovens. If you place your baking pan on a lower shelf, the temperature is warmer than if you place it on a higher shelf. If you stir the mixture more vigorously than I do, you could affect the required baking time by a minute or more.

The best way to gauge the heat of your particular oven is to purchase an oven temperature gauge that hangs in the oven. These can be found in any discount store or kitchen equipment store, and if you're going to be cooking and baking regularly, it's a good idea to own one. Set the oven to 350 degrees, and when the oven indicates that it has reached that temperature, check the reading on the gauge. If it's less than 350 degrees, you know your oven cooks cooler and you need to add a few minutes to the cooking time *or* set your oven at a higher temperature. If it's more than 350 degrees, your oven is warmer and you need to subtract a few minutes from the cooking time. In any event, always treat the suggested baking time as approximate. Check on your baked product at the earliest suggested time. You can always continue baking a few minutes more if needed, but you can't unbake it once you've cooked it too long.

Miscellaneous Ingredients and Tips

I use reduced-sodium **canned chicken broth** in place of dry bouillon to lower the sodium content. The intended flavor is still present in the prepared dish. As a reduced-sodium beef broth is not currently available (at least not in DeWitt, Iowa), I use the canned regular beef broth. The sodium content is still lower than regular dry bouillon.

Whenever **cooked rice or pasta** is an ingredient, follow the package directions, but eliminate the salt and/or margarine called for. This helps lower the sodium and fat content. It tastes just fine; trust me on this.

Here's another tip: When **cooking rice or noodles**, why not cook extra "for the pot"? After you use what you need, store leftover rice in a covered container (where it will keep for a couple of days). With noodles like spaghetti or macaroni, first rinse and drain as usual, then measure out what you need. Put the leftovers in a bowl covered with water, then store in the refrigerator, covered, until they're needed. Then, measure out what you need, rinse and drain, and they're ready to go.

Does your **pita bread** often tear before you can make a sandwich? Here's my tip to make them open easily: Cut the bread in half, put the halves in the microwave for about 15 seconds, and they will open up by themselves. *Voilà!*

When **chunky salsa** is listed as an ingredient, I leave the degree of "heat" up to your personal taste. In our house, I'm considered a wimp. I go for the "mild" while my husband, Cliff, prefers "extra-hot." How do we compromise? I prepare the recipe with mild salsa because he can always add a spoonful or two of the hotter version to his serving, but I can't enjoy the dish if it's too spicy for me.

You can make purchased **fat-free salad dressings taste more like the "real thing"** by adding a small amount of fat-free mayonnaise and a pinch of sugar substitute to the diet dressing. Start with 2 tablespoons of salad dressing (such as Ranch), add 1 teaspoon fat-free mayo and sugar substitute to equal ½ teaspoon sugar. Mix well and spoon over your salad. Unless you remind yourself you're eating the fat-free version, you may just fool yourself into thinking you reached for the high-fat counterpart instead!

Milk, Yogurt, and More

Take it from me—nonfat dry milk powder is great! I *do not* use it for drinking, but I *do* use it for cooking. Three good reasons why:

1. It is very **inexpensive**.

2. It does not **sour** because you use it only as needed. Store the box in your refrigerator or freezer and it will keep almost forever.

3. You can easily **add extra calcium** to just about any recipe without added liquid.

I consider nonfat dry milk powder one of Mother Nature's modern-day miracles of convenience. But do purchase a good national name brand (Carnation), and keep it fresh by proper storage.

I've said many times, "Give me my mixing bowl, my wire

whisk, and a box of nonfat dry milk powder, and I can conquer the world!" Here are some of my favorite ways to use dry milk powder:

1. You can make a **pudding** with the nutrients of 2 cups fat-free milk, but the liquid of only 1¼ to 1½ cups by using ⅔ cup nonfat dry milk powder, a 4-serving package of sugar-free instant pudding, and the lesser amount of water. This makes the pudding taste much creamier and more like homemade. Also, pie filling made my way will set up in minutes. If company is knocking at your door, you can prepare a pie for them almost as fast as you can open the door and invite them in. And if by chance you have leftovers, the filling will not separate the way it does when you use the 2 cups fat-free milk suggested on the package. (If you absolutely refuse to use this handy powdered milk, you can substitute fat-free milk in the amount of water I call for. Your pie won't be as creamy, and will likely get runny if you have leftovers.)

2. You can make your own **"sour cream"** by combining ¾ cup plain fat-free yogurt with ⅓ cup nonfat dry milk powder. What you did by doing this is fourfold: (1) The dry milk stabilizes the yogurt and keeps the whey from separating. (2) The dry milk slightly helps to cut the tartness of the yogurt. (3) It's still virtually fat-free. (4) The calcium has been increased by 100 percent. Isn't it great how we can make that distant relative of sour cream a first kissin' cousin by adding the nonfat dry milk powder? Or if you place 1 cup plain fat-free yogurt in a sieve lined with a coffee filter, place the sieve over a small bowl, and refrigerate for about 6 hours, you will end up with a very good alternative for sour cream. To **stabilize yogurt** when cooking or baking with it, just add 1 teaspoon cornstarch to every ¾ cup yogurt.

3. You can make **evaporated fat-free milk** by using ⅓ cup nonfat dry milk powder and ½ cup water for every ½ cup evaporated fat-free milk you need. This is handy to know when you want to prepare a recipe calling for evaporated fat-free milk and you don't have any in the cupboard. And

if you are using a recipe that requires only 1 cup evaporated fat-free milk, you don't have to worry about what to
do with the leftover milk in the can.

4. You can make **sugar-free and fat-free sweetened condensed milk** by using 1⅓ cups nonfat dry milk powder
   mixed with ½ cup cold water, microwaved on HIGH until
   the mixture is hot but not boiling. Then stir in ½ cup
   Splenda or pourable Sugar Twin. Cover and chill at least 4
   hours.

5. For any recipe that calls for **buttermilk**, you might want to
   try **JO's Buttermilk**: Blend 1 cup water and ⅔ cup nonfat
   dry milk powder (the nutrients of 2 cups of fat-free milk).
   It'll be thicker than this mixed-up milk usually is, because
   it's doubled. Add 1 teaspoon white vinegar and stir, then
   let it sit for at least 10 minutes.

What else? Nonfat dry milk powder adds calcium without fuss
to many recipes, and it can be stored for months in your refrigerator or freezer.

And for **a different taste when preparing sugar-free instant
pudding mixes**, use ¾ cup plain fat-free yogurt for one of the
required cups of milk. Blend as usual. It will be thicker and
creamier—and no, it doesn't taste like yogurt.

Another **variation for the sugar-free instant vanilla pudding**
is to use 1 cup fat-free milk and 1 cup crushed pineapple with
juice. Mix as usual.

Soup Substitutes

One of my subscribers was looking for a way to further restrict salt
intake and needed a substitute for **cream of mushroom soup**. For
many of my recipes, I use Healthy Request Cream of Mushroom
Soup, as it is a reduced-sodium product. The label suggests two
servings per can, but I usually incorporate the soup into a recipe
serving at least four. By doing this, I've reduced the sodium in the
soup by half again.

But if you must restrict your sodium even more, try making

my Healthy Exchanges **Creamy Mushroom Sauce.** Place 1½ cups evaporated fat-free milk and 3 tablespoons flour in a covered jar. Shake well and pour the mixture into a medium saucepan sprayed with butter-flavored cooking spray. Add ½ cup canned sliced mushrooms, rinsed and drained. Cook over medium heat, stirring often, until the mixture thickens. Add any seasonings of your choice. You can use this sauce in any recipe that calls for one 10¾-ounce can of cream of mushroom soup.

Why did I choose these proportions and ingredients?

- 1½ cups evaporated fat-free milk is the amount in one can.

- It's equal to three Fat-Free Milk choices or exchanges.

- It's the perfect amount of liquid and flour for a medium cream sauce.

- 3 tablespoons flour is equal to one Bread/Starch choice or exchange.

- Any leftovers will reheat beautifully with a flour-based sauce, but not with a cornstarch base.

- The mushrooms are one Vegetable choice or exchange.

- This sauce is virtually fat-free, sugar-free, and sodium-free.

Proteins

Eggs

I use eggs in moderation. I enjoy the real thing on an average of three to four times a week. So, my recipes are calculated on using whole eggs. However, if you choose to use egg substitute in place of the egg, the finished product will turn out just fine and the fat grams per serving will be even lower than those listed.

If you like the look, taste, and feel of **hard-boiled eggs** in salads but haven't been using them because of the cholesterol in the yolk, I have a couple of alternatives for you: (1) Pour an 8-ounce carton of egg substitute into a medium skillet sprayed with cooking spray. Cover the skillet tightly and cook over low heat until substitute is just set, about 10 minutes. Remove from heat and let set, still covered, for 10 minutes more. Uncover and cool completely. Chop the set mixture. This will make about 1 cup of chopped egg. (2) Even easier is to hard-boil "real eggs," toss the yolk away, and chop the white. Either way, you don't deprive yourself of the pleasure of egg in your salad.

In most recipes calling for **egg substitutes**, you can use 2 egg whites in place of the equivalent of 1 egg substitute. Just break the eggs open and toss the yolks away. I can hear some of you already saying, "But that's wasteful!" Well, take a look at the price on the egg substitute package (which usually has the equivalent of 4 eggs in it), then look at the price of a dozen eggs, from which you'd get the equivalent of 6 egg substitutes. Now, what's wasteful about that?

Meats

Whenever I include **cooked chicken** in a recipe, I use roasted white meat without skin. Whenever I include **roast beef or pork** in a recipe, I use the loin cuts because they are much leaner. However, most of the time, I do my roasting of all these meats at the local deli. I just ask for a chunk of their lean roasted meat, 6 or 8 ounces, and ask them not to slice it. When I get home, I cube or dice the meat and am ready to use it in my recipe. The reason I do this is threefold: (1) I'm getting just the amount I need without leftovers; (2) I don't have the expense of heating the oven; and (3) I'm not throwing away the bone, gristle, and fat I'd be cutting off the meat. Overall, it is probably cheaper to "roast" it the way I do.

Did you know that you can make an acceptable meatloaf without using egg for the binding? Just replace every egg with ¼ cup of liquid. You could use beef broth, tomato sauce, even applesauce, to name just a few. For a meatloaf to serve 6, I always use 1 pound of extra-lean ground beef or turkey, 6 tablespoons of dried fine bread crumbs, and ¼ cup of the liquid, plus anything else healthy that strikes my fancy at the time. I mix well and place the mixture in an 8-by-8-inch baking dish or 9-by-5-inch loaf pan sprayed with cooking spray. Bake uncovered at 350 degrees for 35 to 50 minutes (depending on the added ingredients). You will never miss the egg.

Anytime you are **browning ground meat** for a casserole and want to get rid of almost all the excess fat, loosely place the uncooked meat in a plastic colander. Set the colander in a glass pie plate. Place in microwave and cook on HIGH for 3 to 6 minutes (depending on the amount being browned), stirring often. Use as you would for any casserole. You can also chop onions and brown them with the meat if you want.

To **brown meat for any Italian dish** (and add some extra "zip"), simply pour a couple of tablespoons of fat-free Italian dressing into a skillet and add your ingredients to be browned. The dressing acts almost like olive oil in the process and adds a touch of flavor as well. And to make an **Italian Sloppy Joe**, brown 16 ounces extra-lean ground meat and 1 cup chopped onion in ¼ cup fat-free Italian dressing, then add 1 cup tomato sauce, lower heat, and simmer for 10 minutes. *Bravo!*

Remember, always opt for the leanest ground beef or turkey you can find. Here in DeWitt, we can buy 95% extra-lean ground sirloin, which provides about 8 to 10 grams fat in a 2- to 3-ounce serving. Lean ground turkey provides about 5 to 7 grams of fat. But cheaper cuts can "cost" you up to 20 grams of fat per serving. It's standard practice to grind the skin into inexpensive ground turkey found in most one-pound frozen packages, so beware.

Gravy and Mashed Potatoes

For **gravy** with all the "old time" flavor but without the extra fat, try this almost effortless way to prepare it. First, pour your pan drippings (from roasted turkey, roast beef, or roast pork) into a large cake pan and set the pan in your freezer for at least 15 to 20 minutes so that the fat can congeal on the top and be skimmed off. Use a large pan even if you only have a small amount of drippings so that you get maximum air exposure for quick congealing. (If you prefer, you can purchase one of those fat separator pitchers that separates the fat from the juice.)

Pour your defatted juice into a large skillet. This recipe begins with about one cup of "stock." Now, pour either one cup of potato water (water that potatoes were boiled in before mashing) or regular water into a large jar. Potato water is my first choice because it's loaded with nutrients so I use it whenever I'm making fresh mashed potatoes to go with my homemade gravy. Add 3 tablespoons of all-purpose flour, screw the lid on, and shake until the mixture is well blended. This easy step assures that you won't get lumps in your gravy!

Pour the mixture into the skillet with defatted stock and add any seasonings you like. Cook over medium heat, stirring constantly with a wire whisk, until mixture thickens and starts to boil. (The whisk is another "secret" for lump-free gravy.) Now pour the gravy into your prettiest gravy bowl and serve with pride!

Why did I use flour instead of cornstarch? Because any leftovers will reheat nicely with the flour base and would not with a cornstarch base. Also, 3 tablespoons of flour works out to 1 Bread/Starch exchange. This virtually fat-free gravy makes about 2 cups, so you could spoon about ½ cup gravy on your low-fat mashed potatoes and only have to count your gravy as ¼ Bread/Starch exchange.

Here's how to make the **best low-fat mashed potatoes**: For a 6-serving batch, quarter 6 medium potatoes and boil in just enough water to cover them until they are tender. Drain the potatoes, but *do not* throw the water away. Return the potatoes to the saucepan, whip them gently with an electric mixer, then add about ½ cup of the reserved potato water, ⅓ cup Carnation nonfat dry milk powder, and 2 tablespoons fat-free sour cream. Continue whipping with the mixer until smooth. You're sure to be begged to share the "secret" of your creamy mashed potatoes!

Fruits and Vegetables

If you want to enjoy a **"fruit shake"** with some pizzazz, just combine soda water and unsweetened fruit juice in a blender. Add crushed ice. Blend on HIGH until thick. Refreshment without guilt.

You'll see that many recipes use ordinary **canned vegetables.** They're much cheaper than reduced-sodium versions, and once you rinse and drain them, the sodium is reduced anyway. I believe in saving money wherever possible so we can afford the best fat-free and sugar-free products as they come onto the market.

All three kinds of **vegetables—fresh, frozen, and canned—** have their place in a healthy diet. My husband, Cliff, hates the taste of frozen or fresh green beans, thinks the texture is all wrong, so I use canned green beans instead. In this case, canned vegetables have their proper place when I'm feeding my husband. If someone in your family has a similar concern, it's important to respond to it so everyone can be happy and enjoy the meal.

When I use **fruits or vegetables** like apples, cucumbers, and zucchini, I wash them really well and **leave the skin on.** It provides added color, fiber, and attractiveness to any dish. And because I use processed flour in my cooking, I like to increase the fiber in my diet by eating my fruits and vegetables in their closest-to-natural state.

To help **keep fresh fruits and veggies fresh**, just give them a quick "shower" with lemon juice. The easiest way to do this is to pour purchased lemon juice into a kitchen spray bottle and store in the refrigerator. Then, every time you use fresh fruits or vegetables in a salad or dessert, simply give them a quick spray with your "lemon spritzer." You just might be amazed by how this little trick keeps your produce from turning brown so fast.

Another great way to **keep fruits from turning brown:** Try dipping them in Diet Mountain Dew!

Here's a way to enjoy cranberries all year round: Buy a few extra bags while they are in season and freeze them for future use. By the way, cranberries chop better when frozen!

The next time you warm canned vegetables such as carrots or green beans, drain and heat the vegetables in ¼ cup beef or chicken broth. It gives a nice variation to an old standby. Here's a simple **white sauce** for vegetables and casseroles without using added fat that can be made by spraying a medium saucepan with butter-flavored cooking spray. Place 1½ cups evaporated fat-free milk and 3 tablespoons flour in a covered jar. Shake well. Pour into the sprayed saucepan and cook over medium heat until thick, stirring constantly. Add salt and pepper to taste. You can also add ½ cup canned drained mushrooms and/or 3 ounces (¾ cup) shredded reduced-fat cheese. Continue cooking until the cheese melts.

Zip up canned or frozen green beans with **chunky salsa:** ½ cup to 2 cups beans. Heat thoroughly. Chunky salsa also makes a wonderful dressing on lettuce salads. It only counts as a vegetable, so enjoy.

Another wonderful **South of the Border dressing** can be stirred up by using ½ cup chunky salsa and ¼ cup fat-free ranch dressing. Cover and store in your refrigerator. Use as a dressing for salads or as a topping for baked potatoes.

To **"roast" green or red peppers,** pierce a whole pepper in four or six places with the tines of a fork, then place the pepper in a glass pie plate and microwave on HIGH for 10 to 12 minutes, turning after every 4 minutes. Cover and let set for 5 minutes. Then, remove the seeds and peel the skin off and cut into strips. Use right away or freeze for future use.

Delightful Dessert Ideas

For a special treat that tastes anything but "diet," try placing **spreadable fruit** in a container and microwave for about 15 seconds. Then pour the melted fruit spread over a serving of nonfat ice cream or frozen yogurt. One tablespoon of spreadable fruit is equal to 1 Fruit choice or exchange. Some combinations to get you started are apricot over chocolate ice cream, strawberry over strawberry ice cream, or any flavor over vanilla.

Another way I use spreadable fruit is to make a delicious **topping for a cheesecake or angel food cake.** I take ½ cup fruit and ½ cup Cool Whip Lite and blend the two together with a teaspoon of coconut extract.

Here's a really **good topping** for the fall of the year. Place 1½ cups unsweetened applesauce in a medium saucepan or 4-cup glass measure. Stir in 2 tablespoons raisins, 1 teaspoon apple pie spice, and 2 tablespoons Cary's Sugar Free Maple Syrup. Cook over medium heat on the stovetop or microwave on HIGH until warm. Then, spoon about ½ cup of the warm mixture over pancakes, French toast, or sugar- and fat-free vanilla ice cream. It's as close as you will get to guilt-free apple pie!

Do you love hot fudge sundaes as much as I do? Here's my secret for making **Almost Sinless Hot Fudge Sauce.** Just combine the contents of a 4-serving package of JELL-O sugar-free chocolate cook-and-serve pudding with ⅔ cup Carnation Nonfat Dry Milk Powder in a medium saucepan. Add 1¼ cups water. Cook over medium heat, stirring constantly with a wire whisk, until the mixture thickens and starts to boil. Remove from heat and stir in 1 teaspoon vanilla extract, 2 teaspoons reduced-calorie margarine, and ½ cup miniature marshmallows. This makes six ¼ cup servings. Any leftovers can be refrigerated and reheated later in the microwave. Yes, you can buy fat-free chocolate syrup nowadays, but have you checked the sugar content? For a ¼-cup serving of store-bought syrup (and you show me any true hot fudge sundae lover who would settle for less than ¼ cup) it clocks in at over 150 calories with 39 grams of sugar! Hershey's Lite Syrup, while better, still has 100 calories and 10 grams of sugar. But this "homemade" version costs you only 60 calories, less than ½ gram of fat, and just 6 grams of sugar for the same ¼-cup serving. For an occasional squirt on something where 1 teaspoon is enough, I'll use Hershey's Lite Syrup. But when I crave a hot fudge sundae, I scoop out some sugar- and fat-free ice cream, then spoon my Almost Sinless Hot Fudge Sauce over the top, and smile with pleasure.

A quick yet tasty way to prepare **strawberries for shortcake** is to place about ¾ cup sliced strawberries, 2 tablespoons Diet Mountain Dew, and sugar substitute to equal ¼ cup sugar in a blender container. Process on BLEND until mixture is smooth. Pour the mixture into bowl. Add 1¼ cups sliced strawberries and mix well. Cover and refrigerate until ready to serve with shortcakes. This tastes just like the strawberry sauce I remember my mother making when I was a child.

Here's a wonderful secret for **making shortcakes**: Just follow the recipe for shortcakes on the Bisquick Reduced-Fat Baking Mix box, but substitute Splenda or pourable Sugar Twin for the sugar, fat-free milk for the regular milk, and fat-free sour cream for the margarine. When you serve these light and tasty shortcakes to your loved ones, I defy any of them to notice the difference between your version and the original!

Have you tried **thawing Cool Whip Lite** by stirring it? Don't! You'll get a runny mess and ruin the look and taste of your dessert. You can *never* treat Cool Whip Lite the same way you did regular Cool Whip because the "lite" version just doesn't contain enough fat. Thaw your Cool Whip Lite by placing it in your refrigerator at least two hours before you need to use it. When they took the excess fat out of Cool Whip to make it "lite," they replaced it with air. When you stir the living daylights out of it to hurry up the thawing, you also stir out the air. You also can't thaw your Cool

Whip Lite in the microwave, or you'll end up with Cool Whip Soup!

Always have a thawed container of Cool Whip Lite in your refrigerator, as it keeps well for up to two weeks. It actually freezes and thaws and freezes and thaws again quite well, so if you won't be using it soon, you could refreeze your leftovers. Just remember to take it out a few hours before you need it, so it'll be creamy and soft and ready to use.

Remember, anytime you see the words "fat-free" or "reduced-fat" on the labels of cream cheese, sour cream, or whipped topping, handle it gently. The fat has been replaced by air or water, and the product has to be treated with special care.

How can you **frost an entire pie with just ½ cup whipped topping?** First, don't use an inexpensive brand. I use Cool Whip Lite or La Creme Lite. Make sure the topping is fully thawed. Always spread from the center to the sides using a rubber spatula. This way, ½ cup topping will cover an entire pie. Remember, the operative word is *frost,* not pile the entire container on top of the pie!

Here's my vote for the easiest **crumb topping** ever! Simply combine 3 tablespoons of purchased graham cracker crumbs (or three 2½-inch squares made into fine crumbs) with 2 teaspoons reduced-calorie margarine and 1 tablespoon (if desired) chopped nuts. Mix this well and sprinkle evenly over the top of your fruit pie and bake as you normally would. You can use either a purchased graham cracker piecrust or an unbaked refrigerated regular piecrust. Another almost effortless crumb topping can be made by combining 6 tablespoons Bisquick Reduced-Fat Baking Mix and 2 tablespoons Splenda or pourable Sugar Twin with 2 teaspoons of reduced-calorie margarine until the mixture becomes crumbly. Again, you can stir in 1 tablespoon of chopped nuts if you wish. Evenly sprinkle this mixture over your fruit filling and bake as usual. This works best with a purchased unbaked refrigerated piecrust.

Another trick I often use is to include tiny amounts of "real people" food, such as coconut, but **extend the flavor by using extracts**. Try it—you will be surprised by how little of the real thing you can use and still feel you are not being deprived.

If you are preparing a pie filling that has ample moisture, just line the bottom of a 9-by-9-inch cake pan with **graham crackers**. Pour the filling over the top of the crackers. Cover and refrigerate until the moisture has enough time to soften the crackers. Overnight is best. This eliminates the added **fats and sugars of a piecrust.**

One of my readers provided a smart and easy way to enjoy a **two-crust pie** without all the fat that usually comes along with those two crusts. Just use one Pillsbury refrigerated piecrust. Let it set at room temperature for about 20 minutes. Cut the crust in half on the folded line. Gently roll each half into a ball. Wipe your counter with a wet cloth and place a sheet of wax paper on it. Put one of the balls on the wax paper, cover with another piece of wax paper, and roll it out with your rolling pin. Carefully remove the wax paper on one side and place that side into your 8- or 9-inch pie plate. Fill with your usual pie filling, then repeat the process for the top crust. Bake as usual. Enjoy!

Here's a good tip for **avoiding a "doughy" taste when using a refrigerated piecrust.** Make sure you take the piecrust out of the refrigerator and let it sit on the counter for at least ten minutes before putting it in the pie plate and baking it. If you put the piecrust into the plate before it has a chance to "warm up," it will be stiffer than if you let it come to room temperature before using. This means that the tiny amount of flour clinging to the crust doesn't have a chance to become "one" with the crust, making the finished product "doughier."

When you are preparing a pie that uses a purchased piecrust, simply tear out the paper label on the plastic cover (but do check it for a coupon good on a future purchase) and turn the cover upside down over the prepared pie. You now have a cover that protects your beautifully garnished pie from having anything fall on top of it. It makes the pie very portable when it's your turn to bring dessert to a get-together.

And for **"picture-perfect" presentation** when using a purchased piecrust, just remove the protective plastic cover, place a pizza pan over the top of the crust, invert the "tin pan" and carefully remove it so the bottom of the crust is exposed. Then, replace the "tin pan" with an attractive pottery pie plate and, with one hand holding each pan in place, flip the piecrust so that the piecrust is now sitting securely in the pottery plate. Remove the pizza pan and fill with your favorite Healthy Exchanges pie filling. This is easier than it sounds, and it makes your dessert look extra-special!

Did you know you can make your own **fruit-flavored yogurt?** Mix 1 tablespoon of any flavor of spreadable fruit spread with ¾ cup plain yogurt. It's every bit as tasty and much cheaper. You can also make your own **lemon yogurt** by combining 3 cups plain fat-free yogurt with 1 tub Crystal Light lemonade powder. Mix well, cover, and store in the refrigerator. I think you will be pleasantly surprised by the ease, cost, and flavor of this "made from scratch" calcium-rich treat. P.S.: You can make any flavor you like by using any of the Crystal Light mixes—Cranberry? Iced Tea? You decide.

Other Smart Substitutions

Many people have inquired about **substituting applesauce and artificial sweetener for butter and sugar**, but what if you aren't satisfied with the result? One woman wrote to me about a recipe for her grandmother's cookies that called for 1 cup of butter and 1½ cups of sugar. Well, any recipe that depends on as much butter and sugar as this one does is generally not a good candidate for "healthy exchanges." The original recipe needed a large quantity of fat to produce a crisp cookie just like Grandma made.

Applesauce can often be used instead of vegetable oil but generally doesn't work well as a replacement for butter, margarine, or lard. If a recipe calls for ½ cup of vegetable oil or less and your recipe is for a bar cookie, quick bread, muffin, or cake mix, you can try substituting an equal amount of unsweetened applesauce. If the recipe calls for more, try using ½ cup applesauce and the rest oil. You're cutting down the fat but shouldn't end up with a taste disaster! This "applesauce shortening" works great in many recipes, but so far I haven't been able to figure out a way to deep-fat fry with it!

Another rule for healthy substitution: Up to ½ cup sugar or less can be replaced by an artificial sweetener that can withstand the heat of baking, like pourable Sugar Twin or Splenda. If it requires more than ½ cup sugar, cut the amount needed by 75 percent and use ½ cup sugar substitute and sugar for the rest. Other options: Reduce the butter and sugar by 25 percent and see if the finished product still satisfies you in taste and appearance. Or, make the cookies just like Grandma did, realizing they are part of your family's holiday tradition. Enjoy a *moderate* serving of a couple of cookies once or twice during the season, and just forget about them the rest of the year.

Did you know that you can replace the fat in many quick breads, muffins, and shortcakes with **fat-free mayonnaise** or **fat-free sour cream?** This can work if the original recipe doesn't call for a lot of fat *and* sugar. If the recipe is truly fat- and sugar-dependent, such as traditional sugar cookies, cupcakes, or pastries, it won't work. Those recipes require the large amounts of sugar and fat to make love in the dark of the oven in order to produce a tender finished product. But if you have a favorite quick bread that doesn't call for a lot of sugar or fat, why don't you give one of these substitutes a try?

If you enjoy beverage mixes like those from Alba, here are my Healthy Exchanges versions:

For **chocolate flavored,** use ⅓ cup nonfat dry milk powder and 2 tablespoons Nestlé Sugar-Free Chocolate Flavored Quik. Mix well and use as usual. Or, use ⅓ cup nonfat dry milk powder, 1 teaspoon unsweetened cocoa, and sugar substitute to equal 3 tablespoons sugar. Mix well and use as usual.

For **vanilla flavored,** use ⅓ cup nonfat dry milk powder, sugar substitute to equal 2 tablespoons sugar, and add 1 teaspoon vanilla extract when adding liquid.

For **strawberry flavored,** use ⅓ cup nonfat dry milk powder, sugar substitute to equal 2 tablespoons sugar, and add 1 teaspoon strawberry extract and 3–4 drops red food coloring when adding liquid.

Each of these makes one packet of drink mix. If you need to double the recipe, double everything but the extract. Use 1½ teaspoons of extract or it will be too strong. Use 1 cup cold water with one recipe mix to make a glass of flavored milk. If you want to make a shake, combine the mix, water, and 3–4 ice cubes in your blender, then process on BLEND till smooth.

A handy tip when making **healthy punch** for a party: Prepare a few extra cups of your chosen drink, freeze it in cubes in a couple of ice trays, then keep your punch from "watering down" by cooling it with punch cubes instead of ice cubes.

What should you do if you can't find the product listed in a

Healthy Exchanges recipe? You can substitute in some cases—use Lemon JELL-O if you can't find Hawaiian Pineapple, for example. But if you're determined to track down the product you need, and your own store manager hasn't been able to order it for you, why not use one of the new online grocers and order exactly what you need, no matter where you live. Try **http://www.netgrocer.com**

Not all low-fat cooking products are interchangeable, as one of my readers recently discovered when she tried to cook pancakes on her griddle using I Can't Believe It's Not Butter! spray—and they stuck! This butter-flavored spray is wonderful for a quick squirt on air-popped popcorn or corn on the cob, and it's great for topping your pancakes once they're cooked. In fact, my tastebuds have to check twice because it tastes so much like real butter! (And this is high praise from someone who once thought butter was the most perfect food ever created.)

But I Can't Believe It's Not Butter! doesn't work well for sautéing or browning. After trying to fry an egg with it and cooking up a disaster, I knew this product had its limitations. So I decided to continue using Pam or Weight Watchers butter-flavored cooking spray whenever I'm browning anything in a skillet or on a griddle.

Many of my readers have reported difficulty finding a product I use in many recipes: JELL-O cook-and-serve puddings. I have three suggestions for those of you with this problem:

1. **Work with your grocery store manager to get this product into your store,** and then make sure you and everyone you know buys it by the bagful! Products that sell well are reordered and kept in stock, especially with today's computerized cash registers that record what's purchased. You may also want to write or call Kraft General Foods and ask for their help. They can be reached at (800) 431–1001 weekdays from 9 A.M. to 4 P.M. (EST).

2. **You can prepare a recipe that calls for cook-and-serve pudding by using instant pudding of the same flavor.** Yes, that's right, you **can** cook with the instant when making my recipes. The finished product won't be quite as wonderful, but still at least a 3 on a 4-star scale. You can never do the opposite—never use cook-and-serve in a

recipe that calls for instant! One time at a cooking demonstration, I could not understand why my Blueberry Mountain Cheesecake never did set up. Then I spotted the box in the trash and noticed I'd picked the wrong type of pudding mix. Be careful—the boxes are both blue, but the instant has pudding on a silver spoon, and the cook-and-serve has a stream of milk running down the front into a bowl with a wooden spoon.

3. **You can make JO's Sugar-Free Vanilla Cook-and-Serve Pudding Mix instead of using JELL-O's.** Here's my recipe: 2 tablespoons cornstarch, ½ cup pourable Sugar Twin or Splenda, ⅔ cup Carnation Nonfat Dry Milk Powder, 1½ cups water, 2 teaspoons vanilla extract, and 4 to 5 drops yellow food coloring. Combine all this in a medium saucepan and cook over medium heat, stirring constantly, until the mixture comes to a full boil and thickens. This is for basic cooked vanilla sugar-free pudding. For a chocolate version, the recipe is 2 tablespoons cornstarch, ¼ cup pourable Sugar Twin or Splenda, 2 tablespoons sugar-free chocolate-flavored Nestlé's Quik, 1½ cups water, and 1 teaspoon vanilla extract. Follow the same cooking instructions as for the vanilla.

If you're preparing this as part of a recipe that also calls for adding a package of gelatin, just stir that into the mix.

Adapting a favorite family cake recipe? Here's something to try: Replace an egg and oil in the original with ⅓ cup fat-free yogurt and ¼ cup fat-free mayonnaise. Blend these two ingredients with your liquids in a separate bowl, then add the yogurt mixture to the flour mixture and mix gently just to combine. (You don't want to overmix or you'll release the gluten in the batter and end up with a tough batter.)

Want a tasty coffee creamer without all the fat? You could use Carnation's Fat Free Coffee-Mate, which is 10 calories per teaspoon, but if you drink several cups a day with several teaspoons each, that adds up quickly to nearly 100 calories a day! Why not try my version? It's not quite as creamy, but it is good. Simply combine ⅓ cup Carnation Nonfat Dry Milk Powder and ¼ cup Splenda or pourable Sugar Twin. Cover and store in your cupboard or refrigerator. At 3 calories per teaspoon, you can enjoy three teaspoons for less than the calories of one teaspoon of the purchased variety.

Some Helpful Hints

Sugar-free puddings and gelatins are important to many of my recipes, but if you prefer to avoid sugar substitutes, you could still prepare the recipes with regular puddings or gelatins. The calories would be higher, but you would still be cooking low-fat.

When a recipe calls for **chopped nuts** (and you only have whole ones), who wants to dirty the food processor just for a couple of tablespoonsful? You could try to chop them using your cutting board, but be prepared for bits and pieces to fly all over the kitchen. I use "Grandma's food processor." I take the biggest nuts I can find, put them in a small glass bowl, and chop them into chunks just the right size using a metal biscuit cutter.

To quickly **toast nuts** without any fuss, spread about ½ cup of nuts (any kind) in a glass pie plate and microwave on HIGH (100% power) for 6 to 7 minutes or until golden. Stir after the first 3 minutes, then after each minute until done. Store them in an airtight container in your refrigerator. Toasting nuts really brings out their flavor, so it seems as if you used a whole treeful instead of tiny amounts.

A quick hint about **reduced-fat peanut butter:** Don't store it in the refrigerator. Because the fat has been reduced, it won't spread as easily when it's cold. Keep it in your cupboard and a little will spread a lot further.

Crushing **graham crackers** for topping? A self-seal sandwich bag works great!

An eleven-year-old fan e-mailed me with a great tip recently: If you can't find the **mini chocolate chips** I use in many recipes, simply purchase the regular size and put them in a nut grinder to coarsely chop them.

If you have a **leftover muffin** and are looking for something a little different for breakfast, you can make **a "breakfast sundae."** Crumble the muffin into a cereal bowl. Sprinkle a serving of fresh fruit over it and top with a couple of tablespoons of plain fat-free yogurt sweetened with sugar substitute and your choice of extract. The thought of it just might make you jump out of bed with a smile on your face. (Speaking of muffins, did you know that if you fill the unused muffin wells with water when baking muffins, you help ensure more even baking and protect the muffin pan at the same time?) Another muffin hint: Lightly spray the inside of paper baking cups with butter-flavored cooking spray before spooning the muffin batter into them. Then you won't end up with paper clinging to your fresh-baked muffins.

The secret of making **good meringues** without sugar is to use 1 tablespoon of Splenda or pourable Sugar Twin for every egg white, and a small amount of extract. Use ½ to 1 teaspoon for the batch. Almond, vanilla, and coconut are all good choices. Use the same amount of cream of tartar you usually do. Bake the meringue in the same way. Even if you can't eat sugar, you can enjoy a healthy meringue pie when it's prepared *The Healthy Exchanges Way*. (Remember that egg whites whip up best at room temperature.)

Try **storing your Bisquick Reduced Fat Baking Mix** in the freezer. It won't freeze, and it *will* stay fresh much longer. (It works for coffee, doesn't it?)

To check if your **baking powder** is fresh, put 1 teaspoonful in a bowl and pour 2 tablespoons of very hot tap water over it. If it's fresh, it will bubble very actively. If it doesn't bubble, then it's time to replace your old can with a new one.

If you've ever wondered about **changing ingredients** in one of my recipes, the answer is that some things can be changed to suit your family's tastes, but others should not be tampered with. **Don't change**: the amount of flour, bread crumbs, reduced-fat baking mix, baking soda, baking powder, or liquid or dry milk powder. And if I include a small amount of salt, it's necessary for the recipe to turn out correctly. **What you can change**: an extract flavor (if you don't like coconut, choose vanilla or almond instead), a spreadable fruit flavor, the type of fruit in a pie filling (but be careful about substituting fresh for frozen and vice versa—sometimes it works, but it may not), the flavor of pudding or gelatin. As long as package sizes and amounts are the same, go for it. It will never hurt my feelings if you change a recipe, so please your family—don't worry about me!

Because I always say that "good enough" isn't good enough for me anymore, here's a way to make your cup of **fat-free and sugar-**

free hot cocoa more special. After combining the hot chocolate mix and hot water, stir in ½ teaspoon vanilla extract and a light sprinkle of cinnamon. If you really want to feel decadent, add a tablespoon of Cool Whip Lite. Isn't life grand?

If you must limit your sugar intake, but you love the idea of sprinkling **powdered sugar** on dessert crepes or burritos, here's a pretty good substitute: Place 1 cup Splenda or pourable Sugar Twin and 1 teaspoon cornstarch in a blender container, then cover and process on HIGH until the mixture resembles powdered sugar in texture, about 45 to 60 seconds. Store in an airtight container and use whenever you want a dusting of "powdered sugar" on any dessert.

Want my "almost instant" pies to set up even more quickly? Do as one of my readers does: Freeze your Keebler piecrusts. Then, when you stir up one of my pies and pour the filling into the frozen crust, it sets up within seconds.

Some of my "island-inspired" recipes call for **rum or brandy extracts**, which provide the "essence" of liquor without the real thing. I'm a teetotaler by choice, so I choose not to include real liquor in any of my recipes. Extracts are cheaper than liquor and you won't feel the need to shoo your kids away from the goodies. If you prefer not to use liquor extracts in your cooking, you can always substitute vanilla extract.

Did you know you can make your own single-serving bags of microwave popcorn? Spoon 2 tablespoons of popping kernels into a paper lunch bag, folding the top over twice to seal and placing the sealed bag in the microwave. Microwave on HIGH for 2 to 3 minutes, or until the popping stops. Then pour the popcorn into a large bowl and lightly spritz with I Can't Believe It's Not Butter! Spray. You'll have 3 cups of virtually fat-free popcorn to munch on at a fraction of the price of purchased microwave popcorn.

Some Healthy Cooking Challenges and How I Solved 'Em

When you stir up one of my pie fillings, do you ever have a problem with **lumps?** Here's an easy solution for all of you "careful" cooks out there. Lumps occur when the pudding starts to set up before you can get the dry milk powder incorporated into the mixture. I always advise you to dump, pour, and stir fast with that wire whisk, letting no more than 30 seconds elapse from beginning to end.

But if you are still having problems, you can always combine the dry milk powder and the water in a separate bowl before adding the pudding mix and whisking quickly. Why don't I suggest this right from the beginning? Because that would mean an extra dish to wash every time—and you know I hate to wash dishes! With a little practice and a light touch, you should soon get the hang of my original method. But now you've got an alternative way to lose those lumps!

I love the chemistry of foods, and so I've gotten great pleasure from analyzing what makes fat-free products tick. By dissecting these "miracle" products, I've learned how to make them work best. They require different handling than the high-fat products we're used to, but if treated properly, these slimmed-down versions can produce delicious results!

Fat-free sour cream: This product is wonderful on a hot baked potato, but have you noticed that it tends to be much gummier than regular sour cream? If you want to use it in a stroganoff dish or baked product, you must stir a tablespoon or two of fat-free milk into the fat-free sour cream before adding it to other ingredients.

Cool Whip Free: When the fat went out of the formula, air was stirred in to fill the void. So, if you stir it too vigorously, you release the air and *decrease* the volume. Handle it with kid gloves—gently. Since the manufacturer forgot to ask for my input, I'll share with you how to make it taste almost the same as it used to. Let the container thaw in the refrigerator, then ever so gently stir in 1 teaspoon vanilla extract. Now, put the lid back on and enjoy it a tablespoon at a time, the same way you did Cool Whip Lite.

Fat-free cream cheese: When the fat was removed from this product, water replaced it. So don't ever use an electric mixer on the fat-free version, or you risk releasing the water and having your finished product look more like dip than cheesecake! Stirring it gently with a sturdy spoon in a glass bowl with a handle will soften it just as much as it needs to be. (A glass bowl with a handle lets you see what's going on; the handle gives you control as you stir. This "user-friendly" method is good for tired cooks, young cooks, and cooks with arthritis!) And don't be alarmed if the cream cheese gets caught in your wire whisk when you start combining the pudding mix and other ingredients. Just keep knocking it back down into the bowl by hitting the whisk against the rim of the bowl, and as you continue blending, it will soften even more and drop off the whisk. When it's time to pour the filling into your crust, your whisk shouldn't have anything much clinging to it.

Reduced-fat margarine: Again, the fat was replaced by water. If you try to use the reduced-fat kind in your cookie recipe spoon for spoon, you will end up with a cakelike cookie instead of the crisp kind most of us enjoy. You have to take into consideration that some water will be released as the product bakes. Use less liquid than the recipe calls for (when re-creating family recipes *only*—I've figured that into Healthy Exchanges recipes). And never, never, never use fat-*free* margarine and expect anyone to ask for seconds!

When every minute counts, and you need 2 cups cooked noodles for a casserole, how do you **figure out how much of a box of pasta to prepare**? Here's a handy guide that should help. While your final amount might vary slightly because of how loosely or tightly you "stuff" your measuring cup, this will make life easier.

Type	Start with this amount uncooked	If you want this amount cooked
Noodles	1 cup	1 cup
(thin, medium,	1¼ cups	1½ cups
wide, and mini	1¾ cups	2 cups
lasagne)	2¼ cups	2½ cups
	2½ cups	3 cups
Macaroni	⅓ cup	½ cup
(medium shells	⅔ cup	1 cup
and elbow)	1 cup	1½ cups
	1⅓ cups	2 cups
	2 cups	3 cups
Spaghetti,	¾ cup	1 cup
fettuccine,	1 cup	1½ cups
and rotini	1½ cups	2 cups
pasta	2½ cups	3 cups

Type	Start with this amount uncooked	If you want this amount cooked
Rice (instant)	⅓ cup	½ cup
	⅔ cup	1 cup
	1 cup	1½ cups
	1⅓ cups	2 cups
	2 cups	3 cups
Rice (regular)	¼ cup	½ cup
	½ cup	1 cup
	1 cup	2 cups
	1½ cups	3 cups

Here's a handy idea for **keeping your cookbooks open** to a certain page while cooking: Use two rubber bands, one wrapped vertically around the left side of the book, another on the right side. And to **keep your cookbooks clean**, try slipping the rubber-banded book into a gallon-sized Ziploc bag. (Though I'd consider it a compliment to know that the pages of my cookbooks were all splattered, because it would mean that you are really using the recipes!)

Homemade or Store-Bought?

I've been asked which is better for you: homemade from scratch or purchased foods. My answer is *both!* Each has a place in a healthy lifestyle, and what that place is has everything to do with you.

Take **piecrusts**, for instance. If you love spending your spare time in the kitchen preparing foods, and you're using low-fat, low-sugar, and reasonably low-sodium ingredients, go for it! But if, like so many people, your time is limited and you've learned to read labels, you could be better off using purchased foods.

I know that when I prepare a pie (and I experiment with a couple of pies each week, because this is Cliff's favorite dessert), I use a purchased crust. Why? Mainly because I can't make a good-tasting piecrust that is lower in fat than the brands I use. Also, purchased piecrusts fit my rule of "If it takes longer to fix than to eat, forget it!"

I've checked the nutrient information for the purchased piecrusts against recipes for traditional and "diet" piecrusts, using my computer software program. The purchased crust calculated lower in both fat and calories! I have tried some low-fat and low-sugar recipes, but they just didn't spark my tastebuds, or were so complicated you needed an engineering degree just to get the crust in the pie plate.

I'm very happy with the purchased piecrusts in my recipes, because the finished product rarely, if ever, has more than 30 percent of total calories coming from fats. I also believe that we have to prepare foods our families and friends will eat with us on a regular basis and not feel deprived, or we've wasted time, energy, and money.

I could use a purchased "lite" **pie filling**, but instead I make my own. Here I can save both fat and sugar, and still make the filling almost as fast as opening a can. The bottom line: Know what you have to spend when it comes to both time and fat/sugar calories, then make the best decision you can for you and your family. And don't go without an occasional piece of pie because you think it isn't *necessary*. A delicious pie prepared in a healthy way is one of the simple pleasures of life. It's a little thing, but it can make all the difference between just getting by with the bare minimum and living a full and healthy lifestyle.

I'm sure you'll add to this list of cooking tips as you begin preparing Healthy Exchanges recipes and discover how easy it can be to adapt your own favorite recipes using these ideas and your own common sense.

A Peek into My Pantry and My Favorite Brands

Everyone asks me what foods I keep on hand and what brands I use. There are lots of good products on the grocery shelves today—many more than we dreamed about even a year or two ago. And I can't wait to see what's out there 12 months from now. The following are my staples and, where appropriate, my favorites *at this time.* I feel these products are healthier, tastier, easy to get—and deliver the most flavor for the least amount of fat, sugar, or calories. If you find others you like as well or better, please use them. This is only a guide to make your grocery shopping and cooking easier.

***Following this list, you'll find my list of nonperishable ingredients that make cooking on the go a pleasure!

Fat-free plain yogurt (*Dannon*)
Nonfat dry milk powder (*Carnation*)
Evaporated fat-free milk (*Carnation*)
Fat-free milk
Fat-free cottage cheese
Fat-free cream cheese (*Philadelphia*)
Fat-free mayonnaise (*Kraft*)
Fat-free salad dressings (*Kraft and Hendrickson's*)
No-fat sour cream (*Land O Lakes*)
Reduced-calorie margarine (*I Can't Believe It's Not Butter! Light*)
Cooking sprays
    Olive oil–flavored (*Pam*)

Butter-flavored (Pam)
Butter-flavored for spritzing after cooking (I Can't Believe
It's Not Butter)
Cooking oil (Puritan Canola Oil)
Reduced-calorie whipped topping (Cool Whip Lite or Cool
Whip Free)
Sugar substitute:
White sugar substitute (Splenda)
Brown sugar substitute (Brown Sugar Twin)
Sugar-free gelatin and pudding mixes (JELL-O)
Baking mix (Bisquick Reduced Fat)
Pancake mix (Aunt Jemima Reduced Calorie)
Sugar-free pancake syrup (Log Cabin or Cary's)
Parmesan cheese (Kraft Reduced Fat Parmesan Style Grated
Topping)
Reduced-fat cheese (shredded and sliced) (Kraft 2% Reduced
Fat)
Shredded frozen potatoes (Mr. Dell's or Ore Ida)
Spreadable fruit spread (Welch's or Smucker's)
Peanut butter (Peter Pan reduced-fat, Jif reduced-fat, or Skippy
reduced-fat)
Chicken broth (Healthy Request)
Beef broth (Swanson)
Tomato sauce (Hunt's)
Canned soups (Healthy Request)
Reduced sodium tomato juice
Reduced sodium ketchup
Piecrust
Unbaked (Pillsbury—in dairy case)
Graham cracker, shortbread, and chocolate (Keebler)
Crescent rolls (Pillsbury Reduced Fat)
Pastrami and corned beef (Carl Buddig Lean)
Luncheon meats (Healthy Choice or Oscar Mayer)
Ham (Dubuque 97% fat-free and reduced-sodium or Healthy
Choice)
Bacon bits (Hormel or Oscar Mayer)
Kielbasa sausage and frankfurters (Healthy Choice or Oscar
Mayer Light)
Canned white chicken, packed in water (Swanson)

Canned tuna, packed in water (Starkist)
95 to 97 percent ground sirloin beef or turkey breast
Crackers (Nabisco Soda Fat Free and Ritz Reduced Fat)
Reduced-calorie bread—40 calories per slice or less
Small hamburger buns—80 calories per bun
Rice—instant, regular, brown, and wild (Minute Rice)
Instant potato flakes
Noodles, spaghetti, macaroni, and rotini pasta
Salsa
Pickle relish—dill, sweet, and hot dog
Mustard—Dijon, prepared yellow, and spicy
Unsweetened apple and orange juice
Reduced-calorie cranberry juice cocktail (Ocean Spray)
Unsweetened applesauce (Musselman's)
Fruit—fresh, frozen (no sugar added), and canned in juice
Pie filling (Lucky Leaf No Sugar Added Cherry and Apple)
Spices (JO's Spices or any national brand)
Vinegar—cider and distilled white
Lemon and lime juice (in small plastic fruit-shaped bottles
   found in the produce section)
Instant fruit beverage mixes (Crystal Light)
Sugar-free hot chocolate beverage mixes (Swiss Miss or
   Nesquik)
Sugar-free and fat-free ice cream (Wells' Blue Bunny)

The items on my shopping list are everyday foods found in just about any grocery store in America. But all are as low in fat, sugar, calories, and sodium as I can find—and still taste good! I can make any recipe in my cookbooks and newsletters as long as I have my cupboards and refrigerator stocked with these items. Whenever I use the last of any one item, I just make sure I pick up another supply the next time I'm at the store.

If your grocer does not stock these items, why not ask if they can be ordered on a trial basis? If the store agrees to do so, be sure to tell your friends to stop by, so that sales are good enough to warrant restocking the new products. Competition for shelf space is fierce, so only products that sell well stay around.

The Healthy Exchanges Kitchen

When I first started creating Healthy Exchanges recipes, I had a tiny galley kitchen with room for only one person. But it never stopped me from feeling the sky was the limit when it came to seeking out great healthy taste! Even though I have a bigger kitchen now, what I learned in those early days still holds true. I'll say it again: Don't waste space on equipment you don't really need. Here's a list of what I consider worth having (in addition to your double-sided electric contact grill, of course!). You can probably find most of what you need at a local discount store or garage sale. You'll find you can prepare healthy, quick, and delicious food with just the "basics."

Kitchen Equipment Recommendations

Good-quality nonstick skillet (10-inch with a lid)
Good-quality nonstick saucepans (small, medium, large, with lids) (If you choose all Teflon-coated pans and skillets, your clean-up time will be greatly reduced.)
An electric skillet is a nice addition.
8-by-8-inch baking dish
Disposable aluminum 9-by-9-inch baking pans
Rimmed cookie sheet (make sure it fits into YOUR oven with room to spare)
Heavy duty plastic set of 3 mixing bowls (the kind that nest inside each other)

Empty Cool Whip Lite containers and lids for refrigerator
   food storage
Plastic liquid measuring cups (1-cup and 4-cup)
Sharp knives (paring and butcher)
Cutting board
Rubber spatulas
Wire whisk
Measuring spoons
Dry measuring cups
Large slotted spoon
Tea kettle
Vegetable parer
Wire racks
Covered jar
Kitchen timer
Can opener

You're stocked, you're set—let's go!

The Recipes

How to Read a Healthy Exchanges Recipe

The Healthy Exchanges Nutritional Analysis

Before using these recipes, you may wish to consult your physician or health-care provider to be sure they are appropriate for you. The information in this book is not intended to take the place of any medical advice. It reflects my experiences, studies, research, and opinions regarding healthy eating.

Each recipe includes nutritional information calculated in three ways:

> Healthy Exchanges Weight Loss Choices™ or Exchanges
> Calories; Fat, Protein, Carbohydrates, and Fiber in grams;
>   Sodium and Calcium in milligrams
> Diabetic Exchanges

In every Healthy Exchanges recipe, the Diabetic Exchanges have been calculated by a registered dietitian. All the other calculations were done by computer, using the Food Processor II software. When the ingredient listing gives more than one choice, the first ingredient listed is the one used in the recipe analysis. Due to inevitable variations in the ingredients you choose to use, the nutritional values should be considered approximate.

The annotation "(limited)" following Protein counts in some recipes indicates that consumption of whole eggs should be limited to four per week.

Please note the following symbols:

☆ This star means that you should read the recipe's directions carefully for special instructions about **division** of ingredients.

❋ This symbol indicates **FREEZES WELL.**

Savory Soups

D o you find yourself saying, "If I only had the time, I'd make delicious homemade soups all year long"? Hearty, healthy soups remind us of cozy kitchens and the warmth of family, but many recipes—with their long lists of ingredients and cooking steps—may seem like just too much trouble. How can I make preparing soup from scratch worth your while? How can I get you to choose homemade over convenient canned soups? Well, it will require a little extra ingenuity on my part, but I've always liked a challenge. Here, with the help of the manufacturers who've brought slow cookers into the twenty-first century, I'm ready to demonstrate just how simple and scrumptious soup can be!

No matter what cuisine you choose, soup is a wonderful way to start a meal or make a meal complete. For a taste of Tuscany, my **Italian Cream of Tomato Soup** is almost as good as a plane ticket, and **James's Pastafazool** is as satisfying to eat as it is to say! For an Oktoberfest revel that has nothing to do with beer gardens, try my **Bavarian Borscht**, and then compare it with my **Iowa-Style Borscht** for a celebration of flavors that easily crosses national borders. And if your heart does somersaults at the idea of inviting friends over for a chili cookoff, you're all set with my **Nothing-to-It Chili**, my **Beefy Chili**, and, oh yes, **Hawaiian Chili!**

Creamy Mushroom Soup

For years, nutritionists have warned us that if something on a menu says "creamy," avoid it—or expect to increase your hips and your risk of a heart attack! Well, here's my gift for fans of soups so luscious and creamy they make you feel guilty with every spoonful you devour: a rich but utterly "sinless" mushroom soup that's downright irresistible!   ☻   Serves 4 (1 cup)

> 1 (10¾-ounce) can Cream of Mushroom Soup
> 1½ cups (one 12-fluid-ounce can) Carnation Evaporated Skim Milk
> 3 cups chopped fresh mushrooms
> ½ cup finely chopped onion
> ¼ teaspoon dried minced garlic
> ½ teaspoon dried basil

Spray a slow cooker container with butter-flavored cooking spray. In prepared container, combine mushroom soup and evaporated skim milk. Stir in mushrooms, onion, garlic, and basil. Cover and cook on LOW for 6 to 8 hours. Mix well before serving.

Each serving equals:

HE: 1 Vegetable • ¾ Skim Milk • ½ Slider •
5 Optional Calories

---

138 Calories • 2 gm Fat • 8 gm Protein •
22 gm Carbohydrate • 418 mg Sodium •
314 mg Calcium • 1 gm Fiber

DIABETIC: 1 Vegetable • 1 Skim Milk •
½ Starch/Carbohydrate

Potato Corn Chowder

As a native Iowan, I've created more corn chowder recipes than anyone else I know! But I'm always thinking about how to make my "state soup" even more delicious—and here's my latest brainstorm, a meal-in-a-bowl full of potatoes and just a hint of bacon.

● Serves 6 (1 cup)

> 1 cup (one 8-ounce can) cream-style corn
> 1 cup frozen whole-kernel corn, thawed
> 1½ cups (one 12-fluid-ounce can) Carnation Evaporated Skim Milk
> ½ cup Land O Lakes Fat Free Half & Half
> 1½ cups diced cooked potatoes
> ½ cup finely chopped celery
> 1 cup chopped onion
> 6 tablespoons Hormel Bacon Bits
> ⅛ teaspoon black pepper

Spray a slow cooker container with butter-flavored cooking spray. In prepared container, combine cream-style corn, whole-kernel corn, evaporated skim milk, and half & half. Stir in potatoes, celery, and onion. Add bacon bits and black pepper. Mix well to combine. Cover and cook on HIGH for 2 hours. Mix well before serving.

HINT: Thaw whole-kernel corn by placing in a colander and rinsing under hot water for one minute.

Each serving equals:

HE: 1 Bread • ½ Vegetable • ½ Skim Milk • ½ Slider • 3 Optional Calories

187 Calories • 3 gm Fat • 10 gm Protein • 30 gm Carbohydrate • 467 mg Sodium • 207 mg Calcium • 2 gm Fiber

DIABETIC: 1½ Starch • ½ Skim Milk • ½ Vegetable

Zucchini Tomato Rice Soup

Of course I grow zucchini—doesn't everyone? Or maybe it just seems that way, since this healthy green squash appears to be in endless supply! I suggest this savory partnership with tomatoes makes a winning combination, especially when you add Parmesan cheese just before serving.　●　Serves 6 (1 cup)

1 (10¾-ounce) can Healthy Request Tomato Soup

1 cup (one 8-ounce can) tomatoes, finely chopped and undrained

1 cup reduced-sodium tomato juice

1½ cups (one 12-fluid-ounce can) Carnation Evaporated Skim Milk

1½ cups chopped unpeeled zucchini

1 cup chopped onion

⅓ cup uncooked instant rice

1 tablespoon pourable Splenda or Sugar Twin

1 teaspoon dried basil leaves

6 tablespoons grated Kraft fat-free Parmesan cheese

Spray a slow cooker container with olive oil–flavored cooking spray. In prepared container, combine tomato soup, undrained tomatoes, tomato juice, and evaporated skim milk. Stir in zucchini and onion. Add uncooked rice, Splenda, and basil. Mix well to combine. Cover and cook on HIGH for 3 to 4 hours. Mix well before serving. When serving, top each bowl with 1 tablespoon Parmesan cheese.

Each serving equals:

HE: 1½ Vegetable • ½ Skim Milk • ½ Slider • ¼ Protein • 3 Optional Calories

168 Calories • 2 gm Fat • 7 gm Protein • 30 gm Carbohydrate • 420 mg Sodium • 220 mg Calcium • 2 gm Fiber

DIABETIC: 1½ Vegetable • 1 Starch • ½ Skim Milk

Frenchy Green Bean Soup

Cliff's favorite veggies, green beans, are often on my mind as we head out in the car. He does the driving, I do the recipe creating—and this one was born to warm his heart (and the rest of him, too!). It's rich and creamy, and it shows off the French-style green bean in a fresh and fun way. ☻ Serves 6 (1½ cups)

> 1 (10¾-ounce) can Healthy Request Tomato Soup
> 1½ cups (one 12-fluid-ounce can) Carnation Evaporated Skim Milk
> 1 cup (one 8-ounce can) tomatoes, finely chopped and undrained
> 4 cups (two 16-ounce cans) French-style green beans, rinsed and drained
> 1 cup cooked noodles, rinsed and drained
> ½ cup (2 ounces) cubed Velveeta Light processed cheese
> 1½ teaspoons dried parsley flakes
> ⅛ teaspoon black pepper

Spray a slow cooker container with butter-flavored cooking spray. In prepared container, combine tomato soup, evaporated skim milk, and undrained tomatoes. Stir in green beans and noodles. Add Velveeta cheese, parsley flakes, and black pepper. Mix well to combine. Cover and cook on HIGH for 3 to 4 hours. Mix well before serving.

HINT: Usually a scant 1 cup uncooked noodles cooks to about 1 cup.

Each serving equals:

HE: 1½ Vegetable • ½ Skim Milk • ⅓ Bread •
⅓ Protein • ¼ Slider • 10 Optional Calories

---

166 Calories • 2 gm Fat • 9 gm Protein •
28 gm Carbohydrate • 905 mg Sodium •
247 mg Calcium • 3 gm Fiber

DIABETIC: 1½ Vegetable • 1 Starch/Carbohydrate •
½ Skim Milk

Iowa-Style Borscht

"But wait," I can hear you saying as you read the list of ingredients for this soup, "there aren't any beets!" Can you make a borscht that doesn't include them, you may wonder. Well, in Iowa, you can—as long as you stir in some corn. Borscht is a traditional Russian beet soup, but its true identity is that of a rosy vegetable soup, and here tomatoes take the place of beets.   ☻   Serves 6 (1½ cups)

1¾ cups (one 14.5-ounce can) diced tomatoes, undrained

1½ cups reduced-sodium tomato juice

2 tablespoons pourable Splenda or Sugar Twin

1½ teaspoons dried parsley flakes

½ teaspoon dried basil

3 cups shredded cabbage

1½ cups finely chopped carrots

½ cup finely chopped onion

2 cups finely chopped unpeeled raw potatoes

1 cup frozen whole-kernel corn, thawed

Spray a slow cooker container with butter-flavored cooking spray. In prepared container, combine undrained tomatoes, tomato juice, Splenda, parsley flakes, and basil. Add cabbage, carrots, onion, and potatoes. Mix well to combine. Stir in corn. Cover and cook on LOW for 8 hours. Mix well before serving.

HINT: Thaw corn by placing in a colander and rinsing under hot water for 1 minute.

Each serving equals:

HE: 2 Vegetable • ⅔ Bread • 2 Optional Calories

---

128 Calories • 0 gm Fat • 4 gm Protein •
28 gm Carbohydrate • 231 mg Sodium •
55 mg Calcium • 4 gm Fiber

DIABETIC: 2 Vegetable • 1 Starch

Tuscan Bean Soup

A summer supper in Tuscany often consists of little more than a hearty bowl of bean soup (like this one) and a hunk of crusty fresh bread. Even if your passport has never been stamped "Italy," you can journey there in spirit when you dine on this high-fiber soup that delivers "delicioso" flavor in every spoonful!

○ Serves 6 (1⅓ cups)

> 20 ounces (two 16-ounce cans) great northern beans,
>   rinsed and drained
> 1½ cups chopped onion
> 1 (10¾-ounce) can Healthy Request Tomato Soup
> 1¾ cups (one 14.5-ounce can) diced tomatoes, undrained
> 1¼ cups reduced-sodium tomato juice
> ¼ cup Kraft Fat Free Italian Dressing
> ¼ teaspoon dried minced garlic

Spray a slow cooker container with olive oil–flavored cooking spray. In prepared container, combine great northern beans and onion. Add tomato soup, undrained tomatoes, and tomato juice. Mix well to combine. Stir in Italian dressing and garlic. Cover and cook on LOW for 6 to 8 hours. Mix well before serving.

Each serving equals:

HE: 1½ Vegetable • 1 Bread • 1 Protein •
¼ Slider • 14 Optional Calories

---

189 Calories • 1 gm Fat • 9 gm Protein •
36 gm Carbohydrate • 503 mg Sodium •
78 mg Calcium • 6 gm Fiber

DIABETIC: 1½ Vegetable • 1½ Starch • 1 Meat

Italian Cream of Tomato Soup

If you grew up enjoying lunches of tomato soup and a sandwich, you're about ready to experience a remarkable flavorfest that will launch you into a new millennium of taste! The magic involves some spices and handy canned tomatoes, along with my favorite secret ingredient for making cream soups (evaporated skim milk).

○ Serves 6 (1 cup)

> 1 (10¾-ounce) can Healthy Request Tomato Soup
> 1¾ cups (one 14.5-ounce can) diced tomatoes, undrained
> 1¼ cups reduced-sodium tomato juice
> 1½ cups (one 12-fluid-ounce can) Carnation Evaporated Skim Milk
> 1 cup finely chopped onion
> ½ cup (one 2.5-ounce jar) sliced mushrooms, drained
> 1½ teaspoons Italian seasoning
> ⅛ teaspoon black pepper

Spray a slow cooker container with olive oil–flavored cooking spray. In prepared container, combine tomato soup, undrained tomatoes, tomato juice, and evaporated skim milk. Stir in onion, mushrooms, Italian seasoning, and black pepper. Cover and cook on LOW for 4 to 6 hours. Mix well before serving.

Each serving equals:

> HE: 1½ Vegetable • ½ Skim Milk • ¼ Slider •
> 10 Optional Calories
>
> ---
>
> 129 Calories • 1 gm Fat • 6 gm Protein •
> 24 gm Carbohydrate • 511 mg Sodium •
> 182 mg Calcium • 2 gm Fiber
>
> ---
>
> DIABETIC: 1½ Vegetable • ½ Skim Milk •
> ½ Starch/Carbohydrate

Old World Minestrone

One of the true pleasures of minestrone soup is what I like to think of as a hunt for treasure—the joyful discovery in every spoonful of the varied ingredients that join hands to make this peasant dish truly soul-satisfying. The hunt is on—go for it!

◐ Serves 6 (1⅓ cups)

2 cups (one 16-ounce can) Healthy Request Chicken Broth
1½ cups reduced-sodium tomato juice
1¾ cups (one 14.5-ounce can) diced tomatoes, undrained
1½ cups shredded carrots
1 cup chopped celery
½ cup frozen peas, thawed
1 cup diced raw potatoes
1 cup chopped onion
⅓ cup uncooked tiny shell pasta
1½ teaspoons Italian seasoning
1½ cups finely shredded fresh spinach

Spray a slow cooker container with olive oil–flavored cooking spray. In prepared container, combine chicken broth, tomato juice, and undrained tomatoes. Stir in carrots, celery, peas, potatoes, and onion. Add uncooked shell pasta and Italian seasoning. Mix well to combine. Cover and cook on LOW for 8 hours. Just before serving, stir in spinach.

HINT: Thaw peas by placing in a colander and rinsing under hot water for one minute.

Each serving equals:

HE: 2½ Vegetable • ½ Bread • 5 Optional Calories

104 Calories • 0 gm Fat • 4 gm Protein • 22 gm Carbohydrate • 378 mg Sodium • 42 mg Calcium • 4 gm Fiber

DIABETIC: 2 Vegetable • ½ Starch

Thick and Hearty Minestrone

Minestrone is a great kitchen-sink kind of soup—the experienced cook tosses in bits and pieces of all kinds of vegetables, confident that the end result will be a magnificent mélange of flavors sure to please every palate. The beans add healthy protein and even more fiber, for a dish just right for a chilly winter night.

☻ Serves 6 (1½ cups)

> 1¾ cups (one 14½-ounce can) Swanson Beef Broth
>
> 1 cup (one 8-ounce can) Hunt's Tomato Sauce
>
> 1 cup reduced-sodium tomato juice
>
> 1 cup water
>
> 1 cup (one 8-ounce can) tomatoes, finely chopped and undrained
>
> ½ cup chopped onion
>
> 1½ cups thinly sliced carrots
>
> 1 cup chopped celery
>
> ½ cup chopped red bell pepper
>
> 1 cup sliced unpeeled zucchini
>
> 10 ounces (one 16-ounce can) red kidney beans, rinsed and drained
>
> 1 cup uncooked instant rice
>
> 1½ teaspoons Italian seasoning
>
> ¼ cup (¾ ounce) grated Kraft fat-free Parmesan cheese
>
> 1 tablespoon pourable Splenda or Sugar Twin

Spray a slow cooker container with olive oil–flavored cooking spray. In prepared container, combine beef broth, tomato sauce, tomato juice, water, and undrained tomatoes. Add onion, carrots, celery, red pepper, zucchini, kidney beans, and uncooked rice. Mix well to combine. Stir in Italian seasoning, Parmesan cheese, and Splenda. Cover and cook on LOW for 6 to 8 hours. Mix well before serving.

Each serving equals:

HE: 2½ Vegetable • 1 Bread • ½ Protein •
6 Optional Calories

170 Calories • 2 gm Fat • 6 gm Protein •
32 gm Carbohydrate • 806 mg Sodium •
77 mg Calcium • 6 gm Fiber

DIABETIC: 2 Vegetable • 1½ Starch • 1 Meat

Vegetable Rice Soup with Bacon

If you're a bacon lover (and there are many of us around), you know that just a bit of this richly flavored smoked meat packs a lot of taste in every mouthful. But who wants to cook up a slice or two of bacon from scratch every time you want that great flavor? As long as you keep a jar of real bacon bits in your refrigerator, you can enjoy it often and with ease!   ☻   Serves 4 (1½ cups)

1¾ cups (one 14.5-ounce can)
    diced tomatoes, undrained
2½ cups reduced-sodium
    tomato juice
1 cup frozen cut green beans,
    thawed
¾ cup chopped onion
1 cup chopped celery

1 cup frozen sliced carrots,
    thawed
⅓ cup uncooked instant rice
¼ cup Hormel Bacon Bits
2 tablespoons pourable Splenda
    or Sugar Twin
1 teaspoon dried parsley flakes

Spray a slow cooker container with butter-flavored cooking spray. In prepared container, combine undrained tomatoes and tomato juice. Stir in green beans, onion, celery, and carrots. Add uncooked rice, bacon bits, Splenda, and parsley flakes. Mix well to combine. Cover and cook on LOW for 8 hours. Mix well before serving.

HINT: Thaw green beans and carrots by placing in a colander and rinsing under hot water for one minute.

Each serving equals:

HE: 3½ Vegetable • ¼ Bread • ¼ Slider •
6 Optional Calories

148 Calories • 2 gm Fat • 6 gm Protein •
26 gm Carbohydrate • 608 mg Sodium •
68 mg Calcium • 5 gm Fiber

DIABETIC: 3 Vegetable • ½ Starch • ½ Meat

Bavarian Borscht

It's amazing how a few little additions to a traditional recipe can alert your tastebuds that something special is passing by. In the case of this beet soup, I've taken a Russian recipe and woven in some German delights by adding cabbage and caraway seeds. I think you'll be surprised to taste what a difference it makes!

◐ Serves 4 (1¼ cups)

> 1¾ cups (one 14½-ounce can) Swanson Beef Broth
> 2 cups (one 16-ounce can) beets, coarsely chopped, drained, and
>   ¼ cup liquid reserved
> 3 cups shredded cabbage
> 1 cup chopped onion
> 1½ cups diced cooked potatoes
> 1 tablespoon pourable Splenda or Sugar Twin
> ½ teaspoon caraway seed
> ⅛ teaspoon black pepper
> ¼ cup Land O Lakes No-Fat Sour Cream

Spray a slow cooker container with butter-flavored cooking spray. In prepared container, combine beef broth and reserved beet juice. Stir in beets, cabbage, onion, and potatoes. Add Splenda, caraway seed, and black pepper. Mix well to combine. Cover and cook on LOW for 6 to 8 hours. Mix well before serving. When serving, top each bowl with 1 tablespoon sour cream.

Each serving equals:

HE: 2¼ Vegetable • ½ Bread • ¼ Slider • 4 Optional Calories

---

133 Calories • 1 gm Fat • 4 gm Protein • 27 gm Carbohydrate • 506 mg Sodium • 76 mg Calcium • 4 gm Fiber

---

DIABETIC: 2 Vegetable • 1 Starch

Cheesy Tuna Noodle Chowder

A recent health news report informed us that even eating fish once or twice a month can have a valuable effect on our health, so that's yet another good reason to put this "fishy" chowder on your menu sometime soon. Because I've added lots of tuna and noodles to the pot, you'll feel supremely satisfied—and energized, too!

○ Serves 6 (1 cup)

> 1 (10¾-ounce) can Healthy Request Cream of
>   Mushroom Soup
> 1½ cups (one 12-fluid-ounce can) Carnation Evaporated
>   Skim Milk
> ¾ cup water
> 2 (6-ounce) cans white tuna, packed in water,
>   drained and flaked
> 1 cup frozen peas, thawed
> ¼ cup (one 2-ounce jar) chopped pimiento, drained
> 1 cup diced Velveeta Light processed cheese
> 2 cups cooked noodles, rinsed and drained
> 1 teaspoon dried onion flakes
> 1 teaspoon dried parsley flakes
> ⅛ teaspoon black pepper

Spray a slow cooker container with butter-flavored cooking spray. In prepared container, combine mushroom soup, evaporated skim milk, and water. Stir in tuna, peas, and pimiento. Add Velveeta cheese, noodles, onion flakes, parsley flakes, and black pepper. Mix well to combine. Cover and cook on HIGH for 3 to 4 hours. Mix well before serving.

HINTS: 1. Thaw peas by placing in a colander and rinsing under hot water for 1 minute.
2. Usually 1¾ cups uncooked noodles cooks to about 2 cups.

Each serving equals:

HE: 2 Protein • 1 Bread • ½ Skim Milk • ¼ Slider • 7 Optional Calories

261 Calories • 5 gm Fat • 24 gm Protein • 30 gm Carbohydrate • 765 mg Sodium • 329 mg Calcium • 2 gm Fiber

DIABETIC: 2½ Meat • 1½ Starch • ½ Skim Milk

Becky's Burrito Chicken Soup

My daughter loves the tangy tastes of Mexican cooking, so for her I've created a bit of "Olé" in a bowl—the scrumptious flavor of burritos in a thick, rich chicken soup that's sure to please every busy mom (and dad) out there!   ☻   Serves 6 (1 full cup)

> 2 cups (one 16-ounce can) Healthy Request
>   Chicken Broth
> 1 (10¾-ounce) can Healthy Request Cream of
>   Chicken Soup
> 1 cup (one 8-ounce can) stewed tomatoes, coarsely chopped
>   and undrained
> 1½ cups frozen whole-kernel corn, thawed
> ½ cup chopped red bell pepper
> ½ cup chopped green bell pepper
> 1 cup chopped onion
> 2 full cups (12 ounces) diced cooked chicken breast
> 6 ounces (one 8-ounce can) red kidney beans,
>   rinsed and drained
> 2 teaspoons taco seasoning
> ⅛ teaspoon black pepper

Spray a slow cooker container with butter-flavored cooking spray. In prepared container, combine chicken broth, chicken soup, and undrained stewed tomatoes. Stir in corn, red bell pepper, green bell pepper, and onion. Add chicken, kidney beans, taco seasoning, and black pepper. Mix well to combine. Cover and cook on LOW for 6 to 8 hours. Mix well before serving.

HINTS: 1. Thaw corn by placing it in a colander and rinsing under hot water for 1 minute.
      2. If you don't have leftovers, purchase a chunk of cooked chicken breast from your local deli.

Each serving equals:

HE: 2 Protein • 1 Vegetable • ¾ Bread •
11 Optional Calories

---

219 Calories • 3 gm Fat • 23 gm Protein •
25 gm Carbohydrate • 607 mg Sodium •
33 mg Calcium • 4 gm Fiber

DIABETIC: 2 Meat • 1 Vegetable • 1 Starch

Cheesy Broccoli Chicken and Noodle Soup

So many restaurants offer broccoli-cheese soup on their menus, but I kept wondering about fun ways to add some fresh excitement to this basic bowl of soup. My solution: creamy chicken soup and old-fashioned noodles, for a taste that's new and oh-so-good!

☻ Serves 6 (1 full cup)

> 2 cups (one 16-ounce can) Healthy Request
>   Chicken Broth
> 2½ cups frozen chopped broccoli, thawed
> ½ cup chopped onion
> 1 (10¾-ounce) can Healthy Request Cream of
>   Chicken Soup
> 1½ cups (one 12-fluid-ounce can) Carnation Evaporated
>   Skim Milk
> 1¼ cups (2¼ ounces) uncooked noodles
> 2 full cups (12 ounces) diced cooked chicken breast
> ½ teaspoon lemon pepper
> ¾ cup (3 ounces) shredded Kraft reduced-fat
>   Cheddar cheese

Spray a slow cooker container with butter-flavored cooking spray. In prepared container, combine chicken broth, broccoli, and onion. Cover and cook on LOW for 3 hours. Stir in chicken soup, evaporated skim milk, uncooked noodles, chicken, and lemon pepper. Cover and continue cooking on LOW for 2 to 3 hours. Stir in Cheddar cheese. Continue stirring until cheese melts. Serve at once.

HINTS: 1. Thaw broccoli by placing in a colander and rinsing under hot water for one minute.
2. If you don't have leftover chicken, purchase a chunk of cooked chicken breast from your local deli.

Each serving equals:

HE: 2½ Protein • 1 Vegetable • ½ Skim Milk •
½ Bread • ¼ Slider • 15 Optional Calories

270 Calories • 6 gm Fat • 30 gm Protein •
24 gm Carbohydrate • 513 mg Sodium •
311 mg Calcium • 2 gm Fiber

DIABETIC: 2½ Meat • 1 Vegetable • 1 Starch •
½ Skim Milk

Rosy Chicken Rice Soup

Maybe you've grown up believing that all chicken soups had to be pale yellow or something wasn't right. If that sounds like you, it's time for a change of pace—time to stir some terrific tomatoes into a chicken rice soup. Your family may wonder at first what's going on, but one taste will convince them to put on their "rose-colored glasses" when it comes to mealtime!

◐ Serves 4 (1½ cups)

2 cups (one 16-ounce can) Healthy Request Chicken Broth

1 cup reduced-sodium tomato juice

1¾ cups (one 14.5-ounce can) diced tomatoes, undrained

1 cup (one 8-ounce can) Hunt's Tomato Sauce

⅔ cup uncooked instant rice

1½ cups (8 ounces) diced cooked chicken breast

¼ cup finely chopped onion

1 tablespoon pourable Splenda or Sugar Twin

1 teaspoon dried parsley flakes

⅛ teaspoon black pepper

Spray a slow cooker container with butter-flavored cooking spray. In prepared container, combine chicken broth, tomato juice, undrained tomatoes, and tomato sauce. Stir in uncooked rice, chicken, and onion. Add Splenda, parsley flakes, and black pepper. Mix well to combine. Cover and cook on LOW for 6 to 8 hours. Mix well before serving.

HINT: If you don't have leftovers, purchase a chunk of cooked chicken breast from your local deli.

Each serving equals:

HE: 2½ Vegetable • 2 Protein • ½ Bread • 9 Optional Calories

206 Calories • 2 gm Fat • 22 gm Protein • 25 gm Carbohydrate • 805 mg Sodium • 45 mg Calcium • 3 gm Fiber

DIABETIC: 2 Vegetable • 2 Meat • 1 Starch

Mom's Chicken Corn Soup

There are an awful lot of "C's" in this winner of a soup, from chicken and corn to carrots and celery, and don't forget about the cheese. When my family tasted it, they declared it a "champion" among chicken soups—and I hope you'll agree.

❍   Serves 6 (1½ cups)

16 ounces skinned and boned
    uncooked chicken breast,
    cut into 36 pieces
2 cups (one 16-ounce can)
    Healthy Request Chicken
    Broth
1 cup water
1 cup chopped onion
1 cup sliced carrots
1 cup chopped celery

1 cup (one 8-ounce can)
    cream-style corn
1½ cups frozen whole-kernel
    corn, thawed
1 cup diced raw potatoes
1 cup (4 ounces) diced Velveeta
    Light processed cheese
1 teaspoon dried parsley flakes
⅛ teaspoon black pepper

Spray a slow cooker container with butter-flavored cooking spray. In prepared container, combine chicken pieces, chicken broth, water, onion, carrots, and celery. Add cream-style corn, whole-kernel corn, and potatoes. Mix well to combine. Stir in Velveeta cheese, parsley flakes, and black pepper. Cover and cook on LOW for 8 hours. Mix well before serving.

HINT: Thaw whole-kernel corn by placing in a colander and rinsing under hot water for one minute.

Each serving equals:

HE: 2½ Protein • 1 Bread • 1 Vegetable •
5 Optional Calories

220 Calories • 4 gm Fat • 22 gm Protein •
24 gm Carbohydrate • 602 mg Sodium •
139 mg Calcium • 3 gm Fiber

DIABETIC: 2½ Meat • 1 Starch • 1 Vegetable

Chicken, Corn, and Rice Chowder

There's been a lot of talk recently about whether we should be cutting back on carbohydrates, and as I was testing this yummy recipe, I thought about how I felt on the subject. The simple truth is, healthy carbs fuel our bodies and deliver lots of good nutrition. As long as we vary our diets, we can eat well and feel good for a lifetime without eliminating any important nutrients.

○ Serves 6 (1 full cup)

> 2 cups (one 16-ounce can) Healthy Request Chicken Broth
> 1 (10³⁄₄-ounce) can Healthy Request Cream of Chicken Soup
> 1¹⁄₂ cups (one 12-fluid-ounce can) Carnation Evaporated Skim Milk
> 1 cup chopped celery
> ¹⁄₂ cup chopped onion
> 2 full cups (12 ounces) diced cooked chicken breast
> 1 cup frozen whole-kernel corn, thawed
> ¹⁄₃ cup uncooked instant rice
> 1 teaspoon dried parsley flakes
> ¹⁄₈ teaspoon black pepper

Spray a slow cooker container with butter-flavored cooking spray. In prepared container, combine chicken broth, chicken soup, and evaporated skim milk. Stir in celery, onion, chicken, and corn. Add uncooked rice, parsley flakes, and black pepper. Mix well to combine. Cover and cook on HIGH for 3 to 4 hours. Mix well before serving.

HINTS: 1. If you don't have leftovers, purchase a chunk of cooked chicken breast from your local deli.
2. Thaw corn by placing in a colander and rinsing under hot water for one minute.

Each serving equals:

HE: 2 Protein • ½ Skim Milk • ½ Bread •
½ Vegetable • ¼ Slider • 15 Optional Calories

---

223 Calories • 3 gm Fat • 25 gm Protein •
24 gm Carbohydrate • 476 mg Sodium •
182 mg Calcium • 1 gm Fiber

DIABETIC: 2 Meat • 1 Starch • ½ Skim Milk

Tom's Chicken Vegetable Soup

My son Tom always liked soup, even as a little boy, and now that he's a father and a brilliant businessman (my mother's pride is showing!), he still enjoys a bowl of soup for a quick meal starter or an anytime snack. This is one of his new favorites, he informed me, so I named it after him! ☻ Serves 6 (1½ cups)

16 ounces skinned and boned
  uncooked chicken breast,
  cut into 36 pieces
1 (10¾-ounce) can Healthy
  Request Tomato Soup
1 cup reduced-sodium tomato
  juice
1¾ cups (one 14.5-ounce can)
  stewed tomatoes, chopped
  and undrained

2 cups diced raw potatoes
1 cup frozen whole-kernel
  corn, thawed
1 cup frozen cut green beans,
  thawed
¾ cup chopped onion
1 teaspoon dried parsley flakes
⅛ teaspoon black pepper

Spray a slow cooker container with butter-flavored cooking spray. In prepared container, combine chicken pieces, tomato soup, tomato juice, and undrained stewed tomatoes. Add potatoes, corn, green beans, and onion. Mix well to combine. Stir in parsley flakes and black pepper. Cover and cook on LOW for 6 to 8 hours. Mix well before serving.

HINT: Thaw corn and green beans by placing in a colander and rinsing under hot water for one minute.

Each serving equals:

HE: 2 Protein • 1½ Vegetable • ⅔ Bread • ¼ Slider •
10 Optional Calories

223 Calories • 3 gm Fat • 19 gm Protein •
30 gm Carbohydrate • 505 mg Sodium •
39 mg Calcium • 4 gm Fiber

DIABETIC: 2 Meat • 1½ Vegetable • 1 Starch

Southwest Chicken and Corn Chowder

Cliff loves salsa so much, I thought about putting a salsa dispenser in my kitchen to save time opening all those jars! (Of course, we'd need two of them, since I like it mild and he likes it hot-hot-hot!) Salsa is a wonderful way to add flavor to just about any dish, and now that we can choose from so many different varieties, life is never dull! ❍ Serves 6 (1½ cups)

> 2 cups (one 16-ounce can) Healthy Request Chicken Broth
> 1 (10¾-ounce) can Healthy Request Cream of Chicken Soup
> ¾ cup chunky salsa (mild, medium, or hot)
> 2 cups (one 16-ounce can) cream-style corn
> 16 ounces skinned and boned uncooked chicken breast,
>   cut into 42 pieces
> ½ cup frozen whole-kernel corn, thawed
> 1 cup diced raw potatoes
> 1 teaspoon dried parsley flakes

Spray a slow cooker container with butter-flavored cooking spray. In prepared container, combine chicken broth, chicken soup, and salsa. Stir in cream-style corn. Add chicken, whole-kernel corn, potatoes, and parsley flakes. Mix well to combine. Cover and cook on LOW for 6 to 8 hours. Mix well before serving.

HINT: Thaw frozen corn by placing in a colander and rinsing under hot water for one minute.

Each serving equals:

HE: 2 Protein • 1 Bread • ¼ Vegetable • ¼ Slider • 15 Optional Calories

219 Calories • 3 gm Fat • 20 gm Protein • 28 gm Carbohydrate • 809 mg Sodium • 12 mg Calcium • 2 gm Fiber

DIABETIC: 2 Meat • 1½ Starch

Chinese Chicken and Cabbage Stew

Here's a quick (3–4 hours instead of all day long) slow cooker recipe that will please anyone who loves the tangy flavors of the Orient! The ingredients blend beautifully as the pot bubbles merrily away, and the end result is oh-so-satisfying!

○ Serves 4 (1½ cups)

> 1 (10¾-ounce) can Healthy Request Cream of Chicken
>   Soup
> 1 cup water
> 2 tablespoons reduced-sodium soy sauce
> 3 cups chopped cabbage
> 1 cup shredded carrots
> ½ cup chopped onion
> ½ cup (one 2.5-ounce jar) sliced mushrooms,
>   drained
> 1½ cups (8 ounces) diced cooked chicken breast
> 2 cups cooked spaghetti, rinsed and drained
> 1 teaspoon parsley flakes
> ⅛ teaspoon black pepper

Spray a slow cooker container with butter-flavored cooking spray. In prepared container, combine chicken soup, water, and soy sauce. Add cabbage, carrots, onion, and mushrooms. Mix well to combine. Stir in chicken, spaghetti, parsley flakes, and black pepper. Cover and cook on HIGH for 3 to 4 hours. Mix well before serving.

HINTS: 1. If you don't have leftovers, purchase a chunk of cooked chicken breast from your local deli.
2. Usually 1½ cups broken uncooked spaghetti cooks to about 2 cups.

Each serving equals:

HE: 2 Protein • 1¾ Vegetable • 1 Bread • ½ Slider •
5 Optional Calories

---

280 Calories • 4 gm Fat • 25 gm Protein •
36 gm Carbohydrate • 694 mg Sodium •
60 mg Calcium • 4 gm Fiber

DIABETIC: 2 Meat • 1½ Vegetable •
1½ Starch/Carbohydrate

Rustic Chicken Pot Stew

Have you always loved chicken pot pies, searching happily for peas and bits of carrot among the creamy chicken chunks? This recipe was certainly inspired by those memories, but I've added a few more veggies and even made the carrots bigger than those tiny chunks you recall. This old-fashioned dish tastes like it was ladled from a pot over a roaring fire in a country farmhouse.

☻ Serves 6 (1½ cups)

1 (10¾-ounce) can Healthy
    Request Cream of
    Chicken Soup
1½ teaspoons dried parsley
    flakes
⅛ teaspoon black pepper
16 ounces skinned and boned
    uncooked chicken breast,
    cut into 28 pieces

1 cup coarsely chopped onion
1½ cups baby carrots
3 cups diced raw potatoes
½ cup (one 2.5-ounce jar)
    sliced mushrooms,
    drained
1 cup frozen whole-kernel
    corn, thawed
½ cup frozen peas, thawed

Spray a slow cooker container with butter-flavored cooking spray. In prepared container, combine chicken soup, parsley flakes, and black pepper. Stir in chicken pieces, onion, carrots, and potatoes. Add mushrooms, corn, and peas. Mix well to combine. Cover and cook on LOW for 6 to 8 hours. Mix well before serving.

HINT: Thaw corn and peas by placing in a colander and rinsing under hot water for one minute.

Each serving equals:

HE: 2 Protein • 1 Bread • 1 Vegetable • ¼ Slider • 10 Optional Calories

231 Calories • 3 gm Fat • 20 gm Protein • 31 gm Carbohydrate • 320 mg Sodium • 36 mg Calcium • 4 gm Fiber

DIABETIC: 2 Meat • 1½ Starch • 1 Vegetable

Turkey Noodle Soup

Most people never think of making turkey soup except right after Thanksgiving, when leftover turkey persuades us to stir up a pot. But instead of choosing chicken soup the rest of the year, consider giving good-for-you turkey a more frequent place of honor at your table. I think you'll agree it has a heartier flavor, its own particular pleasures that are too good to savor only once or twice a year!

○ Serves 4 (1½ cups)

2 cups (one 16-ounce can)
   Healthy Request
   Chicken Broth
1½ cups water
1 cup chopped celery
1 cup sliced carrots
½ cup chopped onion

1½ cups (8 ounces) diced
   cooked turkey breast
1 cup uncooked noodles
½ cup frozen peas, thawed
½ teaspoon dried thyme
⅛ teaspoon black pepper

Spray a slow cooker container with butter-flavored cooking spray. In prepared container, combine chicken broth and water. Stir in celery, carrots, onion, and turkey. Add uncooked noodles, peas, thyme, and black pepper. Mix well to combine. Cover and cook on HIGH for 4 hours. Mix well before serving.

HINTS: 1. If you don't have leftovers, purchase a chunk of cooked turkey breast from your local deli.
2. Thaw peas by placing in a colander and rinsing under hot water for one minute.

Each serving equals:

HE: 2 Protein • 1¼ Vegetable • ¾ Bread •
8 Optional Calories

---

158 Calories • 2 gm Fat • 21 gm Protein •
14 gm Carbohydrate • 297 mg Sodium •
41 mg Calcium • 3 gm Fiber

DIABETIC: 2 Meat • 1 Vegetable • 1 Starch

Abram's Turkey Veggie Soup

I'm willing to bet that every grandma, no matter how busy, will quickly pull out a pot and start cooking when one of her beloved grandkids asks for "that turkey soup I like a lot!" This is a favorite of one of my little guys, but I'm equally sure that yours will share his passion for it.   ☻   Serves 6 (1½ cups)

> 2 cups (one 16-ounce can) Healthy Request Chicken Broth
> 1 (10¾-ounce) can Healthy Request Cream of Chicken Soup
> 1 cup water
> ½ teaspoon lemon pepper
> 2 full cups (12 ounces) diced cooked turkey breast
> 2 cups frozen sliced carrots, thawed
> 1½ cups frozen cut green beans, thawed
> ½ cup chopped onion
> ½ cup (one 2.5-ounce jar) sliced mushrooms, drained

Spray a slow cooker container with butter-flavored cooking spray. In prepared container, combine chicken broth, chicken soup, water, and lemon pepper. Add turkey, carrots, green beans, onion, and mushrooms. Mix well to combine. Cover and cook on LOW for 6 to 8 hours. Mix well before serving.

HINTS: 1. If you don't have leftovers, purchase a chunk of cooked turkey breast from your local deli.
2. Thaw carrots and green beans by placing in a colander and rinsing under hot water for one minute.

Each serving equals:

HE: 2 Protein • 1½ Vegetable • ¼ Slider • 15 Optional Calories

173 Calories • 5 gm Fat • 19 gm Protein • 13 gm Carbohydrate • 491 mg Sodium • 43 mg Calcium • 3 gm Fiber

DIABETIC: 2 Meat • 1½ Vegetable • ½ Starch/Carbohydrate

Old World Cabbage-Rice Soup

Cabbage soup recipes abound in many different cultures, probably because it's an inexpensive ingredient that packs a lot of flavor and fiber in every bite. If you're handy with the knife, you can buy it by the head and chop it yourself, but if you're a busy student who wants to stop eating so much take-out, buy it already chopped at the market and stir up a pot of this traditional soup that is perfect for today's busy lifestyles!   ☻   Serves 4 (1½ cups)

8 ounces extra-lean ground
    turkey or beef
1 (10¾-ounce) can Healthy
    Request Tomato Soup
1 cup (one 8-ounce can) Hunt's
    Tomato Sauce
1 cup (one 8-ounce can)
    tomatoes, finely chopped
    and undrained

2 cups water
1 teaspoon Worcestershire
    sauce
1½ cups shredded cabbage
¾ cup chopped onion
⅓ cup uncooked instant rice
1½ teaspoons dried parsley
    flakes

In a large skillet sprayed with butter-flavored cooking spray, brown meat. Spray a slow cooker container with butter-flavored cooking spray. In prepared container, combine browned turkey, tomato soup, tomato sauce, undrained tomatoes, water, and Worcestershire sauce. Stir in cabbage and onion. Add uncooked rice and parsley flakes. Mix well to combine. Cover and cook on LOW for 6 to 8 hours. Mix well before serving.

Each serving equals:

HE: 2¼ Vegetable • 1½ Protein • ¼ Bread • ½ Slider • 5 Optional Calories

196 Calories • 4 gm Fat • 14 gm Protein • 26 gm Carbohydrate • 783 mg Sodium • 44 mg Calcium • 3 gm Fiber

DIABETIC: 1½ Meat • 1½ Vegetable • 1 Starch

James's Pastafazool

When I first made this Italian bean and noodle soup for my kids when they were young, James couldn't stop saying its name out loud because he found it so funny. Now that he's made me a grandma (several times, in fact), he still loves its hearty goodness—and I still stir it up when he comes for a visit with his family.

☻ Serves 6 (1⅓ cups)

> 16 ounces extra-lean ground turkey or beef
> 1 cup (one 8-ounce can) Hunt's Tomato Sauce
> 1¾ cups (one 14.5-ounce can) diced tomatoes,
>   undrained
> 1¾ cups (one 14.5-ounce can) Swanson Beef Broth
> 6 ounces (one 8-ounce can) red kidney beans,
>   rinsed and drained
> 1 cup shredded carrots
> ½ cup finely chopped onion
> 1½ cups cooked elbow macaroni, rinsed and
>   drained
> 1 tablespoon chili seasoning
> 1 tablespoon Italian seasoning
> 6 tablespoons grated Kraft fat-free Parmesan Cheese

In a large skillet sprayed with olive oil–flavored cooking spray, brown meat. Spray a slow cooker container with olive oil–flavored cooking spray. In prepared container, combine browned meat, tomato sauce, undrained tomatoes, and beef broth. Stir in kidney beans, carrots, and onion. Add macaroni, chili seasoning, and Italian seasoning. Mix well to combine. Cover and cook on HIGH for 3 to 4 hours. Mix well before serving. When serving, top each bowl with 1 tablespoon Parmesan cheese.

HINT: Usually 1 full cup uncooked elbow macaroni cooks to about 1½ cups.

Each serving equals:

HE: 2½ Protein • 1¾ Vegetable • ¾ Bread •
5 Optional Calories

253 Calories • 5 gm Fat • 22 gm Protein •
30 gm Carbohydrate • 649 mg Sodium •
75 mg Calcium • 5 gm Fiber

DIABETIC: 3 Meat • 1½ Starch • 1 Vegetable

...ie of those dishes that can take hours (even days) to prepare in some parts of the nation, but for those of us who can't devote that much time to cutting up exactly the right kind of beef, mixing up a secret blend of spices, or stirring in some surprise ingredient (cinnamon? coffee? or even stranger ones?!), here's a simple but spectacularly good chili that anyone can fix in a jiffy.

◐ Serves 4 (1¼ cups)

8 ounces extra-lean ground turkey or beef

1 cup (one 8-ounce can) Hunt's Tomato Sauce

1 cup (one 8-ounce can) tomatoes, finely chopped and undrained

1¾ cups (one 14½-ounce can) Swanson Beef Broth

½ cup chopped onion

½ cup (one 2.5-ounce jar) sliced mushrooms, drained

10 ounces (one 16-ounce can) red kidney beans, rinsed and drained

1 tablespoon chili seasoning

2 teaspoons pourable Splenda or Sugar Twin

⅛ teaspoon black pepper

In a large skillet sprayed with butter-flavored cooking spray, brown meat. Spray a slow cooker container with butter-flavored cooking spray. In prepared container, combine browned meat, tomato sauce, undrained tomatoes, and beef broth. Stir in onion, mushrooms, and kidney beans. Add chili seasoning, Splenda, and black pepper. Mix well to combine. Cover and cook on LOW for 6 to 8 hours. Mix well before serving.

Each serving equals:

HE: 2 Vegetable • 1¾ Protein • ½ Bread • 9 Optional Calories

---

192 Calories • 4 gm Fat • 17 gm Protein • 22 gm Carbohydrate • 984 mg Sodium • 39 mg Calcium • 7 gm Fiber

---

DIABETIC: 2 Meat • 1 Vegetable • 1 Starch

Full of Beans Soup

I always loved the expression "full of beans" when it was used to refer to someone with a lot of energy, opinions, and enthusiasm for a subject, so when I was searching for just the right name for a delectable bean soup, it came to mind. This dish is rich in fiber, rich in flavor, and rich in the kinds of satisfied comments you're bound to receive when you serve it to your family!

◑ Serves 6 (1 full cup)

8 ounces extra-lean ground turkey or beef
2 cups reduced-sodium tomato juice
1 cup water
½ cup chopped onion
2 cups (one 16-ounce can) cut green beans, rinsed and drained
10 ounces (one 16-ounce can) butter beans, rinsed and drained
10 ounces (one 16-ounce can) red kidney beans, rinsed and drained
¼ cup Hormel Bacon Bits
2 tablespoons pourable Splenda or Sugar Twin
1 teaspoon prepared yellow mustard
⅛ teaspoon black pepper

In a large skillet sprayed with butter-flavored cooking spray, brown meat. Spray a slow cooker container with butter-flavored cooking spray. In prepared container, combine browned meat, tomato juice, and water. Add onion, green beans, butter beans, and kidney beans. Mix well to combine. Stir in bacon bits, Splenda, mustard, and black pepper. Cover and cook on LOW for 6 to 8 hours. Mix well before serving.

Each serving equals:

HE: 1½ Vegetable • 1½ Protein • 1 Bread • 19 Optional Calories

175 Calories • 3 gm Fat • 15 gm Protein • 22 gm Carbohydrate • 816 mg Sodium • 51 mg Calcium • 5 gm Fiber

DIABETIC: 2½ Meat • 1½ Vegetable • 1 Starch

Farm-Style Vegetable Beef Soup

Few Americans raise everything they eat these days, but recipes like this one recall the pioneers who did just that! This soup celebrates the best of what American farmers provide the rest of us, so that we can never forget what down-home cooking should taste like.

● Serves 6 (1½ cups)

> 16 ounces extra-lean ground turkey or beef
> ¾ cup chopped onion
> 1¾ cups (one 14½-ounce can) stewed tomatoes,
>   undrained
> 1 (10¾-ounce) can Healthy Request
>   Tomato Soup
> 1 cup water
> 1¾ cups (one 14½-ounce can) Swanson
>   Beef Broth
> 2 cups frozen cut carrots, thawed
> 1½ cups frozen cut green beans, thawed
> 1 cup frozen peas, thawed
> 1 cup diced raw potatoes
> 1 tablespoon pourable Splenda or Sugar Twin
> 1½ teaspoons dried parsley flakes
> ⅛ teaspoon black pepper

In a large skillet sprayed with butter-flavored cooking spray, brown meat and onion. Spray a slow cooker container with butter-flavored cooking spray. In prepared container, combine browned meat mixture, undrained stewed tomatoes, tomato soup, water, and beef broth. Add carrots, green beans, peas, and potatoes. Mix well to combine. Stir in Splenda, parsley flakes, and black pepper. Cover and cook on LOW for 6 to 8 hours. Mix well before serving.

HINT: Thaw vegetables by placing in a colander and rinsing under hot water for one minute.

Each serving equals:

HE: 2 Protein • 2 Vegetable • ½ Bread • ¼ Slider •
16 Optional Calories

233 Calories • 5 gm Fat • 19 gm Protein •
28 gm Carbohydrate • 721 mg Sodium •
49 mg Calcium • 4 gm Fiber

DIABETIC: 2 Meat • 2 Vegetable • 1 Starch

Almost Too Easy
Vegetable Beef Soup

Years ago, cake mix manufacturers simplified the process so much that all the home cook had to do was add water—but that turned out to be a big mistake. Those cake bakers needed to break an egg to feel they were "baking," so the process was changed. Now, is this soup recipe too easy for you? I wonder. Well, you have to brown the meat, you have to open a can and a package, and even slice an onion. Nope, it's just right. It's *almost* too easy, but just that.

☻ Serves 4 (1½ cups)

> 8 ounces extra-lean ground turkey or beef
> 1¾ cups (one 14½-ounce can) Swanson Beef Broth
> 1 cup reduced-sodium tomato juice
> 1 (10-ounce) package frozen mixed vegetables, thawed
> ½ cup chopped onion
> 1 teaspoon dried parsley flakes
> ⅛ teaspoon black pepper

In a large skillet sprayed with butter-flavored cooking spray, brown meat. Spray a slow cooker container with butter-flavored cooking spray. In prepared container, combine browned meat, beef broth, and tomato juice. Add mixed vegetables, onion, parsley flakes, and black pepper. Mix well to combine. Cover and cook on LOW for 6 to 8 hours. Mix well before serving.

HINT: Thaw mixed vegetables by placing in a colander and rinsing under hot water for one minute.

Each serving equals:

> HE: 1¾ Vegetable • 1½ Protein • ½ Bread • 9 Optional Calories
>
> ---
>
> 139 Calories • 3 gm Fat • 14 gm Protein • 14 gm Carbohydrate • 545 mg Sodium • 28 mg Calcium • 3 gm Fiber
>
> ---
>
> DIABETIC: 1½ Meat • 1 Vegetable • ½ Starch

Vegetable Beef and Noodle Soup

Here's another quick-and-easy dish that even your kids can prepare without too much effort! It's one of the best reasons to own and use a slow cooker—a recipe that tells you to stir all your ingredients into a pot, turn on the heat, and leave the house for 3 hours. Returning home to a hearty meal feels like a reward.

Serves 6 (1 full cup)

16 ounces extra-lean ground turkey or beef
1 cup chopped onion
1 (10-ounce) package frozen mixed vegetables, thawed
2 cups reduced-sodium tomato juice
¼ cup reduced-sodium ketchup
1¾ cups (one 14½-ounce can) Swanson Beef Broth
1 cup uncooked noodles

In a large skillet sprayed with butter-flavored cooking spray, brown meat and onion. Spray a slow cooker container with butter-flavored cooking spray. In prepared container, combine browned meat mixture and mixed vegetables. Add tomato juice, ketchup, and beef broth. Mix well to combine. Stir in uncooked noodles. Cover and cook on HIGH for 3 hours. Mix well before serving.

HINT: Thaw mixed vegetables by placing in a colander and rinsing under hot water for one minute.

Each serving equals:

HE: 2 Protein • 1½ Vegetable • ½ Bread • 15 Optional Calories

184 Calories • 4 gm Fat • 18 gm Protein • 19 gm Carbohydrate • 468 mg Sodium • 27 mg Calcium • 3 gm Fiber

DIABETIC: 2 Meat • 1½ Vegetable • ½ Starch

Tex-Mex Vegetable Beef Soup

Before the Internet existed, finding unusual ingredients was nearly impossible if you, like me, lived in a small Midwestern town. Now, you've got the world to choose from if your taste runs to the more exotic or spicy. Choose the chili seasoning that pleases you and your family, whether it's the handy mix you find at the supermarket or a hotter one you can mail order from closer to the Rio Grande. Either way, you'll enjoy some Texas-size sizzle with this soup.

● Serves 6 (1⅓ cups)

> 16 ounces extra-lean ground turkey or beef
> 1¾ cups (one 14.5-ounce can) diced tomatoes,
>   undrained
> 1 cup (one 8-ounce can) Hunt's Tomato Sauce
> 1¾ cups (one 14½-ounce can) Swanson Beef Broth
> 1¼ cups chopped onion
> 1 cup diced celery
> 1½ cups frozen sliced carrots, thawed
> 1½ cups frozen cut green beans, thawed
> 1½ cups frozen whole-kernel corn, thawed
> 2 tablespoons pourable Splenda or Sugar Twin
> 1½ teaspoons chili seasoning
> 1 teaspoon dried parsley flakes

In a large skillet sprayed with butter-flavored cooking spray, brown meat. Spray a slow cooker container with butter-flavored cooking spray. In prepared container, combine browned meat, undrained tomatoes, tomato sauce, and beef broth. Stir in onion, celery, carrots, green beans, and corn. Add Splenda, chili seasoning, and parsley flakes. Mix well to combine. Cover and cook on LOW for 8 hours. Mix well before serving.

HINT: Thaw frozen vegetables by placing in a colander and rinsing under hot water for one minute.

Each serving equals:

HE: 3 Vegetable • 2 Protein • ½ Bread •
6 Optional Calories

208 Calories • 4 gm Fat • 19 gm Protein •
24 gm Carbohydrate • 650 mg Sodium •
60 mg Calcium • 5 gm Fiber

DIABETIC: 2½ Vegetable • 2 Meat • ½ Starch

Santa Fe Beef Soup

In that enchanted land called New Mexico, the sun must shine a little brighter—or maybe it's all those spices that manage to convince us that it does! This combination of beef, veggies, and beans will win over the hungriest husband and kids in town (or just fill you up before you head out for an evening of holiday shopping!).

Serves 6 (1⅓ cups)

> 8 ounces extra-lean ground turkey or beef
> 1¾ cups (one 14.5-ounce can) diced tomatoes, undrained
> 2¾ cups reduced-sodium tomato juice
> 1 cup chopped onion
> ½ cup chopped green bell pepper
> 10 ounces (one 16-ounce can) red kidney beans, rinsed and drained
> 1½ cups frozen whole-kernel corn, thawed
> 1 tablespoon taco seasoning
> 1½ cups (6 ounces) cubed Velveeta Light processed cheese

In a large skillet sprayed with butter-flavored cooking spray, brown meat. Spray a slow cooker container with butter-flavored cooking spray. In prepared container, combine browned meat, undrained tomatoes, and tomato juice. Stir in onion, green pepper, kidney beans, corn, and taco seasoning. Add Velveeta cheese. Mix well to combine. Cover and cook on HIGH for 3 to 4 hours. Mix well before serving.

HINT: Thaw corn by placing in a colander and rinsing under hot water for one minute.

Each serving equals:

HE: 2 Protein • 2 Vegetable • 1 Bread

---

262 Calories • 6 gm Fat • 20 gm Protein •
32 gm Carbohydrate • 991 mg Sodium •
256 mg Calcium • 6 gm Fiber

DIABETIC: 3 Meat • 2 Vegetable • 1½ Starch

Hearty Vegetable Beef Soup

If you're a real meat lover who prefers chunks of beef rather than the crumbled kind, here's the soup to soothe your hunger every time! With a base of rich beefy broth, this soup provides an ideal setting for all that STEAK. Enjoy! ☻   Serves 6 (1⅓ cups)

> 1¾ cups (one 14.5-ounce can) diced tomatoes, undrained
> 1¾ cups (one 14½-ounce can) Swanson Beef Broth
> 16 ounces lean round steak, cut into 36 pieces
> 1½ cups frozen whole-kernel corn, thawed
> 1¾ cups frozen cut green beans, thawed
> 1½ cups frozen peas, thawed
> 1 cup frozen sliced carrots, thawed
> 1½ teaspoons dried parsley flakes
> ⅛ teaspoon black pepper

Spray a slow cooker container with butter-flavored cooking spray. In prepared container, combine undrained tomatoes and beef broth. Stir in steak pieces. Add corn, green beans, peas, carrots, parsley flakes, and black pepper. Mix well to combine. Cover and cook on LOW for 6 to 8 hours. Mix well before serving.

HINT: Thaw frozen vegetables by placing in a colander and rinsing under hot water for one minute.

Each serving equals:

HE: 2 Protein • 1½ Vegetable • 1 Bread •
5 Optional Calories

---

195 Calories • 3 gm Fat • 21 gm Protein •
21 gm Carbohydrate • 412 mg Sodium •
45 mg Calcium • 5 gm Fiber

DIABETIC: 2 Meat • 1½ Vegetable • 1 Starch

Cliff's Vegetable Beef Soup

Over the years, Cliff has tasted so many different soups and stews, it sometimes amazes me that he's so good at telling them apart—and telling me what he likes (or doesn't!) about them. This one got his highest rating recently, and when asked to explain why he liked it so much, he simply said, "Lots of everything in it—meat, corn, peas, carrots, beans." This one's for you, Cliff!

☺ Serves 6 (1½ cups)

> 1¾ cups (one 14.5-ounce can) Swanson
>   Beef Broth
> 1¾ cups (one 14.5-ounce can) stewed tomatoes,
>   undrained
> 16 ounces lean round steak, cut into 36 pieces
> 2 cups chopped cabbage
> 1½ cups frozen cut green beans, thawed
> 1½ cups frozen sliced carrots, thawed
> 1½ cups frozen whole-kernel corn, thawed
> 1½ cups frozen peas, thawed
> ½ cup chopped onion
> 1 tablespoon pourable Splenda or Sugar Twin
> ⅛ teaspoon black pepper

Spray a slow cooker container with butter-flavored cooking spray. In prepared container, combine beef broth and undrained stewed tomatoes. Stir in steak pieces, cabbage, green beans, and carrots. Add corn, peas, onion, Splenda, and black pepper. Mix well to combine. Cover and cook on LOW for 6 to 8 hours. Mix well before serving.

HINT: Thaw frozen vegetables by placing in a colander and rinsing under hot water for one minute.

Each serving equals:

HE: 2 Protein • 1½ Vegetable • 1 Bread •
6 Optional Calories

---

228 Calories • 4 gm Fat • 22 gm Protein •
26 gm Carbohydrate • 533 mg Sodium •
63 mg Calcium • 5 gm Fiber

DIABETIC: 2 Meat • 2 Vegetable • 1 Starch

Beefy French Onion Soup

On French menus, when you see the word *boeuf*, you know you're getting BEEF in all its glory. In this recipe, when I combined the ingredients for a traditional French onion soup with a little *boeuf*, I expected my taste testers to go "Ooh-la-la!" Well, you better believe that they did! ☺ Serves 4

1¾ cups (one 14½-ounce can) Swanson Beef Broth
1½ cups water
1½ teaspoons dried parsley flakes
1 teaspoon Worcestershire sauce
¼ cup grated Kraft fat-free Parmesan cheese
4 cups thinly sliced onion
1½ cups (8 ounces) diced lean cooked roast beef
1 cup frozen peas, thawed
4 slices reduced-calorie French or white bread, toasted and cubed

Spray a slow cooker container with butter-flavored cooking spray. In prepared container, combine beef broth, water, parsley flakes, Worcestershire sauce, and Parmesan cheese. Stir in onion, roast beef, and peas. Cover and cook on LOW for 8 hours. For each serving, place ¼ of bread cubes in a bowl and spoon 1½ cups soup mixture over top.

HINT: If you don't have leftovers, purchase a chunk of lean cooked roast beef from your local deli or use Healthy Choice Deli slices.

Each serving equals:

HE: 2 Protein • 2 Vegetable • 1 Bread •
8 Optional Calories

266 Calories • 6 gm Fat • 24 gm Protein •
29 gm Carbohydrate • 597 mg Sodium •
75 mg Calcium • 4 gm Fiber

DIABETIC: 2 Meat • 2 Vegetable • 1 Starch

Creamy Steak Soup

There's some kind of magic when steak and mushrooms get together, so when I set out to create a truly luscious and meaty soup, I knew how to begin. The potatoes add a special richness to this blend of flavors. As they cook on that slow temperature, they reach out and embrace the other ingredients in a kind of savory "hug." The result? A soup splendid enough to serve to company!

○ Serves 6 (1⅓ cups)

1 (10¾-ounce) can Healthy Request Cream of Mushroom Soup
2 cups reduced-sodium V-8 juice
16 ounces lean round steak, cut into 36 pieces
1 cup chopped onion
2 cups diced raw potatoes
1 (10-ounce) package frozen mixed vegetables, thawed
1 teaspoon dried parsley flakes
⅛ teaspoon black pepper

Spray a slow cooker container with butter-flavored cooking spray. In prepared container, combine mushroom soup and V-8 juice. Stir in steak pieces, onion, potatoes, and mixed vegetables. Add parsley flakes and black pepper. Mix well to combine. Cover and cook on LOW for 8 hours. Mix well before serving.

HINT: Thaw mixed vegetables by placing in a colander and rinsing under hot water for one minute.

Each serving equals:

HE: 2 Protein • 1½ Vegetable • ½ Bread • ¼ Slider • 7 Optional Calories

216 Calories • 4 gm Fat • 20 gm Protein • 25 gm Carbohydrate • 407 mg Sodium • 78 mg Calcium • 3 gm Fiber

DIABETIC: 2 Meat • 1½ Vegetable • 1 Starch

Beefy Chili

I imagined this dish being devoured by a long, tall Texan because it contains so much meaty goodness, it might actually satisfy one of those big appetites! The two teaspoons of chili seasoning pleased my family of medium-size Iowans, but you may discover that a little more (or less) is right for your group of chili fans.

● Serves 6 (1½ cups)

1 (10¾-ounce) can Healthy Request Tomato Soup	10 ounces (one 16-ounce can) red kidney beans, rinsed and drained
1 cup reduced-sodium tomato juice	1 cup shredded carrots
1¾ cups (one 14.5-ounce can) diced tomatoes, undrained	1 cup finely chopped celery
	½ cup chopped onion
	¼ cup chopped green bell pepper
½ cup water	
16 ounces lean round steak, cut into 42 pieces	2 teaspoons chili seasoning
	⅛ teaspoon black pepper

Spray a slow cooker container with butter-flavored cooking spray. In prepared container, combine tomato soup, tomato juice, undrained tomatoes, and water. Stir in steak pieces, kidney beans, carrots, celery, onion, and green pepper. Add chili seasoning and black pepper. Mix well to combine. Cover and cook on LOW for 8 hours. Mix well before serving.

Each serving equals:

HE: 1¾ Protein • 1½ Vegetable • ½ Bread • ¼ Slider • 10 Optional Calories

---

216 Calories • 4 gm Fat • 21 gm Protein • 24 gm Carbohydrate • 535 mg Sodium • 49 mg Calcium • 5 gm Fiber

---

DIABETIC: 2 Meat • 1½ Vegetable • 1 Starch

Robust German Stew

The word *robust* makes me think of those hard-working woodsmen who labor in the lush forests of Bavaria, people who arrive at the dinner table hungry with a capital H! For them (and for you, of course), I emphasized intense flavors (*three* kinds of tomato taste) and plenty of meat, then added some sweet and tangy sauerkraut to send you on a culinary journey to those pretty woods.

Serves 6 (1⅓ cups)

1 cup (one 8-ounce can) tomatoes, finely chopped and undrained
1 cup (one 8-ounce can) Hunt's Tomato Sauce
¾ cup reduced-sodium tomato juice
16 ounces lean round steak, cut into 36 pieces
½ cup chopped onion
1 cup uncooked instant rice
1 (14½-ounce) can Frank's Bavarian Style sauerkraut, well drained
1 tablespoon Splenda Granular

Spray a slow cooker container with butter-flavored cooking spray. In prepared container, combine undrained tomatoes, tomato sauce, and tomato juice. Stir in steak pieces, onion, uncooked rice, and sauerkraut. Add Splenda. Mix well to combine. Cover and cook on LOW for 6 to 8 hours. Mix well before serving.

HINT: If you can't find Frank's Bavarian Style sauerkraut, use regular sauerkraut, ½ teaspoon caraway seeds, and 1 teaspoon Brown Sugar Twin.

Each serving equals:

HE: 2 Protein • 2 Vegetable • ½ Bread •
1 Optional Calorie

216 Calories • 4 gm Fat • 18 gm Protein •
27 gm Carbohydrate • 752 mg Sodium •
24 mg Calcium • 1 gm Fiber

DIABETIC: 2 Meat • 1½ Vegetable • 1 Starch

Savory Stew

"Guess what's in it?" I sometimes like to ask my family and friends when I serve a new recipe. Nobody figured out that this hearty stew drew its unique flavor from the addition of a little cider vinegar. Blended with the other ingredients, the cider vinegar turns what might be ordinary into extraordinary. If you don't keep it on hand, consider investing in a small bottle. It's worth the bit of extra trouble! ☻ Serves 6 (1 full cup)

1 (10¾-ounce) can Healthy Request Tomato Soup
½ cup reduced-sodium tomato juice
2 tablespoons cider vinegar
1 teaspoon dried parsley flakes
⅛ teaspoon black pepper
16 ounces lean round steak, cut into 36 pieces
3 cups diced raw potatoes
2 cups sliced carrots
1 cup chopped onion
1 cup chopped celery

Spray a slow cooker container with butter-flavored cooking spray. In prepared container, combine tomato soup, tomato juice, vinegar, parsley flakes, and black pepper. Stir in meat pieces. Add potatoes, carrots, onion, and celery. Mix well to combine. Cover and cook on LOW for 8 hours. Mix well before serving.

Each serving equals:

HE: 2 Protein • 1½ Vegetable • ½ Bread • ¼ Slider • 10 Optional Calories

219 Calories • 3 gm Fat • 19 gm Protein • 29 gm Carbohydrate • 298 mg Sodium • 36 mg Calcium • 3 gm Fiber

DIABETIC: 2 Meat • 1½ Vegetable • 1 Starch

Simmering Stew

There's an important trick to preparing delicious food in your slow cooker—DON'T LIFT THE LID! It's especially tempting to want to inhale the aromas when you see through the glass top that your stew is bubbling away so delectably. (Maybe that's why it's best to leave the house while it cooks!) Your reward will come soon enough, in a dish that delivers fantastic flavor in every bowl!

☻ Serves 6 (1¼ cups)

1 (10¾-ounce) can Healthy
    Request Tomato Soup
1 tablespoon Worcestershire
    sauce
1 cup (one 8-ounce can)
    cream-style corn
1 teaspoon dried parsley
    flakes

⅛ teaspoon black pepper
16 ounces lean round steak,
    cut into 36 pieces
2 cups diced raw potatoes
2 cups sliced carrots
1½ cups chopped celery
1 cup chopped onion
1 cup frozen peas, thawed

Spray a slow cooker container with butter-flavored cooking spray. In prepared container, combine tomato soup, Worcestershire sauce, corn, parsley flakes, and black pepper. Add meat, potatoes, carrots, celery, and onion. Mix well to combine. Stir in peas. Cover and cook on LOW for 8 hours. Mix well before serving.

HINT: Thaw peas by placing in a colander and rinsing under hot water for one minute.

Each serving equals:

HE: 2 Protein • 1½ Vegetable • 1 Bread • ¼ Slider • 10 Optional Calories

244 Calories • 4 gm Fat • 20 gm Protein • 32 gm Carbohydrate • 401 mg Sodium • 33 mg Calcium • 4 gm Fiber

DIABETIC: 2 Meat • 1½ Vegetable • 1½ Starch

Lazy Day Stew

Too tired to cook? Can't bear to think about spending any time in the kitchen today? I've got just the recipe for you. It's an ideal one-pot meal that is terrifically tasty . . . and you get to spend the day with your feet up! ☻ Serves 6 (1½ cups)

1 (10¾-ounce) can Healthy Request Tomato Soup
½ cup reduced-sodium tomato juice
3 tablespoons all-purpose flour
2 teaspoons dried parsley flakes
⅛ teaspoon black pepper
16 ounces lean round steak, cut into 36 pieces
2 cups diced, unpeeled raw potatoes
2 cups cut carrots
1½ cups coarsely cut celery
1½ cups coarsely chopped onion
½ cup (one 2.5-ounce jar) sliced mushrooms, undrained

Spray a slow cooker container with butter-flavored cooking spray. In prepared container, combine tomato soup, tomato juice, flour, parsley flakes, and black pepper. Stir in steak pieces and potatoes. Add carrots, celery, onion, and undrained mushrooms. Mix well to combine. Cover and cook on LOW for 8 hours. Mix well before serving.

Each serving equals:

HE: 2 Protein • 2 Vegetable • ½ Bread • ¼ Slider •
10 Optional Calories

232 Calories • 4 gm Fat • 20 gm Protein •
29 gm Carbohydrate • 360 mg Sodium •
43 mg Calcium • 4 gm Fiber

DIABETIC: 2 Meat • 2 Vegetable • 1 Starch

Hawaiian Chili

So many different culinary cultures combined to create Hawaiian cooking, so why shouldn't all that variety produce a chili recipe that is truly unique? This dish centers on pork instead of beef and finds a clever way to incorporate pineapple into a classic dish.

○ Serves 6 (1½ cups)

16 ounces ground extra-lean
    pork
1 cup (one 8-ounce can) Hunt's
    Tomato Sauce
1¾ cups (one 14.5-ounce can)
    diced tomatoes, undrained
3 cups reduced-sodium
    tomato juice
1 cup (one 8-ounce can)
    crushed pineapple, packed
    in fruit juice, undrained

1¼ cups chopped onion
1½ cups chopped green bell
    pepper
¼ cup (one 2-ounce jar)
    chopped pimiento,
    drained
2 tablespoons pourable
    Splenda or Sugar Twin
1 tablespoon chili seasoning
1 teaspoon dried parsley flakes
⅛ teaspoon black pepper

In a large skillet sprayed with butter-flavored cooking spray, brown pork. Spray a slow cooker container with butter-flavored cooking spray. In prepared container, combine browned pork, tomato sauce, undrained tomatoes, and tomato juice. Stir in undrained pineapple, onion, and green pepper. Add pimiento, Splenda, chili seasoning, parsley flakes, and black pepper. Mix well to combine. Cover and cook on HIGH for 3 to 4 hours. Mix well before serving.

Each serving equals:

HE: 2½ Vegetable • 2 Protein • ⅓ Fruit

188 Calories • 4 gm Fat • 17 gm Protein •
21 gm Carbohydrate • 602 mg Sodium •
50 mg Calcium • 4 gm Fiber

DIABETIC: 2½ Vegetable • 2 Meat

Bahama Pork Stew

Pork responds beautifully to slow cooking, turning amazingly tender as the hours pass. It's a perfect partner for sweet potatoes and corn, transforming every bite into a taste of Caribbean sun!

● Serves 6 (1 full cup)

> 1¾ cups (one 14.5-ounce can) diced tomatoes, undrained
>
> ½ cup reduced-sodium tomato juice
>
> 2 tablespoons pourable Splenda or Sugar Twin
>
> 1½ teaspoons chili seasoning
>
> 16 ounces lean pork tenderloin, cut into 36 pieces
>
> 2 full cups diced raw sweet potatoes
>
> 1½ cups frozen whole-kernel corn, thawed
>
> 1¼ cups frozen cut green beans, thawed
>
> 1 cup chopped onion

Spray a slow cooker container with butter-flavored cooking spray. In prepared container, combine undrained tomatoes, tomato juice, Splenda, and chili seasoning. Stir in pork pieces. Add sweet potatoes, corn, green beans, and onion. Mix well to combine. Cover and cook on LOW for 6 to 8 hours. Mix well before serving.

HINT: Thaw corn and green beans by placing in a colander and rinsing under hot water for one minute.

Each serving equals:

> HE: 2 Protein • 1½ Vegetable • 1 Bread •
> 1 Optional Calorie
> _____
> 211 Calories • 3 gm Fat • 18 gm Protein •
> 28 gm Carbohydrate • 170 mg Sodium •
> 48 mg Calcium • 4 gm Fiber
> _____
> DIABETIC: 2 Meat • 1½ Vegetable • 1 Starch

Continental Bean and Potato Soup

Does it surprise you to know you can enjoy a hearty ham-and-bean soup that's low in fat and fabulously flavored? Slow cooking makes flavors deepen, and a modest amount of meat tastes like a whole lot more!   ○   Serves 6 (1⅓ cups)

> 10 ounces (one 16-ounce can) great northern beans, rinsed and drained
> 2 cups water
> 1¾ cups (one 14.5-ounce can) diced tomatoes, undrained
> 2 full cups (12 ounces) diced Dubuque 97% fat-free ham or any extra-lean ham
> 3 cups diced raw potatoes
> 1¼ cups frozen French-style green beans, thawed
> 1 teaspoon dried parsley flakes
> ⅛ teaspoon black pepper

Spray a slow cooker container with butter-flavored cooking spray. In prepared container, combine great northern beans, water, and undrained tomatoes. Stir in ham, potatoes, green beans, parsley flakes, and black pepper. Cover and cook on LOW for 8 hours. Mix well before serving.

HINT: Thaw green beans by placing in a colander and rinsing under hot water for one minute.

Each serving equals:

HE: 1¼ Protein • 1 Bread • 1 Vegetable

---

198 Calories • 2 gm Fat • 15 gm Protein •
30 gm Carbohydrate • 501 mg Sodium •
57 mg Calcium • 5 gm Fiber

DIABETIC: 2 Meat • 1½ Starch • 1 Vegetable

French Market Ham and Bean Soup

Here's a scrumptious, high-protein, high-fiber soup that delivers a giant wallop of nutrition along with terrific taste! Two kinds of beans join with a little ham for a splendidly savory meal.

● Serves 6 (1½ cups)

> 1 full cup (6 ounces) diced Dubuque 97% fat-free ham or any extra-lean ham
> 10 ounces (one 16-ounce can) great northern beans, rinsed and drained
> 10 ounces (one 16-ounce can) navy beans, rinsed and drained
> 1¾ cups (one 14.5-ounce can) diced tomatoes, undrained
> 1¾ cups reduced-sodium tomato juice
> 1 cup chopped onion
> 1 tablespoon pourable Splenda or Sugar Twin
> 1 teaspoon chili seasoning
> ⅛ teaspoon black pepper

Spray a slow cooker container with butter-flavored cooking spray. In prepared container, combine ham, great northern beans, and navy beans. Add undrained tomatoes, tomato juice, and onion. Stir in Splenda, chili seasoning, and black pepper. Cover and cook on LOW for 6 to 8 hours. Mix well before serving.

Each serving equals:

HE: 2½ Protein • 1½ Vegetable • 1 Optional Calorie

234 Calories • 2 gm Fat • 16 gm Protein •
38 gm Carbohydrate • 610 mg Sodium •
96 mg Calcium • 8 gm Fiber

DIABETIC: 2 Meat • 1½ Starch • 1½ Vegetable

Ham and Cabbage Stew

If you enjoy feeling full but want to make smart choices about calories and fat, this lip-smacking stew will delight you and your family every time! Lots of potatoes in every bite, hearty cabbage, and tangy ham—it's a worthy winner that you'll enjoy often.

○ Serves 6 (1⅓ cups)

> 6 cups shredded cabbage
> 3 cups diced raw potatoes
> 1½ cups thinly sliced carrots
> 1½ cups chopped onion
> 2 full cups (12 ounces) diced Dubuque 97% fat-free ham
>   or any extra-lean ham
> 2 cups water
> 2 teaspoons dried parsley flakes
> ⅛ teaspoon black pepper

Spray a slow cooker container with butter-flavored cooking spray. In prepared container, combine cabbage, potatoes, carrots, onion, and ham. Add water, parsley flakes, and black pepper. Mix well to combine. Cover and cook on LOW for 6 to 8 hours. Mix well before serving.

Each serving equals:

HE: 2 Vegetable • 1½ Protein • ½ Bread

154 Calories • 2 gm Fat • 12 gm Protein •
22 gm Carbohydrate • 478 mg Sodium •
57 mg Calcium • 4 gm Fiber

DIABETIC: 2 Vegetable • 1½ Meat • ½ Starch

Bohemian Potato
Sauerkraut Soup

My ancestors came from Eastern Europe, where there's a long tradition of rich, filling soups, and I think they'd be pleased by the tasty combination of ingredients in this dish. Lean kielbasa doesn't stint on the kind of flavor you expect in a sausage, and the tangy sauerkraut works beautifully with all those potatoes.

○ Serves 6 (1½ cups)

> 1 (16-ounce) package Healthy Choice 97% lean kielbasa sausage,
>   cut into ½-inch pieces
> 3 cups diced raw potatoes
> 1½ cups chopped onion
> 1½ cups chopped carrots
> 2 cups (one 16-ounce can) Healthy Request Chicken Broth
> 1 cup water
> 1 cup (one 8-ounce can) tomatoes, finely chopped and undrained
> 2 cups (one 16-ounce can) sauerkraut, rinsed and well drained
> 1 teaspoon dried parsley flakes

Spray a slow cooker container with butter-flavored cooking spray. In prepared container, combine kielbasa, potatoes, onion, and carrots. Add chicken broth, water, undrained tomatoes, sauerkraut, and parsley flakes. Mix well to combine. Cover and cook on LOW for 8 hours. Mix well before serving.

Each serving equals:

> HE: 2 Protein • 2 Vegetable • ½ Bread •
> 5 Optional Calories
>
> ---
>
> 198 Calories • 2 gm Fat • 13 gm Protein •
> 32 gm Carbohydrate • 997 mg Sodium •
> 78 mg Calcium • 5 gm Fiber
>
> ---
>
> DIABETIC: 2 Meat • 2 Vegetable • 1 Starch

Kielbasa Kale Soup

If you're unfamiliar with kale, let me just say it's a good-for-you green vegetable that makes marvelous soup! Partnered with beans and sausage, it will satisfy the most ravenous diner and provide you with yet another choice when it comes to buying greens.

○ Serves 6 (1½ cups)

> 4 cups (two 16-ounce cans) Healthy Request Chicken Broth
> ½ cup chopped onion
> 1 cup chopped kale
> 2 cups chopped cabbage
> 1 cup chopped carrots
> 8 ounces Healthy Choice 97% lean kielbasa sausage, cut into
>   ½-inch slices
> 10 ounces (one 16-ounce can) red kidney beans, rinsed and
>   drained
> 1½ cups diced unpeeled raw red potatoes
> ⅛ teaspoon black pepper

Spray a slow cooker container with butter-flavored cooking spray. In prepared container, combine chicken broth, onion, kale, cabbage, and carrots. Stir in kielbasa, kidney beans, potatoes, and black pepper. Cover and cook on LOW for 6 to 8 hours. Mix well before serving.

Each serving equals:

> HE: 1½ Protein • 1 Bread • 1 Vegetable •
> 11 Optional Calories
>
> ---
>
> 203 Calories • 3 gm Fat • 12 gm Protein •
> 32 gm Carbohydrate • 725 mg Sodium •
> 79 mg Calcium • 4 gm Fiber
>
> ---
>
> DIABETIC: 1½ Meat • 1 Starch • 1 Vegetable

Kielbasa Potato Stew

Remember not to peel the potatoes in this recipe—those red skins pack lots of delicate, delectable flavor, and they also add some healthy fiber! Potatoes also take on the taste of what surrounds them, so just imagine how good sausage-infused potatoes will be. This is a great choice for a snowy night and a family Scrabble tournament.   ☻   Serves 4 (1½ cups)

> 8 ounces Healthy Choice 97% lean kielbasa sausage, cut into
> ½-inch slices
> 3 cups diced, unpeeled red potatoes
> 1 cup chopped onion
> 1 cup sliced celery
> 1 (10¾-ounce) can Healthy Request Tomato Soup
> ½ cup frozen peas, thawed
> 1 teaspoon dried parsley flakes
> ⅛ teaspoon black pepper

Spray a slow cooker container with butter-flavored cooking spray. In prepared container, combine kielbasa, potatoes, onion, and celery. Stir in tomato soup, peas, parsley flakes, and black pepper. Cover and cook on LOW for 8 hours. Mix well before serving.

HINT: Thaw peas by placing in a colander and rinsing under hot water for one minute.

Each serving equals:

HE: 1½ Protein • 1 Bread • 1 Vegetable • ½ Slider • 5 Optional Calories

227 Calories • 3 gm Fat • 12 gm Protein • 38 gm Carbohydrate • 817 mg Sodium • 53 mg Calcium • 4 gm Fiber

DIABETIC: 1½ Meat • 1 Starch • 1 Vegetable

Chipped Beef and Cauliflower Soup

Maybe you've never eaten chipped beef, but it's a favorite choice of many men I've met who first tasted it while in the service. In this dish, the cream cheese transforms those bits of beef into the most luscious "gravy" you can imagine. When combined with cheese and cauliflower (very tasty all by themselves), the end result is a hearty meal sure to produce happy smiles all around!

● Serves 6 (1⅓ cups)

3½ cups hot water
1 (8-ounce) package
    Philadelphia fat-free
    cream cheese
4 cups frozen chopped
    cauliflower, thawed
½ cup chopped onion

1 (5-ounce) jar Hormel Lean
    dried chipped beef, rinsed
    and shredded
1½ cups (6 ounces) cubed
    Velveeta Light processed
    cheese
1 cup instant potato flakes

Spray a slow cooker container with butter-flavored cooking spray. In prepared container, combine hot water and cream cheese. Mix well to dissolve cream cheese. Stir in cauliflower and onion. Add chipped beef, Velveeta cheese, and dry potato flakes. Mix well to combine. Cover and cook on LOW for 2 to 3 hours. Mix well before serving.

HINT: Thaw cauliflower by placing in a colander and rinsing under hot water for one minute.

Each serving equals:

HE: 1½ Protein • 1½ Vegetable • ½ Bread

180 Calories • 4 gm Fat • 19 gm Protein • 17 gm Carbohydrate • 983 mg Sodium • 356 mg Calcium • 2 gm Fiber

DIABETIC: 1½ Meat • 1½ Vegetable • ½ Starch

Sensational
Side Dishes

Too often, we omit the flavorful side dishes that can add so much to a meal. When you choose your slow cooker as your kitchen "partner," you get more than a cooking tool—you actually get an assistant that saves time and money while providing delightful variety at your table. Most of these recipes turn you into a vegetable chef par excellence by making it easy to transform everyday veggies into party food and special-occasion treats.

Here's a splendid selection of sides from A to Z and back again. When your garden overflows with zucchini, don't cope by leaving baskets of them on neighbors' doorsteps and running away! Instead, try my **Zucchini and Carrot Bake** or my **Zucchini Tomato Pot**. If you feel (as I sometimes have) that you just can't make another green bean side dish because you've run out of ideas, here I come to the rescue with **Dutchman's Green Beans and Tomatoes** and **Barbequed Green Beans**. And if you and your family could eat potatoes three times a day, I offer an abundance of recipes that will satisfy that urge, from **Scalloped Pizza Potatoes** to **Candied Sweet Potatoes**.

Grande Vegetable Platter

Make a mélange of colorful veggies in your slow cooker and even those family members who usually skip the good-for-you foods will have to make room for a spoonful or two. These keep their color beautifully, so serving them is a pleasure!

○ Serves 4 (1 full cup)

> 1 cup coarsely chopped onion
> 1/2 cup coarsely chopped green bell pepper
> 1/2 cup coarsely chopped red bell pepper
> 3 full cups diced cooked potatoes
> 1 1/2 cups chopped fresh tomatoes
> 1/2 cup chunky salsa (mild, medium, or hot)
> 1 tablespoon pourable Splenda or Sugar Twin
> 1 teaspoon dried parsley flakes
> 1/8 teaspoon black pepper

Spray a slow cooker container with butter-flavored cooking spray. In prepared container, combine onion, green pepper, red pepper, potatoes, and tomatoes. Add salsa, Splenda, parsley flakes, and black pepper. Mix well to combine. Cover and cook on HIGH for 3 to 4 hours. Mix well before serving.

Each serving equals:

HE: 2 Vegetable • 1 Bread • 2 Optional Calories

152 Calories • 0 gm Fat • 4 gm Protein • 34 gm Carbohydrate • 232 mg Sodium • 21 mg Calcium • 5 gm Fiber

DIABETIC: 2 Vegetable • 1 Starch

Slow-Roasted Veggies

Forget the roast, but get that oven-browned flavor in your vegetables in this savory blend. The veggies take on the rich lusciousness of the creamy gravy, so every bite melts in your mouth!

● Serves 6 (¾ cup)

1 (12-ounce) jar Heinz Fat Free Beef Gravy
1 (10¾-ounce) can Healthy Request Cream of Mushroom Soup
3 cups sliced raw potatoes
2 cups sliced carrots
1½ cups chopped celery
1 cup chopped onion
1 teaspoon dried parsley flakes

Spray a slow cooker container with butter-flavored cooking spray. In prepared container, combine beef gravy and mushroom soup. Add potatoes, carrots, celery, and onion. Mix well to combine. Stir in parsley flakes. Cover and cook on LOW for 8 hours. Mix well before serving.

Each serving equals:

HE: 1½ Vegetable • ½ Bread • ¼ Slider •
12 Optional Calories

133 Calories • 1 gm Fat • 4 gm Protein •
27 gm Carbohydrate • 573 mg Sodium •
75 mg Calcium • 3 gm Fiber

DIABETIC: 1½ Vegetable • 1 Starch

Orange-Spiced Glazed Carrots

Celebrate the sweetness of this vibrant root vegetable when you serve up a spicy-sweet side dish that is as pretty as it is appetizing. You've never tasted carrots as succulent as these!

⏾ Serves 6 (¾ cup)

> 6 cups baby carrots
> 6 tablespoons orange marmalade spreadable fruit
> ½ cup pourable Splenda or Sugar Twin
> 2 tablespoons reduced-calorie margarine
> ½ teaspoon apple pie spice

Spray a slow cooker container with butter-flavored cooking spray. In prepared container, combine carrots and spreadable fruit. Add Splenda, margarine, and apple pie spice. Mix well to combine. Cover and cook on LOW for 6 to 8 hours. Mix well before serving.

Each serving equals:

> HE: 2 Vegetable • 1 Fruit • ½ Fat •
> 8 Optional Calories
>
> ---
>
> 118 Calories • 2 gm Fat • 1 gm Protein •
> 24 gm Carbohydrate • 90 mg Sodium •
> 36 mg Calcium • 4 gm Fiber
>
> ---
>
> DIABETIC: 2 Vegetable • 1 Fruit • ½ Fat

Falling Leaves Carrots and Apples

What a wonderful fall combination this is, both sweet and savory all in one dish! The tartness of the apples is the perfect foil for the tender sweetness of the carrots, and even though they cook together for hours, they don't lose their great texture.

○ Serves 4 (1 cup)

> 3 cups frozen sliced carrots, thawed
> 1½ cups (3 small) cored, peeled, and chopped tart cooking apples
> ½ cup unsweetened apple juice
> ¼ cup Hormel Bacon Bits
> ½ cup finely chopped onion
> 1 teaspoon dried parsley flakes

Spray a slow cooker container with butter-flavored cooking spray. In prepared container, combine carrots, apples, and apple juice. Stir in bacon bits, onion, and parsley flakes. Cover and cook on LOW for 6 to 8 hours. Mix well before serving.

HINT: Thaw carrots by placing in a colander and rinsing under hot water for one minute.

Each serving equals:

HE: 1¾ Vegetable • 1 Fruit • ¼ Slider •
5 Optional Calories

118 Calories • 2 gm Fat • 4 gm Protein •
21 gm Carbohydrate • 308 mg Sodium •
40 mg Calcium • 4 gm Fiber

DIABETIC: 2 Vegetable • 1 Fruit • ½ Meat

Sweet and Sour Cabbage

If you've never had a chance to taste a sweet and sour vegetable dish, you're in for a wonderful surprise! I like serving this with pork tenderloins or another roasted meat dish, just as my ancestors did back in the old country.   ☙   Serves 6 (1 cup)

> 6 cups shredded cabbage
> 2 cups (4 small) cored, peeled, and coarsely chopped cooking
>   apples
> 1½ cups chopped onion
> ¼ cup seedless raisins
> ¼ cup cider vinegar
> ¼ cup pourable Splenda or Sugar Twin

Spray a slow cooker container with butter-flavored cooking spray. In prepared container, combine cabbage, apples, onion, and raisins. In a small bowl, combine vinegar and Splenda. Pour liquid mixture evenly over cabbage mixture. Mix well to combine. Cover and cook on LOW for 6 to 8 hours. Mix well before serving.

Each serving equals:

HE: 1½ Vegetable • 1 Fruit • 4 Optional Calories

88 Calories • 0 gm Fat • 2 gm Protein •
20 gm Carbohydrate • 18 mg Sodium •
56 mg Calcium • 4 gm Fiber

DIABETIC: 1½ Vegetable • 1 Fruit

Cheesy Cabbage-Carrot Side Dish

When you swirl all of these ingredients together, you may wonder what kind of magic will pull them together into a scrumptious side dish—but a little heat and a lot of time work wonders! The creamy-cheesy sauce is so irresistible, you'll be tempted to lick the pot.

○ Serves 8 (1 full cup)

9 cups shredded cabbage
3 cups shredded carrots
½ cup chopped onion
1 (10¾-ounce) can Healthy Request Cream of Mushroom Soup
2 cups cubed Velveeta Light processed cheese
1 teaspoon dried parsley flakes
⅛ teaspoon black pepper

Spray a slow cooker container with butter-flavored cooking spray. In prepared container, combine cabbage, carrots, and onion. In a medium bowl, combine mushroom soup, Velveeta cheese, parsley flakes, and black pepper. Pour soup mixture evenly over cabbage mixture. Mix well to combine. Cover and cook on LOW for 3 to 4 hours. Mix well before serving.

Each serving equals:

HE: 2 Vegetable • 1 Protein • ¼ Slider • 1 Optional Calorie

140 Calories • 4 gm Fat • 8 gm Protein • 18 gm Carbohydrate • 680 mg Sodium • 263 mg Calcium • 3 gm Fiber

DIABETIC: 2 Vegetable • 1 Meat

Green Bean Almondine Pot

Originally from France, string beans almondine combines textures and flavors in a truly memorable dish. I've taken it a step or two further here, joining the beans and nuts in a luscious cheese sauce that is definitely *delicieux* (delicious)! ◐ Serves 6 (½ cup)

> 4½ cups frozen cut green beans, thawed
> 1 (10¾-ounce) can Healthy Request Cream of Chicken Soup
> 21 small fat-free saltine crackers, made into crumbs
> 1 cup cubed Velveeta Light processed cheese
> ½ cup slivered almonds

Spray a slow cooker container with butter-flavored cooking spray. In prepared container, combine green beans, chicken soup, and cracker crumbs. Stir in Velveeta cheese and almonds. Cover and cook on LOW for 4 to 6 hours. Mix well before serving.

HINTS: 1. Thaw green beans by placing in a colander and rinsing under hot water for one minute.
2. A self-seal sandwich bag works great for crushing crackers.

Each serving equals:

HE: 1 Protein • 1 Vegetable • ⅔ Fat • ½ Bread • ¼ Slider • 10 Optional Calories

212 Calories • 8 gm Fat • 10 gm Protein • 25 gm Carbohydrate • 626 mg Sodium • 176 mg Calcium • 3 gm Fiber

DIABETIC: 1½ Vegetable • 1 Meat • 1 Starch • 1 Fat

Green Beans with Onion-Mushroom Sauce

I've met so many people who feel that a festive table isn't complete without a string bean dish topped with French fried onions. If you feel the same way, this one's for you! Of course, good enough is never good enough for me, so I've added fresh mushrooms and sour cream to make a dish that tastes like a party all by itself.

● Serves 6 (1 cup)

1 (10¾-ounce) can Healthy Request Cream of Mushroom Soup
¼ cup Land O Lakes no-fat sour cream
½ teaspoon dried thyme
⅛ teaspoon black pepper
2 (16-ounce) cans cut green beans, rinsed and drained
1½ cups chopped fresh mushrooms
½ cup finely chopped onion
½ cup canned French's Fried Onion Rings

Spray a slow cooker container with butter-flavored cooking spray. In prepared container, combine mushroom soup, sour cream, thyme, and black pepper. Add green beans, mushrooms, and chopped onion. Mix well to combine. Stir in onion rings. Cover and cook on LOW for 3 to 4 hours. Mix well before serving.

Each serving equals:

HE: 2 Vegetable • ¾ Slider • 8 Optional Calories
___
103 Calories • 3 gm Fat • 3 gm Protein •
16 gm Carbohydrate • 694 mg Sodium •
89 mg Calcium • 3 gm Fiber
___
DIABETIC: 1½ Vegetable • 1 Starch

Dutchman's Green Beans and Tomatoes

I've always enjoyed reading cookbooks from around the world, and paging through recipes for all that food inspires me to create my own versions. Here's a dish that would be right at home on an Amsterdam dining table, where sweet and tangy go together like tulips and wooden shoes. ☻ Serves 6 (1 full cup)

1½ cups (9 ounces) diced Dubuque 97% fat-free ham or any
    extra-lean ham
6½ cups frozen cut green beans, thawed
1½ cups finely chopped onion
1¾ cups (one 14½-ounce can) stewed tomatoes, chopped and
    undrained
1 cup (one 8-ounce can) Hunt's Tomato Sauce
1 tablespoon pourable Splenda or Sugar Twin
⅛ teaspoon black pepper

Spray a slow cooker container with butter-flavored cooking spray. In prepared container, combine ham, green beans, and onion. Stir in undrained stewed tomatoes, tomato sauce, Splenda, and black pepper. Cover and cook on LOW for 6 to 8 hours. Mix well before serving.

HINT: Thaw green beans by placing in a colander and rinsing under hot water for one minute.

Each serving equals:

HE: 4 Vegetable • 1 Protein

161 Calories • 1 gm Fat • 11 gm Protein •
27 gm Carbohydrate • 929 mg Sodium •
91 mg Calcium • 6 gm Fiber

DIABETIC: 4 Vegetable • 1 Meat

Special Green Beans
and Carrots

Do you remember your grandmother cooking the vegetables in the same dish as her roast, so that the veggies would take on some of that meaty flavor as they cooked? Now you can get that same savory flavor in your slow cooker, and some help from a truly luscious fat-free gravy. ☺ Serves 6 (1 cup)

1 (12-ounce) jar Heinz Fat Free Beef Gravy
6 tablespoons Hormel Bacon Bits
3½ cups frozen cut green beans, thawed
3 cups frozen sliced carrots, thawed
1 cup finely chopped onion
⅛ teaspoon black pepper

Spray a slow cooker container with butter-flavored cooking spray. In prepared container, combine beef gravy and bacon bits. Add green beans, carrots, and onion. Mix well to combine. Stir in black pepper. Cover and cook on HIGH for 4 hours. Mix well before serving.

HINT: Thaw green beans and carrots by placing in a colander and rinsing under hot water for one minute.

Each serving equals:

HE: 2½ Vegetable • ½ Slider • 4 Optional Calories

110 Calories • 2 gm Fat • 6 gm Protein •
17 gm Carbohydrate • 621 mg Sodium •
56 mg Calcium • 4 gm Fiber

DIABETIC: 2½ Vegetable • ½ Meat

Barbequed Green Beans

Okay, I know you can't toss your string beans on the grill, but wouldn't it be great to have that barbecued flavor mixed in with your vegetables? I stirred and blended and tested these sauce ingredients until I made myself believe the beans had come right off the fire! ☺ Serves 6 (½ cup)

1 cup (one 8-ounce can) Hunt's Tomato Sauce
½ cup pourable Splenda or Sugar Twin
1 tablespoon Worcestershire sauce
⅛ teaspoon black pepper
6 tablespoons Hormel Bacon Bits
5 cups frozen cut green beans, thawed
½ cup chopped onion

Spray a slow cooker container with butter-flavored cooking spray. In prepared container, combine tomato sauce, Splenda, Worcestershire sauce, and black pepper. Stir in bacon bits. Add green beans and onion. Mix well to combine. Cover and cook on LOW for 6 to 8 hours. Mix well before serving.

HINT: Thaw green beans by placing in a colander and rinsing under hot water for 1 minute.

Each serving equals:

HE: 2½ Vegetable • ¼ Slider • 13 Optional Calories

98 Calories • 2 gm Fat • 5 gm Protein •
15 gm Carbohydrate • 509 mg Sodium •
54 mg Calcium • 3 gm Fiber

DIABETIC: 2½ Vegetable • ½ Meat

Octoberfest Kraut

If you're a sauerkraut lover but only enjoy the treat on top of hot dogs at the ballpark, you're really missing out on one of my special favorites. Here's a terrific way to savor the flavor you love without the distraction of the game!   ☉   Serves 6 (1 cup)

> 1 cup (one 8-ounce can) tomatoes, finely chopped and undrained
> 2 tablespoons pourable Splenda or Sugar Twin
> 1 teaspoon Worcestershire sauce
> 1/4 cup Hormel Bacon Bits
> 3 1/2 cups (two 14 1/2-ounce cans) Frank's Bavarian Style
>   sauerkraut, well drained
> 1 1/2 cups finely chopped onion

Spray a slow cooker container with butter-flavored cooking spray. In prepared container, combine undrained tomatoes, Splenda, Worcestershire sauce, and bacon bits. Add sauerkraut and onion. Mix well to combine. Cover and cook on LOW for 6 to 8 hours. Mix well before serving.

HINT: If you can't find Frank's Bavarian sauerkraut, use regular sauerkraut, 1/2 teaspoon caraway seeds, and 1 teaspoon Brown Sugar Twin.

Each serving equals:

HE: 1 1/2 Vegetable • 19 Optional Calories

61 Calories • 1 gm Fat • 3 gm Protein •
10 gm Carbohydrate • 610 mg Sodium •
15 mg Calcium • 1 gm Fiber

DIABETIC: 2 Vegetable

Zucchini Special

Imagine a sort of pizza on a plate, starring zucchini as the center attraction, coupled with a scrumptious tomato sauce and luscious strands of cheese. Got the picture? Good. That's what makes this dish so special! ☻ Serves 6 (1 full cup)

> 3 cups chopped unpeeled zucchini
> ½ cup chopped onion
> 1¾ cups (one 14½-ounce can) stewed tomatoes, undrained
> 1 cup (one 8-ounce can) Hunt's Tomato Sauce
> 1 tablespoon pourable Splenda or Sugar Twin
> 1 teaspoon dried basil
> 1½ cups (6 ounces) shredded Kraft reduced-fat mozzarella cheese

Spray a slow cooker container with olive oil–flavored cooking spray. In prepared container, combine zucchini, onion, undrained stewed tomatoes, and tomato sauce. Stir in Splenda, basil, and mozzarella cheese. Cover and cook on LOW for 6 to 8 hours. Mix well before serving.

Each serving equals:

HE: 2½ Vegetable • 1⅓ Protein • 1 Optional Calorie

133 Calories • 5 gm Fat • 11 gm Protein •
11 gm Carbohydrate • 592 mg Sodium •
250 mg Calcium • 2 gm Fiber

DIABETIC: 2½ Vegetable • 1 Meat

Zucchini Tomato Pot

I decided to celebrate the glories of the garden in this superb side dish that makes beautiful use of all your fresh tomatoes and zucchini. Don't have a garden of your own? Not a problem. Your nearest farmers' market or supermarket will have just what you need at terrific prices all summer long. ☻ Serves 4 (¾ cup)

2 cups chopped unpeeled zucchini
2 cups peeled and chopped fresh tomatoes
½ cup chopped onion
2 tablespoons Kraft Fat Free Italian Dressing
2 tablespoons pourable Splenda or Sugar Twin
2 teaspoons chopped fresh basil or ½ teaspoon dried basil
¾ cup (3 ounces) shredded Kraft reduced-fat mozzarella cheese

Spray a slow cooker container with olive oil–flavored cooking spray. In prepared container, combine zucchini, tomatoes, and onion. Stir in Italian dressing, Splenda, and basil. Add mozzarella cheese. Mix gently to combine. Cover and cook on LOW for 4 to 6 hours. Mix well before serving.

Each serving equals:

HE: 2¼ Vegetable • 1 Protein • 6 Optional Calories

108 Calories • 4 gm Fat • 9 gm Protein •
9 gm Carbohydrate • 275 mg Sodium •
177 mg Calcium • 2 gm Fiber

DIABETIC: 2 Vegetable • 1 Meat

Zucchini Cheddar Cheese Side Dish

Is it a soufflé? Is it a veggie pot pie? Is it something entirely unique and original you've never seen before? Well, you tell me. All I can promise you is that it's wonderfully aromatic and downright mouthwatering. ☻ Serves 6 (1 cup)

1 cup + 2 tablespoons Bisquick Reduced Fat Baking Mix

1 tablespoon pourable Splenda or Sugar Twin

1/4 cup Kraft Fat Free Italian Dressing

3 eggs, beaten, or equivalent in egg substitute

3 cups finely chopped unpeeled zucchini

3/4 cup chopped onion

3/4 cup (3 ounces) shredded Kraft reduced-fat Cheddar cheese

1/4 cup (one 2-ounce jar) chopped pimiento, drained

Spray a slow cooker container with olive oil–flavored cooking spray. In prepared container, combine baking mix, Splenda, Italian dressing, and eggs. Stir in zucchini and onion. Add Cheddar cheese and pimiento. Mix well to combine. Cover and cook on LOW for 6 to 8 hours. Mix well before serving.

Each serving equals:

HE: 1 1/4 Vegetable • 1 Bread • 1 Protein •
5 Optional Calories

187 Calories • 7 gm Fat • 9 gm Protein •
22 gm Carbohydrate • 439 mg Sodium •
153 mg Calcium • 2 gm Fiber

DIABETIC: 1 Vegetable • 1 Starch • 1 Meat

Zucchini and Carrot Bake

I've always been a big fan of bread pudding, and not just because it's a great way to use up leftover stale bread. I tried to do a little something like that here, with carrots and zucchini, using cheddar cheese and sour cream to sauce it up and make it as rich and yummy as possible. ☻ Serves 6 (1 cup)

1 (10¾-ounce) can Healthy Request Tomato Soup
¼ cup Land O Lakes no-fat sour cream
3 cups unpeeled chopped zucchini
1 cup chopped onion
2 cups shredded carrots
2 cups (3 ounces) unseasoned dry bread cubes
¾ cup (3 ounces) shredded Kraft reduced-fat Cheddar cheese
⅛ teaspoon black pepper

Spray a slow cooker container with butter-flavored cooking spray. In prepared container, combine tomato soup and sour cream. Stir in zucchini, onion, and carrots. Add bread cubes, Cheddar cheese, and black pepper. Mix well to combine. Cover and cook on LOW for 6 to 8 hours. Mix well before serving.

HINT: Pepperidge Farm bread cubes work great.

Each serving equals:

HE: 2 Vegetable • ⅔ Bread • ½ Protein • ½ Slider

188 Calories • 4 gm Fat • 8 gm Protein •
30 gm Carbohydrate • 388 mg Sodium •
139 mg Calcium • 4 gm Fiber

DIABETIC: 2 Vegetable • 1 Starch • ½ Meat

Broccoli-Corn Casserole

Here's a dish bound to please almost everyone (not Cliff, of course, since he and broccoli just don't mix). It's one of the creamiest veggie dishes I've ever created, and yet it can still be enjoyed by anyone committed to living healthy and happily ever after!

☻ Serves 6 (1 cup)

> 1 (10¾-ounce) can Healthy Request Cream of Broccoli or
>   Mushroom Soup
> 1 cup (one 8-ounce can) cream-style corn
> 3 cups frozen chopped broccoli, thawed
> 2 cups frozen whole-kernel corn, thawed
> ¾ cup finely chopped onion
> 1½ cups (6 ounces) shredded Kraft reduced-fat Cheddar cheese

Spray a slow cooker container with butter-flavored cooking spray. In prepared container, combine broccoli soup and cream-style corn. Add broccoli, whole-kernel corn, and onion. Mix well to combine. Stir in Cheddar cheese. Cover and cook on LOW for 5 to 6 hours. Mix well before serving.

HINT: Thaw broccoli and whole-kernel corn by placing in a colander and rinsing under hot water for one minute.

Each serving equals:

> HE: 1¼ Vegetable • 1 Bread • 1 Protein • ¼ Slider •
> 7 Optional Calories
>
> ───────────────────────────────
> 223 Calories • 7 gm Fat • 12 gm Protein •
> 28 gm Carbohydrate • 318 mg Sodium •
> 291 mg Calcium • 4 gm Fiber
> ───────────────────────────────
> DIABETIC: 1 Vegetable • 1 Starch • 1 Meat

Creamy Corn and Cabbage

Cabbage does especially well in the slow cooker, you'll discover, because it absorbs the delicious flavors of everything else in the pot. The sweetness of the corn is a perfect partner in this scrumptious recipe. ☻ Serves 6 (½ cup)

> 1 (10¾-ounce) can Healthy Request Cream of Mushroom Soup
> ¼ cup (one 2-ounce jar) chopped pimiento, undrained
> 5 cups shredded cabbage
> 3 cups frozen whole-kernel corn, thawed
> ½ cup chopped onion
> 1½ teaspoons dried parsley flakes
> ⅛ teaspoon black pepper

Spray a slow cooker container with butter-flavored cooking spray. In prepared container, combine mushroom soup and undrained pimiento. Add cabbage, corn, and onion. Mix well to combine. Stir in parsley flakes and black pepper. Cover and cook on LOW for 6 to 8 hours. Mix well before serving.

HINT: Thaw corn by placing in a colander and rinsing under hot water for one minute.

Each serving equals:

HE: 1 Bread • 1 Vegetable • ¼ Slider •
7 Optional Calories

138 Calories • 2 gm Fat • 4 gm Protein •
26 gm Carbohydrate • 214 mg Sodium •
83 mg Calcium • 3 gm Fiber

DIABETIC: 1 Starch • 1 Vegetable

Aaron's Cheesy Corn

Of course my grandson Aaron loves corn—he's an Iowan, and it's in our genes! But even he plays favorites sometimes, and this is one he especially adores. Isn't it great to know that a delicious dish can please all the generations at once? I think so!

◑ Serves 8 (½ cup)

> 1 (8-ounce) package Philadelphia fat-free cream cheese
> ¼ cup water
> 1 tablespoon + 1 teaspoon reduced-calorie margarine
> 2 tablespoons pourable Splenda or Sugar Twin
> 4 cups frozen whole-kernel corn, thawed
> 1 cup (4 ounces) shredded Kraft reduced-fat Cheddar cheese

Spray a slow cooker container with butter-flavored cooking spray. In prepared container, combine cream cheese, water, margarine, and Splenda. Add corn and Cheddar cheese. Mix well to combine. Cover and cook on LOW for 4 hours. Mix well before serving.

HINT: Thaw corn by placing in a colander and rinsing under hot water for one minute.

Each serving equals:

HE: 1 Bread • 1 Protein • ¼ Fat • 2 Optional Calories

160 Calories • 4 gm Fat • 10 gm Protein • 21 gm Carbohydrate • 198 mg Sodium • 232 mg Calcium • 2 gm Fiber

DIABETIC: 1 Starch • 1 Meat

Garden Harvest Corn

Red tomatoes, green zucchini, and gorgeous yellow corn as golden as a Midwestern summer sun—if that isn't a recipe for happiness, I don't know what is! Always remember that it's important to please the eye at the same time we satisfy the stomach, so consider color when you compose a meal. ☻ Serves 6 (½ cup)

3 cups fresh or frozen whole-kernel corn, thawed
1 cup peeled and chopped fresh tomatoes
1 cup unpeeled chopped zucchini
1 cup chopped red onion
2 tablespoons pourable Splenda or Sugar Twin
2 tablespoons chopped fresh parsley or 1½ teaspoons dried
    parsley flakes
1 tablespoon reduced-calorie margarine

Spray a slow cooker container with butter-flavored cooking spray. In prepared container, combine corn, tomatoes, zucchini, and onion. Stir in Splenda, parsley, and margarine. Cover and cook on HIGH for 2 to 3 hours. Mix well before serving.

Each serving equals:

HE: 1 Bread • 1 Vegetable • ¼ Fat •
2 Optional Calories

114 Calories • 2 gm Fat • 3 gm Protein •
21 gm Carbohydrate • 30 mg Sodium •
15 mg Calcium • 3 gm Fiber

DIABETIC: 1 Starch • 1 Vegetable

Succulent Succotash

The name "succotash" comes from the Native Americans, who were probably the first to stir up a tasty blend of corn and beans. But back then I doubt they or the first European settlers ever imagined such a scrumptiously creamy-cheesy version. Aren't we lucky to be living now?　　◑　　Serves 6 (1 full cup)

> 3 cups frozen whole-kernel corn, thawed
>
> 3 cups frozen cut green beans, thawed
>
> 2 cups frozen green lima beans, thawed
>
> 1 cup chopped onion
>
> 1 (10¾-ounce) can Healthy Request Cream of Mushroom Soup
>
> ¾ cup (3 ounces) shredded Kraft reduced-fat Cheddar cheese
>
> 2 teaspoons dried parsley flakes
>
> ⅛ teaspoon black pepper

Spray a slow cooker container with butter-flavored cooking spray. In prepared container, combine corn, green beans, lima beans, and onion. Stir in mushroom soup and Cheddar cheese. Add parsley flakes and black pepper. Mix well to combine. Cover and cook on LOW for 6 to 8 hours. Mix well before serving.

HINT: Thaw corn, green beans, and lima beans by placing in a colander and rinsing under hot water for one minute.

Each serving equals:

HE: 2 Vegetable • 1 Bread • ½ Protein • ¼ Slider • 8 Optional Calories

233 Calories • 5 gm Fat • 11 gm Protein • 36 gm Carbohydrate • 218 mg Sodium • 192 mg Calcium • 6 gm Fiber

DIABETIC: 1½ Starch • 1 Vegetable • ½ Meat

Medley of Beans

Three-bean salad is an American tradition, but I figured that blending beans in a warm side dish was bound to be just as popular! Besides being super-high in fiber and fat-free, this dish is downright delectable—try it and see!   ☻   Serves 8 (1 cup)

> 4 cups (two 16-ounce cans) cut green beans, rinsed and drained
> 20 ounces (two 16-ounce cans) great northern beans, rinsed and
>   drained
> 10 ounces (one 16-ounce can) red kidney beans, rinsed and
>   drained
> 1 cup finely chopped onion
> 1 cup chunky salsa (mild, medium, or hot)
> 2 tablespoons reduced-sodium ketchup
> ¼ cup pourable Splenda or Sugar Twin
> ⅛ teaspoon black pepper

Spray a slow cooker container with butter-flavored cooking spray. In prepared container, combine green beans, great northern beans, and kidney beans. Add onion. Mix well to combine. Stir in salsa, ketchup, Splenda, and black pepper. Cover and cook on LOW for 6 to 8 hours. Mix well before serving.

Each serving equals:

HE: 1½ Vegetable • 1¼ Protein • 1 Bread •
3 Optional Calories

184 Calories • 0 gm Fat • 11 gm Protein •
35 gm Carbohydrate • 481 mg Sodium •
86 mg Calcium • 9 gm Fiber

DIABETIC: 1½ Vegetable • 1½ Meat • 1½ Starch

Calico Bean Bake

Here's a kind of kitchen-sink recipe that was as much fun to create as it is to eat! It's a real "pantry pleaser," something you can stir up with almost no notice because most of the ingredients will be on hand. Are you surprised that I would choose to mix in a can of pork & beans? They provide some great ready-made flavor that makes good cooking sense when you don't have a lot of prep time but want something yummy to serve your family.

● Serves 6 (1 cup)

8 ounces extra-lean ground turkey or beef
¾ cup chopped onion
½ cup reduced-sodium ketchup
2 tablespoons cider vinegar
6 tablespoons Hormel Bacon Bits
½ cup pourable Splenda or Sugar Twin

10 ounces (one 16-ounce can) red kidney beans, rinsed and drained
10 ounces (one 15-ounce can) butter beans, rinsed and drained
10 ounces (one 15-ounce can) pork & beans, pork removed and undrained

In a large skillet sprayed with butter-flavored cooking spray, brown meat and onion. Spray a slow cooker container with butter-flavored cooking spray. In prepared container, combine meat mixture, ketchup, and vinegar. Stir in bacon bits and Splenda. Add kidney beans, butter beans, and pork and beans. Mix well to combine. Cover and cook on LOW for 8 hours. Mix well before serving.

Each serving equals:

HE: 2 Protein • 1 Bread • ¼ Vegetable • ¼ Slider • 13 Optional Calories

248 Calories • 4 gm Fat • 19 gm Protein • 34 gm Carbohydrate • 806 mg Sodium • 73 mg Calcium • 8 gm Fiber

DIABETIC: 3 Meat • 1½ Starch

Maple Bean Pot

If you already love baked beans, I'm willing to bet this New England–inspired pot of beans will appeal to your tastebuds. What a sweet and tangy blend to serve alongside burgers or franks!

♥ Serves 6 (¾ cup)

> 2 cups (one 16-ounce can) diced tomatoes, undrained
> ½ cup reduced-sodium ketchup
> ¼ cup Log Cabin or Cary's Sugar Free Maple Syrup
> 2 tablespoons pourable Splenda or Sugar Twin
> 1½ teaspoons dried parsley flakes
> 30 ounces (three 16-ounce cans) great northern beans, rinsed and drained
> 1¼ cups finely chopped onion

Spray a slow cooker container with butter-flavored cooking spray. In prepared container, combine undrained tomatoes, ketchup, maple syrup, Splenda, and parsley flakes. Add great northern beans and onion. Mix well to combine. Cover and cook on HIGH for 3 to 4 hours. Mix well before serving.

Each serving equals:

HE: 1½ Protein • 1 Bread • 1 Vegetable

209 Calories • 1 gm Fat • 12 gm Protein •
38 gm Carbohydrate • 128 mg Sodium •
93 mg Calcium • 8 gm Fiber

DIABETIC: 2 Starch • 1½ Meat • 1 Vegetable

Slow Cooker Beans

Low and slow—meaning low heat and long, slow cooking—is my recommendation to transform some ordinary canned beans into food worth writing home about! The bacon bits let you enjoy rich flavor without the mess of frying up a few slices to blend with the beans. ☻ Serves 6 (½ cup)

20 ounces (two 16-ounce cans) great northern beans, rinsed and
    drained
¾ cup finely chopped onion
½ cup reduced-sodium ketchup
⅓ cup pourable Splenda or Sugar Twin
6 tablespoons Hormel Bacon Bits
⅛ teaspoon black pepper

Spray a slow cooker container with butter-flavored cooking spray. In prepared container, combine great northern beans, onion, and ketchup. Add Splenda, bacon bits, and black pepper. Mix well to combine. Cover and cook on LOW for 3 to 4 hours. Mix well before serving.

Each serving equals:

HE: 1 Bread • 1 Protein • ¼ Vegetable • ½ Slider •
10 Optional Calories

174 Calories • 2 gm Fat • 10 gm Protein •
29 gm Carbohydrate • 258 mg Sodium •
58 mg Calcium • 5 gm Fiber

DIABETIC: 2 Starch • 1½ Meat

Cauliflower and Rice Side Dish

I'm convinced that nothing makes cauliflower "bloom" quite like a rich and cheesy sauce! This is such an easy and delightful way to eat your vegetables, and it tastes so luscious and light, even your kids are likely to love it. Try it and see! ☻ Serves 6 (1 cup)

1 (10¾-ounce) can Healthy
    Request Cream of
    Mushroom Soup
½ cup Land O Lakes no-fat
    sour cream
½ cup water
3 cups frozen cut cauliflower,
    thawed
1 cup chopped onion
½ cup (one 2.5-ounce jar)
    sliced mushrooms, drained

¼ cup (one 2-ounce jar)
    chopped pimiento,
    drained
1 cup uncooked instant rice
1½ cups cubed Velveeta Light
    processed cheese
1 teaspoon dried parsley flakes
⅛ teaspoon black pepper

Spray a slow cooker container with butter-flavored cooking spray. In prepared container, combine mushroom soup, sour cream, and water. Stir in cauliflower, onion, mushrooms, and pimiento. Add uncooked rice, Velveeta cheese, parsley flakes, and black pepper. Mix well to combine. Cover and cook on LOW for 4 to 6 hours. Mix well before serving.

HINT: Thaw cauliflower by placing in a colander and rinsing under hot water for one minute.

Each serving equals:

HE: 1½ Vegetable • 1 Protein • ½ Bread • ½ Slider • 7 Optional Calories

188 Calories • 4 gm Fat • 10 gm Protein • 28 gm Carbohydrate • 747 mg Sodium • 257 mg Calcium • 3 gm Fiber

DIABETIC: 1½ Vegetable • 1½ Starch/Carbohydrate • 1 Meat

Peas and Rice Please

Oh, wouldn't it be nice, eating peas and rice? (Forgive the little poem, but the sentiment seems just right to me!) Cooking rice in chicken broth is just one of the reasons this dish is so tasty.

○ Serves 6 (full ½ cup)

> 2 cups (one 16-ounce can) Healthy Request Chicken Broth
> ½ cup water
> 1 cup uncooked instant rice
> 1½ cups frozen peas, thawed
> ¾ cup chopped onion
> 6 tablespoons grated Kraft fat-free Parmesan cheese
> ½ teaspoon Italian seasoning

Spray a slow cooker container with olive oil–flavored cooking spray. In prepared container, combine chicken broth and water. Add uncooked rice, peas, and onion. Mix well to combine. Stir in Parmesan cheese and Italian seasoning. Cover and cook on LOW for 3 to 4 hours. Mix well before serving.

HINT: Thaw peas by placing in colander and rinsing under hot water for one minute.

Each serving equals:

> HE: 1 Bread • ¼ Protein • ¼ Vegetable •
> 5 Optional Calories
> ___
> 92 Calories • 0 gm Fat • 4 gm Protein •
> 19 gm Carbohydrate • 181 mg Sodium •
> 16 mg Calcium • 2 gm Fiber
> ___
> DIABETIC: 1 Starch

Cheesy Rice and Tomatoes

Rice cooked long and slow drinks up any sauce it's cooked in, making it a natural for slow cooker recipes. This time, the rice will be "sipping" up both cheese and tomatoes, transforming it into something dreamy and oh-so-good.

Serves 6 (1 cup)

1 (10¾-ounce) can Healthy Request Cream of Mushroom Soup
2 cups (one 16-ounce can) diced tomatoes, undrained
1½ cups reduced-sodium tomato juice
2 cups uncooked instant rice
½ cup finely chopped onion
1½ cups (6 ounces) shredded Kraft reduced-fat Cheddar cheese
1½ teaspoons dried parsley flakes

Spray a slow cooker container with butter-flavored cooking spray. In prepared container, combine mushroom soup, undrained tomatoes, and tomato juice. Stir in uncooked rice and onion. Add Cheddar cheese and parsley flakes. Mix well to combine. Cover and cook on LOW for 4 to 6 hours. Mix well before serving.

Each serving equals:

HE: 1⅓ Protein • 1¼ Vegetable • 1 Bread • ¼ Slider • 7 Optional Calories

---

247 Calories • 7 gm Fat • 10 gm Protein • 36 gm Carbohydrate • 404 mg Sodium • 269 mg Calcium • 2 gm Fiber

---

DIABETIC: 1½ Starch • 1 Vegetable • 1 Meat

Cheesy Corn and Macaroni Side Dish

I never listen to people who insist you shouldn't mix starches in one dish—why would I, when it would mean never savoring corn and macaroni at the same time? They're both wonderful on their own, but together they're a Top Ten song rising high on the charts. Add a little cheese, and *wheee*—it's a hit! ☺ Serves 6 (½ cup)

> 1 (10¾-ounce) can Healthy Request Cream of Mushroom Soup
> 1 cup (one 8-ounce can) cream-style corn
> 1½ teaspoons dried parsley flakes
> ⅛ teaspoon black pepper
> 2 cups cooked elbow macaroni, rinsed and drained
> ¾ cup (3 ounces) shredded Kraft reduced-fat Cheddar cheese
> ¼ cup (one 2-ounce jar) chopped pimiento, drained

Spray a slow cooker container with butter-flavored cooking spray. In prepared container, combine mushroom soup, corn, parsley flakes, and black pepper. Add macaroni. Mix well to combine. Stir in Cheddar cheese and pimiento. Cover and cook on HIGH for 3 to 4 hours. Mix well before serving.

HINT: Usually 1⅓ cups uncooked macaroni cooks to about 2 cups.

Each serving equals:

HE: 1 Bread • ½ Protein • ¼ Slider •
7 Optional Calories

---

164 Calories • 4 gm Fat • 7 gm Protein •
25 gm Carbohydrate • 299 mg Sodium •
146 mg Calcium • 1 gm Fiber

DIABETIC: 1½ Starch • ½ Meat

Scalloped Potatoes and Vegetables

Lifting the lid on this colorful side dish, you're sure to smile—and inhale the luscious aroma again and again! From the freezer to the slow cooker, the dish is ready to cook in just minutes, which makes it perfect for your busiest days. ❂ Serves 6 (1 cup)

1 (10¾-ounce) can Healthy Request Cream of Mushroom Soup
2 cups (one 16-ounce can) diced tomatoes, undrained
6 cups shredded loose-packed frozen potatoes

1 cup frozen cut green beans, thawed
1 cup frozen sliced carrots, thawed
¾ cup chopped onion
1 teaspoon dried parsley flakes
⅛ teaspoon black pepper

Spray a slow cooker container with butter-flavored cooking spray. In prepared container, combine mushroom soup and undrained tomatoes. Add potatoes, green beans, carrots, and onion. Mix well to combine. Stir in parsley flakes and black pepper. Cover and cook on LOW for 6 to 8 hours. Mix well before serving.

HINTS: 1. Thaw green beans and carrots by placing in a colander and rinsing under hot water for one minute.
2. Mr. Dell's frozen shredded potatoes are a good choice, or raw shredded potatoes, rinsed and patted dry, may be used in place of frozen potatoes.

Each serving equals:

HE: 1½ Vegetable • ⅔ Bread • ¼ Slider • 8 Optional Calories

133 Calories • 1 gm Fat • 4 gm Protein • 27 gm Carbohydrate • 297 mg Sodium • 81 mg Calcium • 4 gm Fiber

DIABETIC: 1½ Vegetable • 1 Starch

Pam's Pizza Potatoes

My daughter-in-law Pam looked so happy when I told her what I was making for lunch the day she visited. "Potatoes that taste like pizza?" she asked with delight in her voice. "I can't think of anything I'd rather eat right now!" When she finally tasted the dish, she wasn't disappointed. Rather, she was even more enthusiastic, which is why I'm calling it hers.   ☻   Serves 6 (1 full cup)

6 cups thinly sliced unpeeled baking potatoes

1 cup sliced onion

1 cup (one 8-ounce can) Hunt's Tomato Sauce

1/2 cup water

1 1/2 cups (6 ounces) shredded Kraft reduced-fat mozzarella cheese

1 tablespoon pourable Splenda or Sugar Twin

1 1/2 teaspoons pizza or Italian seasoning

Spray a slow cooker container with butter-flavored cooking spray. In prepared container, combine potatoes and onion. In a small bowl, combine tomato sauce, water, mozzarella cheese, Splenda, and pizza seasoning. Pour sauce mixture evenly over potato mixture. Cover and cook on LOW for 8 hours. Mix well before serving.

HINT: This can be turned into a main dish by adding 2 (3.5-ounce) packages Hormel reduced-fat pepperoni or 8 ounces browned extra-lean ground sirloin beef or turkey breast.

Each serving equals:

HE: 1 Bread • 1 Protein • 1 Vegetable • 1 Optional Calorie

208 Calories • 4 gm Fat • 12 gm Protein • 31 gm Carbohydrate • 424 mg Sodium • 204 mg Calcium • 3 gm Fiber

DIABETIC: 1 1/2 Starch • 1 Meat • 1 Vegetable

Scalloped Pizza Potatoes

Yes, I've got two versions of a pizza-potato dish in this cookbook, and why not? Pizza is just about the most popular carry-out food in the United States, and I think such a beloved taste treat deserves to be featured more than once! This time, I "topped" it with cheddar instead of mozzarella because I like both. How about you?

◑ Serves 4 (1 full cup)

6 cups shredded loose-packed frozen potatoes
1 (10¾-ounce) can Healthy Request Tomato Soup
1 teaspoon pizza or Italian seasoning
¼ cup sliced ripe olives
½ cup (one 2.5-ounce jar) sliced mushrooms, drained
1 cup finely chopped onion
¾ cup (3 ounces) shredded Kraft reduced-fat Cheddar cheese

Spray a slow cooker container with olive oil–flavored cooking spray. In prepared container, combine potatoes, tomato soup, and pizza seasoning. Stir in olives, mushrooms, and onion. Add Cheddar cheese. Mix well to combine. Cover and cook on LOW for 6 to 8 hours. Mix well before serving.

HINT: Mr. Dell's frozen shredded potatoes are a good choice, or raw shredded potatoes, rinsed and patted dry, may be used in place of frozen potatoes.

Each serving equals:

HE: 1 Bread • 1 Protein • ½ Vegetable • ¼ Fat • ½ Slider • 10 Optional Calories

246 Calories • 6 gm Fat • 10 gm Protein • 38 gm Carbohydrate • 439 mg Sodium • 180 mg Calcium • 5 gm Fiber

DIABETIC: 2 Starch • 1 Meat • ½ Vegetable

Veggie Hash Browns

It's one sure way to get your kids to eat their vegetables—blend them with some creamy, cheesy hash brown potatoes! Who knows, you might succeed in convincing them that peas and carrots are pretty good even without a potato partner.

◐ Serves 8 (scant 1 cup)

> 9 cups shredded loose-packed frozen potatoes
> 2 cups frozen peas and carrots, thawed
> 1 (10¾-ounce) can Healthy Request Cream of Mushroom Soup
> 1 teaspoon dried parsley flakes
> ⅛ teaspoon black pepper
> 1½ cups cubed Velveeta Light processed cheese

Spray a slow cooker container with butter-flavored cooking spray. In prepared container, combine potatoes and peas and carrots. Add mushroom soup, parsley flakes, and black pepper. Mix well to combine. Stir in Velveeta cheese. Cover and cook on LOW for 4 to 6 hours. Mix well before serving.

HINTS: 1. Mr. Dell's frozen shredded potatoes are a good choice, or raw shredded potatoes, rinsed and patted dry, may be used in place of frozen potatoes.
2. Thaw peas and carrots by placing in a colander and rinsing under hot water for one minute.

Each serving equals:

HE: 1 Bread • ¾ Protein • ¼ Vegetable • ¼ Slider • 1 Optional Calorie

---

167 Calories • 3 gm Fat • 8 gm Protein • 27 gm Carbohydrate • 512 mg Sodium • 172 mg Calcium • 3 gm Fiber

---

DIABETIC: 1½ Starch • 1 Meat

Creamy Hash Browns

Wasn't it Mae West who said, "Too much of a good thing can be wonderful!"? Perhaps she was thinking about potatoes delectably drenched in rich and luscious cheese. Once you've tried hash browns this creamy, you may never be able to eat them plain again!

❂ Serves 8 (1 cup)

9 cups shredded loose-packed frozen potatoes
1 cup finely chopped onion
½ cup Hormel Bacon Bits
1 (10¾-ounce) can Healthy Request Cream of Mushroom Soup
¼ cup Land O Lakes no-fat sour cream
1½ cups cubed Velveeta Light processed cheese
⅛ teaspoon black pepper

Spray a slow cooker container with butter-flavored cooking spray. In prepared container, combine potatoes, onion, and bacon bits. In a medium bowl, combine mushroom soup and sour cream. Stir in Velveeta cheese and black pepper. Add soup mixture to potato mixture. Mix well to combine. Cover and cook on LOW for 4 to 6 hours. Mix well before serving.

HINT: Mr. Dell's frozen shredded potatoes are a good choice, or raw shredded potatoes, rinsed and patted dry, may be used in place of frozen potatoes.

Each serving equals:

HE: ¾ Bread • ¾ Protein • ½ Slider •
13 Optional Calories

180 Calories • 4 gm Fat • 10 gm Protein •
26 gm Carbohydrate • 745 mg Sodium •
176 mg Calcium • 2 gm Fiber

DIABETIC: 1½ Starch/Carbohydrate • 1 Meat

German Potato Salad

Many Americans have been eating potato salad since childhood but have never tasted the warm potato salad German immigrants brought with them to America. Usually made with those wonderful little red potatoes, this tangy dish is a revelation. What a wonderful accompaniment it makes for a pork roast or other meaty main dish!

◑ Serves 6 (1 full cup)

1½ cups water
¼ cup cider vinegar
¼ cup pourable Splenda or Sugar Twin
3 tablespoons all-purpose flour
6 tablespoons Hormel Bacon Bits
1 teaspoon dried parsley flakes
⅛ teaspoon black pepper
5 cups sliced unpeeled raw red potatoes
1½ cups chopped onion
1½ cups chopped celery

Spray a slow cooker container with butter-flavored cooking spray. In a large bowl, combine water, vinegar, Splenda, flour, bacon bits, parsley flakes, and black pepper. Add potatoes, onion, and celery. Mix well to combine. Pour mixture into prepared container. Cover and cook on LOW for 8 hours. Mix gently before serving. Serve warm.

Each serving equals:

HE: 1 Bread • 1 Vegetable • ¼ Slider • 10 Optional Calories

162 Calories • 2 gm Fat • 6 gm Protein • 30 gm Carbohydrate • 285 mg Sodium • 30 mg Calcium • 3 gm Fiber

DIABETIC: 1½ Starch • 1 Vegetable • ½ Meat

Make-Ahead Mashed Potatoes

One of the hardest things about having dinner parties is getting the food ready at the same time you want to be visiting with your guests, right? Well, here's a great way to prepare truly irresistible mashed potatoes in advance, so they can be served whenever you want. Better make plenty if you're having a crowd!

◐ Serves 8 (¾ cup)

> *3 cups hot water*
> *2⅔ cups instant potato flakes*
> *½ cup (4 ounces) Philadelphia fat-free cream cheese*
> *½ cup Land O Lakes no-fat sour cream*
> *1 tablespoon + 1 teaspoon reduced-calorie margarine*
> *1 teaspoon dried onion flakes*
> *⅛ teaspoon black pepper*
> *Paprika*

Spray a slow cooker container with butter-flavored cooking spray. In prepared container, combine water and potatoes, mixing well with a fork. Stir in cream cheese, sour cream, margarine, onion flakes, and black pepper. Lightly sprinkle top with paprika. Cover and cook on LOW for 3 to 4 hours.

Each serving equals:

> HE: 1 Bread • ¼ Protein • ¼ Fat •
> 15 Optional Calories
> _____
> 77 Calories • 1 gm Fat • 4 gm Protein •
> 13 gm Carbohydrate • 138 mg Sodium •
> 85 mg Calcium • 0 gm Fiber
> _____
> DIABETIC: 1 Starch

Candied Sweet Potatoes

They aren't just for Thanksgiving dinner, I'm happy to report. These spicy-sweet potatoes will make you feel you've got something to celebrate, even if it's just any old Wednesday.

○ Serves 6 (½ cup)

> 1 cup (one 8-ounce can) crushed pineapple, packed in fruit juice, undrained
> ¼ cup pourable Splenda or Sugar Twin
> ½ teaspoon apple pie spice
> 1 (17-ounce) can vacuum-packed sweet potatoes, rinsed and thinly sliced

Spray a slow cooker container with butter-flavored cooking spray. In prepared container, combine undrained pineapple, Splenda, and apple pie spice. Stir in sweet potatoes. Cover and cook on HIGH for 4 hours. Mix well before serving.

Each serving equals:

HE: 1 Bread • ⅓ Fruit • 3 Optional Calories

88 Calories • 0 gm Fat • 1 gm Protein •
21 gm Carbohydrate • 43 mg Sodium •
24 mg Calcium • 2 gm Fiber

DIABETIC: 1 Starch

Pasta Rotini Side Dish

What a quick and easy way to offer a tasty pasta appetizer without worrying about boiling water, how long to cook the pasta, and how to make a sauce from scratch! It's stress-free, truly tasty, and can be doubled to serve a larger group. ☻ Serves 4 (½ cup)

1 cup (one 8-ounce can) Hunt's Tomato Sauce
1 cup (one 8-ounce can) tomatoes, finely chopped and undrained
½ cup (one 2.5-ounce jar) sliced mushrooms, drained
1 tablespoon pourable Splenda or Sugar Twin
1 teaspoon Italian seasoning
⅛ teaspoon black pepper
½ cup frozen peas, thawed
1½ cups cooked rotini pasta, rinsed and drained

Spray a slow cooker container with olive oil–flavored cooking spray. In prepared container, combine tomato sauce, undrained tomatoes, and mushrooms. Stir in Splenda, Italian seasoning, and black pepper. Add peas and rotini pasta. Mix well to combine. Cover and cook on HIGH for 3 to 4 hours. Mix well before serving.

HINT: Usually a full 1 cup uncooked rotini pasta cooks to about 1½ cups.

Each serving equals:

HE: 1¾ Vegetable • 1 Bread • 2 Optional Calories

104 Calories • 0 gm Fat • 5 gm Protein • 21 gm Carbohydrate • 550 mg Sodium • 26 mg Calcium • 3 gm Fiber

DIABETIC: 1½ Vegetable • 1 Starch

Cleland's Macaroni and Tomatoes

My father-in-law loves home cooking, especially old-fashioned hearty dishes like this one that are sure to satisfy a hard-working farmer's appetite. It's a pleasure to cook for him and Cliff because I know their plates will be cleaned and my efforts appreciated!

◐ Serves 6 (1 cup)

1 (10¾-ounce) can Healthy Request Cream of Mushroom Soup

2 cups (one 16-ounce can) diced tomatoes, undrained

¼ cup reduced-sodium tomato juice

6 tablespoons Hormel Bacon Bits

1 cup finely chopped onion

3 cups cooked elbow macaroni

½ teaspoon dried basil

Spray a slow cooker container with butter-flavored cooking spray. In prepared container, combine mushroom soup, undrained tomatoes, and tomato juice. Stir in bacon bits and onion. Add macaroni and basil. Mix well to combine. Cover and cook on LOW for 6 to 8 hours. Mix well before serving.

HINT: Usually 2 cups uncooked macaroni cooks to about 3 cups.

Each serving equals:

HE: 1 Bread • 1 Vegetable • ½ Slider • 4 Optional Calories

179 Calories • 3 gm Fat • 7 gm Protein • 31 gm Carbohydrate • 555 mg Sodium • 67 mg Calcium • 2 gm Fiber

DIABETIC: 1½ Starch • 1 Vegetable • ½ Meat

Bountiful Blessings Dressing

I don't believe in waiting for Thanksgiving to express my gratitude to the Lord and to the people I love. Neither do I believe in dining only once a year on savory "dressing" alongside the big turkey. Here's a recipe I hope you'll serve frequently and use its name as a reminder to count your blessings often. I surely do!

● Serves 8 (¾ cup)

2 cups (one 16-ounce can) Healthy Request Chicken Broth
1 (10¾-ounce) can Healthy Request Cream of Mushroom Soup
1 teaspoon ground sage
½ teaspoon poultry seasoning
⅛ teaspoon black pepper
1½ cups finely chopped celery
1½ cups shredded carrots
1 cup chopped onion
16 slices day-old reduced-calorie white bread, cut into cubes

Spray a slow cooker container with butter-flavored cooking spray. In prepared container, combine chicken broth, mushroom soup, sage, poultry seasoning, and black pepper. Stir in celery, carrots, and onion. Add bread cubes. Mix well to combine. Cover and cook on LOW for 6 to 8 hours. Mix well before serving.

Each serving equals:

HE: 1 Bread • 1 Vegetable • ¼ Slider •
5 Optional Calories

138 Calories • 2 gm Fat • 6 gm Protein •
24 gm Carbohydrate • 510 mg Sodium •
88 mg Calcium • 2 gm Fiber

DIABETIC: 1 Starch • 1 Vegetable

Magnificent
Main Dishes

One of the great joys of slow cooker cooking is that these handy appliances are perfectly sized for feeding your family—or making a potful of healthy leftovers you can enjoy all week long. Main dishes are what these cookers were "born for," and there seem to be an infinite number of ways to make scrumptious and satisfying entrées without watching the pot or following complicated recipes. Even if you're used to preparing some of these types of dishes in your skillet or Dutch oven, give these slow cooker versions a try—you may discover that what you've been doing all these years isn't the best or easiest way to get supper on the table!

I've traveled the world in my mind to bring you old classics and new favorites that sparkle when simmered for hours in your slow cooker. You can dine in the French countryside if you like (**Provençal Chicken**) or Barcelona-style (**Olé Spanish Rice**) or in the spirit of Asian cuisine (**Rising Sun Beef and Pepper Pot**), or in even more exotic spots (**South Seas Sweet Potatoes and Ham**). Of course, this section is delectably crammed with all kinds of "Born in the USA" recipes, too, like **BBQ Loose Meat Burgers** and **Grandma's Beef Hash**. From pot roast to pizza, from dumplings to scalloped potatoes, it's all in here!

Cheesy Italian Pasta

Doesn't it seem amazing that you can make a perfect pasta meal without boiling the pasta on your stovetop? The first few times I used my slow cooker all those years ago, I thought that this was a real kitchen miracle, especially for a busy mom and business-woman like me. Times have changed, but I still marvel at that machine's talents! ❤ Serves 4 (1 cup)

1 (10¾-ounce) can Healthy Request Tomato Soup

1 cup (one 8-ounce can) tomatoes, finely chopped and undrained

¼ cup grated Kraft fat-free Parmesan cheese

1½ teaspoons Italian seasoning

½ cup (one 2.5-ounce jar) sliced mushrooms, drained

¼ cup sliced ripe olives

1 cup (4 ounces) shredded Kraft reduced-fat mozzarella cheese

2 cups rotini pasta, rinsed and drained

Spray a slow cooker container with olive oil–flavored cooking spray. In prepared container, combine tomato soup, undrained tomatoes, Parmesan cheese, and Italian seasoning. Stir in mushrooms, olives, and mozzarella cheese. Add rotini pasta. Mix well to combine. Cover and cook on HIGH for 3 to 4 hours. Mix well before serving.

HINT: Usually 1½ cups uncooked rotini pasta cooks to about 2 cups.

Each serving equals:

HE: 1½ Protein • 1 Bread • ¾ Vegetable • ¼ Fat • ½ Slider • 5 Optional Calories

281 Calories • 9 gm Fat • 14 gm Protein • 36 gm Carbohydrate • 887 mg Sodium • 266 mg Calcium • 2 gm Fiber

DIABETIC: 2 Starch/Carbohydrate • 1 Meat • ½ Vegetable

Easy Pasta Primavera

What could be healthier than a simple pasta with veggies, the spirit of spring (as the recipe name promises)? But when you've got so much to do, chopping up some fresh vegetables to toss with your pasta seems too much trouble. Here come those wonderful frozen veggie blends to the rescue! ❂ Serves 4 (1 cup)

1 (10¾-ounce) can Healthy Request Cream of Mushroom Soup
½ cup (one 2.5-ounce jar) sliced mushrooms, drained
1½ cups (6 ounces) cubed Velveeta Light processed cheese
1 (16-ounce) package frozen broccoli, cauliflower, and carrot
  blend, thawed
2 cups cooked rotini pasta, rinsed and drained
⅛ teaspoon black pepper

Spray a slow cooker container with butter-flavored cooking spray. In prepared container, combine mushroom soup, mushrooms, and Velveeta cheese. Stir in vegetable blend, rotini pasta, and black pepper. Cover and cook on HIGH for 2 hours. Mix well before serving.

HINTS: 1. Thaw vegetable blend by placing in a colander and rinsing under hot water for one minute.
    2. Usually 1½ cups uncooked rotini pasta cooks to about 2 cups.

Each serving equals:

HE: 2 Protein • 1½ Vegetable • 1 Bread • ½ Slider •
5 Optional Calories

271 Calories • 7 gm Fat • 16 gm Protein •
36 gm Carbohydrate • 985 mg Sodium •
381 mg Calcium • 4 gm Fiber

DIABETIC: 2 Meat • 1½ Vegetable •
1½ Starch/Carbohydrate

Rice with Tomatoes and Cheese

Did you know that your slow cooker doubles beautifully as a rice cooker as well? It's true, and the gentle action of long-term cooking produces a tender and fluffy result. This rich vegetarian supper dish is a terrific choice for a hungry family! ☻ Serves 6 (1 cup)

> 1 (10¾-ounce) can Healthy Request Tomato Soup
> 3½ cups (two 14.5-ounce cans) diced tomatoes, undrained
> ½ cup reduced-sodium tomato juice
> ¼ cup water
> 2 cups (8 ounces) diced Velveeta Light processed cheese
> 2 cups uncooked instant rice
> ½ cup finely chopped onion
> 1½ teaspoons dried parsley flakes
> ⅛ teaspoon black pepper

Spray a slow cooker container with butter-flavored cooking spray. In prepared container, combine tomato soup, undrained tomatoes, tomato juice, and water. Stir in Velveeta cheese. Add uncooked rice, onion, parsley flakes, and black pepper. Mix well to combine. Cover and cook on LOW for 6 to 8 hours. Mix well before serving.

Each serving equals:

> HE: 1½ Vegetable • 1⅓ Protein • 1 Bread •
> ¼ Slider • 10 Optional Calories
>
> ---
>
> 241 Calories • 5 gm Fat • 11 gm Protein •
> 38 gm Carbohydrate • 914 mg Sodium •
> 293 mg Calcium • 3 gm Fiber
>
> ---
>
> DIABETIC: 1½ Vegetable • 1½ Starch/Carbohydrate •
> 1 Meat

Two-Cheese Cabbage and Rice Main Dish

Here's a recipe that doubles your pleasure in every single bite! I could have used just Cheddar or just mozzarella for a "good enough" result, but I like to push the envelope when it comes to boosting flavor. Maybe it's because at heart I'm like those "we try harder" people—but in this case trying harder produced something special! ☻ Serves 6 (1 full cup)

1 (10¾-ounce) can Healthy Request Cream of Mushroom Soup
1½ cups water
1 cup + 2 tablespoons (4½ ounces) shredded Kraft reduced-fat
    Cheddar cheese
1 cup + 2 tablespoons (4½ ounces) shredded Kraft reduced-fat
    mozzarella cheese
4 cups shredded cabbage
1 cup chopped onion
1 cup uncooked instant rice

Spray a slow cooker container with butter-flavored cooking spray. In prepared container, combine mushroom soup, water, Cheddar cheese, and mozzarella cheese. Stir in cabbage and onion. Add uncooked rice. Mix well to combine. Cover and cook on LOW for 6 to 8 hours. Mix well before serving.

Each serving equals:

HE: 2 Protein • 1 Vegetable • ½ Bread • ¼ Slider •
8 Optional Calories

225 Calories • 9 gm Fat • 14 gm Protein •
22 gm Carbohydrate • 349 mg Sodium •
379 mg Calcium • 2 gm Fiber

DIABETIC: 2 Meat • 1 Vegetable • ½ Starch

Barbequed Tuna Sandwiches

Wasn't there a band called Hot Tuna quite a few years ago? (See, I'm not totally un-hip!) But since my taste runs more to big band than rock band music, this is my kind of "hot tuna"—the scrumptiously savory kind that tastes so good when piled high on top of a bun.

● Serves 6

> 1 (10¾-ounce) can Healthy Request Tomato Soup
> 2 tablespoons Worcestershire sauce
> 2 tablespoons white distilled vinegar
> 1 tablespoon prepared yellow mustard
> ½ cup finely chopped celery
> ½ cup chopped green bell pepper
> ½ cup chopped onion
> 2 (6-ounce) cans white tuna, packed in water, drained and flaked
> ½ teaspoon chili seasoning
> 6 small hamburger buns

Spray a slow cooker container with butter-flavored cooking spray. In prepared container, combine tomato soup, Worcestershire sauce, vinegar, and mustard. Add celery, green pepper, and onion. Mix well to combine. Stir in tuna and chili seasoning. Cover and cook on LOW for 6 to 8 hours. Mix well before serving. For each sandwich, spoon about ½ cup tuna mixture between a hamburger bun.

Each serving equals:

> HE: 1½ Protein • 1 Bread • ½ Vegetable • ¼ Slider • 10 Optional Calories
>
> ---
> 183 Calories • 3 gm Fat • 14 gm Protein • 25 gm Carbohydrate • 621 mg Sodium • 25 mg Calcium • 2 gm Fiber
>
> ---
> DIABETIC: 2 Meat • 1½ Starch/Carbohydrate

Hot Tuna Salad Casserole

I bet this recipe title got a second look from you, didn't it? You never think of cooking a salad dish, or at least you don't most of the time. But a creamy tuna treat as rich as this one is worth a second look just for its luscious flavors—try it and see!

○ Serves 6 (1 cup)

1 (10¾-ounce) can Healthy Request Cream of Celery Soup
½ cup Kraft fat-free mayonnaise
2 (6-ounce) cans white tuna, packed in water, drained and flaked
1 cup finely diced celery
½ cup chopped onion
3 hard-boiled eggs, chopped
1½ cups crushed Tostitos WOW tortilla chips ☆
⅛ teaspoon black pepper

Spray a slow cooker container with butter-flavored cooking spray. In prepared container, combine celery soup and mayonnaise. Add tuna, celery, and onion. Mix well to combine. Stir in chopped eggs, 1¼ cups tortilla chips, and black pepper. Evenly sprinkle remaining ¼ cup tortilla chips over top. Cover and cook on LOW for 6 to 8 hours.

Each serving equals:

HE: 2 Protein • 1½ Vegetable • ½ Bread • ½ Slider • 1 Optional Calorie

170 Calories • 6 gm Fat • 16 gm Protein • 13 gm Carbohydrate • 643 mg Sodium • 102 mg Calcium • 1 gm Fiber

DIABETIC: 2½ Meat • 1 Starch/Carbohydrate

Company Tuna Noodle Casserole

I know, I know, tuna casserole is for those family-only nights when there's no time to sit over a leisurely supper because everyone is running off to choir practice, a soccer game, or a committee meeting. But sprinkle a few almonds on top, add some pretty pimiento, and you've got a dish worthy of your favorite guests!

◑ Serves 6 (1 cup)

> 1 (10¾-ounce) can Healthy Request Cream of Mushroom Soup
> ½ cup (one 2.5-ounce jar) sliced mushrooms, undrained
> ¼ cup (one 2-ounce jar) chopped pimiento, undrained
> 2 (6-ounce) cans white tuna, packed in water, drained and flaked
> 1 cup frozen sliced green beans, thawed
> 3 cups cooked noodles, rinsed and drained
> ¼ cup slivered almonds, toasted

Spray a slow cooker container with butter-flavored cooking spray. In prepared container, combine mushroom soup, undrained mushrooms, and undrained pimiento. Add tuna, green beans, and noodles. Mix well to combine. Evenly sprinkle almonds over top. Cover and cook on LOW for 6 to 8 hours. Mix well before serving.

HINTS: 1. Thaw green beans by placing in a colander and rinsing under hot water for one minute.
2. Usually 2⅔ cups uncooked noodles cooks to about 3 cups.

Each serving equals:

HE: 1⅔ Protein • 1 Bread • ½ Vegetable • ⅓ Fat • ¼ Slider • 8 Optional Calories

230 Calories • 6 gm Fat • 17 gm Protein • 27 gm Carbohydrate • 438 mg Sodium • 82 mg Calcium • 2 gm Fiber

DIABETIC: 2 Meat • 1½ Starch/Carbohydrate • ½ Vegetable • ½ Fat

Macaroni and Tuna with Vegetables

Does seeing a tall stack of tuna cans in the pantry make you feel as if you could weather any blizzard or unexpected crisis? I've met some people who love knowing they're well supplied for just about anything. This recipe is one for just those kinds of times, since the ingredients are probably on your shelf and in your freezer right now! ❍ Serves 6 (1 cup)

> 1 (10¾-ounce) can Healthy Request Cream of Mushroom Soup
> ¼ cup Land O Lakes no-fat sour cream
> 1 teaspoon dried onion flakes
> 2 cups cooked elbow macaroni, rinsed and drained
> ½ cup (one 2.5-ounce jar) sliced mushrooms, drained
> 2½ cups frozen mixed vegetables, thawed
> 2 (6-ounce) cans white tuna, packed in water, drained and flaked

Spray a slow cooker container with butter-flavored cooking spray. In prepared container, combine mushroom soup, sour cream, and onion flakes. Add macaroni, mushrooms, and mixed vegetables. Mix well to combine. Stir in tuna. Cover and cook on HIGH for 3 to 4 hours. Mix well before serving.

HINTS: 1. Usually 1⅓ cups uncooked elbow macaroni cooks to about 2 cups.

2. Thaw mixed vegetables by placing in a colander and rinsing under hot water for one minute.

Each serving equals:

HE: 1½ Protein • 1 Vegetable • ⅔ Bread • ¼ Slider • 13 Optional Calories

207 Calories • 3 gm Fat • 16 gm Protein • 29 gm Carbohydrate • 470 mg Sodium • 85 mg Calcium • 4 gm Fiber

DIABETIC: 2 Meat • 1½ Starch/Carbohydrate • ½ Vegetable

Swiss Tuna Spaghetti Casserole

I've never been to Switzerland, but you've got to agree, those dairy farmers know something special about making cheese! Otherwise, how did they figure out how to make such a tangy, flavorful cheese—and fill it with all those quirky holes? Hmm. I love using Swiss cheese in my cooking, because any dish made the Swiss way just seems to win applause.　❍　Serves 6 (1 cup)

> 1 (10¾-ounce) can Healthy Request Cream of Mushroom Soup
> ¼ cup Land O Lakes no-fat sour cream
> 2 (6-ounce) cans white tuna, packed in water, drained and flaked
> 1 cup finely chopped celery
> ½ cup finely chopped onion
> ½ cup (one 2.5-ounce jar) sliced mushrooms, drained
> ¼ cup (one 2-ounce jar) chopped pimiento, drained
> 6 (¾-ounce) slices Kraft reduced-fat Swiss cheese, shredded
> 3 cups cooked spaghetti, rinsed and drained

Spray a slow cooker container with butter-flavored cooking spray. In prepared container, combine mushroom soup and sour cream. Add tuna, celery, onion, mushrooms, and pimiento. Mix well to combine. Stir in Swiss cheese and spaghetti. Cover and cook on HIGH for 2 to 3 hours. Mix well before serving.

HINT: Usually 2½ cups broken uncooked spaghetti cooks to about 3 cups.

Each serving equals:

HE: 2½ Protein • 1 Bread • ⅔ Vegetable • ¼ Slider • 18 Optional Calories

276 Calories • 8 gm Fat • 22 gm Protein •
29 gm Carbohydrate • 694 mg Sodium •
272 mg Calcium • 2 gm Fiber

DIABETIC: 2½ Meat • 1½ Starch/Carbohydrate •
½ Vegetable

Veggie Mac and Salmon

In our house, salmon was popular as a change of pace from the same old, same old canned tuna in a steamy macaroni dish, but it's deserving of attention just on its own merits. It's vitamin-packed, full of rich bounty from the sea, and besides all that, it's just a beautiful color, especially when you blend it with—yum, yum—sour cream!   ☻   Serves 6 (1 cup)

1 (10¾-ounce) can Healthy Request Cream of Mushroom Soup

2 tablespoons Land O Lakes no-fat sour cream

½ teaspoon dried dill weed

1 (14¾-ounce) can skinless and boneless salmon, packed in water, drained and flaked

1½ cups diced Velveeta Light processed cheese

2 cups (one 16-ounce can) peas and carrots, rinsed and drained

2 cups cooked elbow macaroni, rinsed and drained

½ cup finely chopped onion

⅛ teaspoon black pepper

Spray a slow cooker container with butter-flavored cooking spray. In prepared container, combine mushroom soup, sour cream, and dill weed. Stir in salmon, Velveeta cheese, and peas and carrots. Add macaroni, onion, and black pepper. Mix well to combine. Cover and cook on LOW for 6 to 8 hours. Mix well before serving.

HINT: Usually 1⅓ cups uncooked elbow macaroni cooks to about 2 cups.

Each serving equals:

HE: 3 Protein • 1 Bread • ½ Vegetable • ¼ Slider • 13 Optional Calories

280 Calories • 8 gm Fat • 24 gm Protein • 28 gm Carbohydrate • 941 mg Sodium • 372 mg Calcium • 3 gm Fiber

DIABETIC: 3 Meat • 1½ Starch/Carbohydrate • ½ Vegetable

Salmon Cheese Strata

Just as treasure hunters enjoy the thrill of the hunt almost as much as the actual discovery of their prizes, so, too, will you savor the pleasure of unearthing the layers of creamy, cheesy goodness in this lovely supper or brunch dish. ☻ Serves 6 (¾ cup)

> 1 (14¾-ounce) can skinless and boneless salmon, packed in water, drained and flaked
> 2 eggs, beaten, or equivalent in egg substitute
> ¼ cup Land O Lakes Fat Free Half & Half
> ¾ cup shredded Kraft reduced-fat Cheddar cheese
> 1 cup (one 4-ounce can) sliced mushrooms, drained
> ¼ cup (one 2-ounce jar) chopped pimiento, drained
> ½ cup finely chopped onion
> 3 slices reduced-calorie bread, made into small crumbs
> ¾ teaspoon dried dill weed
> ⅛ teaspoon black pepper

Spray a slow cooker container with butter-flavored cooking spray. In prepared container, combine salmon, eggs, half & half, and Cheddar cheese. Add mushrooms, pimiento, onion, and bread crumbs. Mix well to combine. Stir in dill weed and black pepper. Cover and cook on LOW for 3 to 4 hours.

Each serving equals:

HE: 3 Protein • ½ Vegetable • ¼ Bread

197 Calories • 9 gm Fat • 21 gm Protein •
9 gm Carbohydrate • 567 mg Sodium •
281 mg Calcium • 1 gm Fiber

DIABETIC: 3 Meat • ½ Starch/Carbohydrate

Baked Chicken and Gravy

Long slow cooking is one of the clever cook's best ways to produce truly tender poultry, as this dish perfectly proves. Better still, those hours in the pot create a gravy as good as Grandma's—well, almost!

○ Serves 4

3 tablespoons all-purpose flour
16 ounces skinned and boned uncooked chicken pieces, cut into
    4 pieces
2 teaspoons reduced-calorie margarine
1 (10¾-ounce) can Healthy Request Cream of Chicken Soup
1 teaspoon dried onion flakes
1 teaspoon dried parsley flakes
⅛ teaspoon black pepper

Place flour in a shallow saucer and coat chicken pieces in flour. In a large skillet sprayed with butter-flavored cooking spray, melt margarine. Arrange coated chicken pieces in skillet. Cook chicken for 3 to 4 minutes on each side. Spray a slow cooker container with butter-flavored cooking spray. Evenly arrange browned chicken pieces in prepared container. In a small bowl, combine chicken soup, onion flakes, parsley flakes, black pepper, and any remaining flour. Spoon soup mixture evenly over chicken pieces. Cover and cook on LOW for 6 to 8 hours. When serving, evenly spoon about ½ cup sauce over chicken pieces.

Each serving equals:

HE: 3 Protein • ½ Slider • ¼ Bread • ¼ Fat •
5 Optional Calories

193 Calories • 5 gm Fat • 25 gm Protein •
12 gm Carbohydrate • 372 mg Sodium •
14 mg Calcium • 0 gm Fiber

DIABETIC: 3 Meat • 1 Starch/Carbohydrate

Grandma's Chicken and Dumplings

Old-fashioned goodness in a newfangled appliance—is it possible? Take it from a grandma, it's not only possible, it's a promise! This hearty dish recalls memorable meals with all the family gathered round to celebrate the holidays, a birthday, or just the joy of togetherness.   ☕   Serves 6

> 2 full cups (12 ounces) diced cooked chicken breast
> 1½ cups (one 12-fluid-ounce can) Carnation Evaporated
>   Skim Milk ☆
> 1 (10¾-ounce) can Healthy Request Cream of Chicken
>   Soup
> 2 cups (one 16-ounce can) cut green beans,
>   rinsed and drained
> 1 cup (one 8-ounce can) sliced carrots, rinsed
>   and drained
> 2 teaspoons dried parsley flakes ☆
> 1½ cups Bisquick Reduced Fat Baking Mix

Spray a slow cooker container with butter-flavored cooking spray. In prepared container, combine chicken, 1 cup evaporated skim milk, chicken soup, green beans, carrots, and 1 teaspoon parsley flakes. Cover and cook on LOW for 4 hours. In a medium bowl, combine baking mix, remaining 1 teaspoon parsley flakes, and remaining ½ cup evaporated skim milk. Drop by tablespoonful to form 6 dumplings. Recover and continue cooking on LOW for 45 to 60 minutes. For each serving, place 1 dumpling on a plate and spoon about ¾ cup chicken mixture over top.

HINT: If you don't have leftovers, purchase a chunk of cooked chicken breast from your local deli.

Each serving equals:

HE: 2 Protein • 1⅓ Bread • 1 Vegetable •
½ Skim Milk • ¼ Slider • 10 Optional Calories

293 Calories • 5 gm Fat • 26 gm Protein •
36 gm Carbohydrate • 906 mg Sodium •
227 mg Calcium • 2 gm Fiber

DIABETIC: 2 Meat • 1½ Starch • 1 Vegetable •
½ Skim Milk

Roman Chicken Pot

They conquered the world all those years ago, but the undeniable power of the Roman Empire comes through in this chicken feast just full of vegetables! You may want to experiment with different potatoes to find the ones you like best in this recipe.

○ Serves 6 (1 cup)

1 cup (one 8-ounce can) Hunt's Tomato Sauce
1 cup (one 8-ounce can) tomatoes, finely chopped and undrained
1 tablespoon pourable Splenda or Sugar Twin
1½ teaspoons Italian seasoning
3 cups unpeeled chopped raw potatoes
1 cup chopped celery
1 cup chopped onion
1 cup chopped carrots
⅓ cup sliced ripe olives
16 ounces skinned and boned uncooked chicken breast,
*   cut into 24 pieces*

Spray a slow cooker container with olive oil–flavored cooking spray. In prepared container, combine tomato sauce, undrained tomatoes, Splenda, and Italian seasoning. Stir in potatoes, celery, onion, and carrots. Add olives and chicken pieces. Mix well to combine. Cover and cook on LOW for 6 to 8 hours. Mix well before serving.

Each serving equals:

HE: 2 Protein • 2 Vegetable • ½ Bread • ¼ Fat • 1 Optional Calorie

191 Calories • 3 gm Fat • 18 gm Protein • 23 gm Carbohydrate • 428 mg Sodium • 50 mg Calcium • 4 gm Fiber

DIABETIC: 2 Meat • 2 Vegetable • 1 Starch

Riviera Chicken

Did I feel like Grace Kelly, blonde movie star and future Princess of Monaco, riding in a convertible next to Cary Grant when I dined on this dish? I'll never tell. But see if you don't find yourself transported to the sunny French Riviera when you put this on the menu!

Serves 4

> 1/4 cup Kraft Fat Free French Dressing
> 1 cup (one 8-ounce can) tomatoes, finely chopped and undrained
> 1 cup finely chopped celery
> 1/2 cup chopped onion
> 1/2 cup (one 2.5-ounce jar) sliced mushrooms, drained
> 1 tablespoon chopped fresh parsley or 1 teaspoon dried parsley flakes
> 1/8 teaspoon black pepper
> 16 ounces skinned and boned uncooked chicken breast, cut into 4 pieces

Spray a slow cooker container with butter-flavored cooking spray. In prepared container, combine French dressing, undrained tomatoes, celery, onion, and mushrooms. Add parsley and black pepper. Mix well to combine. Arrange chicken pieces in vegetable mixture. Cover and cook on LOW for 6 to 8 hours. For each serving, place 1 piece of chicken on a plate and spoon about 1/2 cup vegetable mixture over top.

Each serving equals:

HE: 3 Protein • 1 1/2 Vegetable • 1/4 Slider • 5 Optional Calories

167 Calories • 3 gm Fat • 24 gm Protein • 11 gm Carbohydrate • 418 mg Sodium • 40 mg Calcium • 2 gm Fiber

DIABETIC: 3 Meat • 1 Vegetable

John's Chicken and Rice Supper

My son-in-law, John, is a great husband and father who has never failed to appreciate good cooking, whether it's mine or anyone else's. He loved the homecooked coziness of this creamy chicken-and-rice combination. ○ Serves 6 (1⅓ cups)

> 1 (10¾-ounce) can Healthy Request Cream of Chicken Soup
>
> 2 cups water
>
> ½ cup finely chopped onion
>
> 1 cup finely chopped celery
>
> 16 ounces skinned and boned uncooked chicken breast, cut into 36 pieces
>
> ½ cup (one 2.5-ounce jar) sliced mushrooms, drained
>
> 2 cups uncooked instant rice
>
> ¼ cup (one 2-ounce jar) chopped pimiento, drained
>
> 1½ teaspoons dried parsley flakes
>
> ⅛ teaspoon black pepper

Spray a slow cooker container with butter-flavored cooking spray. In prepared container, combine chicken soup and water. Stir in onion, celery, chicken pieces, and mushrooms. Add uncooked rice, pimiento, parsley flakes, and black pepper. Mix well to combine. Cover and cook on LOW for 6 to 8 hours. Mix well before serving.

Each serving equals:

HE: 2 Protein • 1 Bread • ⅔ Vegetable • ¼ Slider • 10 Optional Calories

---

231 Calories • 3 gm Fat • 19 gm Protein • 32 gm Carbohydrate • 311 mg Sodium • 30 mg Calcium • 2 gm Fiber

---

DIABETIC: 2 Meat • 1½ Starch • ½ Vegetable

Provençal Chicken

I've read so many stories about summers in Provence, where cooking is an art and life is lived to the fullest, that even though I haven't visited that region of France, I wanted to celebrate its cooks' commitment to good food. Do chicken breasts have to be boring? *Mais non!* (But no!)   ◑   Serves 4

1 (10¾-ounce) can Healthy Request Cream of Chicken Soup
1 cup (one 8-ounce can) tomatoes, finely chopped and undrained
2 teaspoons Worcestershire sauce
1 tablespoon dried parsley flakes
½ cup (one 2.5-ounce jar) sliced mushrooms, drained
¼ cup (one 2-ounce jar) chopped pimiento, drained
½ cup chopped onion
1 cup (one 8-ounce can) small peas, rinsed and drained
16 ounces skinned and boned uncooked chicken breast, cut into
    4 pieces

Spray a slow cooker container with butter-flavored cooking spray. In a slow cooker container, combine chicken soup, undrained tomatoes, Worcestershire sauce, and parsley flakes. Add mushrooms, pimiento, onion, and peas. Mix well to combine. Evenly arrange chicken pieces in soup mixture. Cover and cook on LOW for 8 hours. When serving, place 1 piece of chicken on a plate and spoon about ¾ cup sauce mixture over top.

Each serving equals:

HE: 3 Protein • 1 Vegetable • ½ Bread • ½ Slider •
5 Optional Calories

212 Calories • 4 gm Fat • 27 gm Protein •
17 gm Carbohydrate • 707 mg Sodium •
39 mg Calcium • 3 gm Fiber

DIABETIC: 3 Meat • 1 Vegetable • 1 Starch

Italian Chicken Dinner

In Italy, many restaurants serve a pasta course before the meat course, but that kind of dining requires a leisurely lifestyle few of us enjoy, except on vacation. Taking that into consideration, I've created a pasta *and* chicken dish brimming with Italian flavor but stream-lined for busy American eaters.   ☻   Serves 4 (1½ cups)

1 (10¾-ounce) can
   Healthy Request
   Tomato Soup
1 cup (one 8-ounce can)
   tomatoes, finely chopped
   and undrained
2 cups (10 ounces) diced
   cooked chicken breast

1 cup (one 4-ounce can) sliced
   mushrooms, drained
2 cups cooked elbow macaroni,
   rinsed and drained
1 teaspoon Italian seasoning
⅛ teaspoon black pepper
¼ cup grated Kraft fat-free
   Parmesan cheese

Spray a slow cooker container with olive oil–flavored cooking spray. In prepared container, combine tomato soup and undrained tomatoes. Stir in chicken, mushrooms, and macaroni. Add Italian seasoning and black pepper. Mix well to combine. Cover and cook on HIGH for 2 to 3 hours. Mix well before serving. When serving, top each with 1 tablespoon Parmesan cheese.

HINTS: 1. If you don't have leftovers, purchase a chunk of cooked chicken breast from your local deli.
2. Usually 1⅓ cups uncooked elbow macaroni cooks to about 2 cups.

Each serving equals:

HE: 2¾ Protein • 1 Bread • 1 Vegetable • ½ Slider • 5 Optional Calories

301 Calories • 5 gm Fat • 28 gm Protein • 36 gm Carbohydrate • 691 mg Sodium • 64 mg Calcium • 3 gm Fiber

DIABETIC: 3 Meat • 1½ Starch/Carbohydrate • 1 Vegetable

Creamy Chicken and Pasta

Each time I visit the supermarket, I'm intrigued by new products, including some pasta shapes I don't recall from when I was a girl. In those days, I think we got to choose between spaghetti and elbow macaroni most of the time. Now you've got all kinds of fun choices, including rotini that comes in different colors and flavors. Would that make this dish taste better? I doubt it, but if you happen to have some on hand, it would certainly look lovely!

❂ Serves 4 (1 cup)

1 (10¾-ounce) can Healthy Request Cream of Chicken Soup
½ cup Land O Lakes Fat Free Half & Half
2 cups (10 ounces) diced cooked chicken breast
½ cup finely chopped onion
1 cup (one 4-ounce can) sliced mushrooms, drained
2 cups cooked rotini pasta, rinsed and drained
1 teaspoon dried parsley flakes

Spray a slow cooker container with butter-flavored cooking spray. In prepared container, combine chicken soup and half & half. Stir in chicken, onion, and mushrooms. Add rotini pasta and parsley flakes. Mix well to combine. Cover and cook on HIGH for 3 to 4 hours. Mix well before serving.

HINTS: 1. If you don't have leftovers, purchase a chunk of cooked chicken breast from your local deli.
2. Usually 1½ cups uncooked rotini pasta cooks to about 2 cups.

Each serving equals:

HE: 2½ Protein • 1 Bread • ¾ Vegetable • ¾ Slider • 9 Optional Calories

268 Calories • 4 gm Fat • 28 gm Protein • 30 gm Carbohydrate • 545 mg Sodium • 71 mg Calcium • 2 gm Fiber

DIABETIC: 2½ Meat • 1½ Starch/Carbohydrate • 1 Vegetable

Cheesy Chicken and Rice

I'm sometimes asked why I choose instant rice instead of the long-cooking kind, as long as I'm going to be cooking the dish for a few hours. First, most of my readers stock instant rice on their kitchen shelves because they like its convenience. Second, the creamy texture of this dish produces about the same result, so why should I ask you to buy an additional product in order to prepare it? Finally, it's what I use myself most often—and remember, Cliff and I eat Healthy Exchanges recipes ourselves. Hope that answers the question!

☻ Serves 4 (1 cup)

1 (10¾-ounce) can Healthy Request Cream of Chicken
    Soup
1 cup water
1½ cups shredded carrots
⅔ cup uncooked instant rice
½ cup finely chopped onion
1½ cups (8 ounces) diced cooked chicken breast
1 cup (4 ounces) diced Velveeta Light processed
    cheese
1 cup frozen peas, thawed
1 teaspoon dried parsley flakes
⅛ teaspoon black pepper

Spray a slow cooker container with butter-flavored cooking spray. In prepared container, combine chicken soup and water. Stir in carrots, uncooked rice, and onion. Add chicken, Velveeta cheese, peas, parsley flakes, and black pepper. Mix well to combine. Cover and cook on LOW for 4 hours. Mix well before serving.

HINTS: 1. If you don't have leftovers, purchase a chunk of cooked chicken breast from your local deli.
2. Thaw peas by placing in a colander and rinsing under hot water for one minute.

Each serving equals:

HE: 3 Protein • 1 Bread • 1 Vegetable • ½ Slider • 5 Optional Calories

---

294 Calories • 6 gm Fat • 28 gm Protein • 32 gm Carbohydrate • 803 mg Sodium • 199 mg Calcium • 2 gm Fiber

---

DIABETIC: 3 Meat • 1½ Starch • 1 Vegetable

Tex-Mex BBQ Chicken over Pasta ❄

Tex-Mex food is perfect for all those fun occasions—Super Bowl parties, teenager birthdays, even a quick supper on bowling night. This is one of my family's favorites, as piquant and spicy as a mariachi dance band. It's a great choice for teens to prepare all by themselves, too. ☻ Serves 6

> 16 ounces skinned and boned uncooked chicken breast,
>   cut into 32 pieces
> 1 (10¾-ounce) can Healthy Request Tomato
>   Soup
> 1 cup chopped onion
> ½ cup chopped green bell pepper
> ¾ cup frozen whole-kernel corn, thawed
> 2 teaspoons chili seasoning
> 1 teaspoon dried parsley flakes
> 3 cups cooked rotini pasta, rinsed and
>   drained
> 6 tablespoons Land O Lakes no-fat
>   sour cream

Spray a slow cooker container with butter-flavored cooking spray. In prepared container, combine chicken pieces and tomato soup. Stir in onion and green pepper. Add corn, chili seasoning, and parsley flakes. Mix well to combine. Cover and cook on LOW for 6 to 8 hours. Mix well before serving. When serving, place ½ cup rotini pasta on a plate, spoon about ⅔ cup chicken mixture over pasta, and top with 1 tablespoon sour cream.

HINTS: 1. Thaw corn by placing in a colander and rinsing under hot water for one minute.
2. Usually 2½ cups uncooked rotini pasta cooks to about 3 cups.

Each serving equals:

HE: 2 Protein • 1¼ Bread • ½ Vegetable • ½ Slider • 5 Optional Calories

---

255 Calories • 3 gm Fat • 21 gm Protein •
36 gm Carbohydrate • 256 mg Sodium •
42 mg Calcium • 3 gm Fiber

DIABETIC: 2 Meat • 1½ Starch/Carbohydrate •
½ Vegetable

Chicken Cacciatore and Rotini Casserole

Doesn't it just seem that Italian families in movies and on TV are always eating something scrumptious? You sit there with your mouth watering, counting the minutes until you can get home and start eating, too! Here's an easy dish any of those families would be proud to serve, but even if your favorite show's in reruns, you're all set! ☻ Serves 6 (1 cup)

1 (10¾-ounce) can Healthy Request
    Tomato Soup
1 cup (one 8-ounce can) tomatoes, finely chopped
    and undrained
¼ cup water
2 tablespoons Splenda granular
1½ teaspoons Italian seasoning
1 cup chopped onion
1½ cups chopped green bell pepper
½ cup (one 2.5-ounce jar) sliced mushrooms,
    drained
16 ounces skinned and boned uncooked chicken breast,
    cut into 36 pieces
1½ cups hot cooked rotini pasta

Spray a slow cooker container with olive oil–flavored cooking spray. In prepared container, combine tomato soup, undrained tomatoes, water, Splenda, and Italian seasoning. Stir in onion, green pepper, and mushrooms. Add chicken pieces. Mix well to combine. Stir in rotini pasta. Cover and cook on HIGH for 4 hours. Mix well before serving.

HINT: Usually 1 full cup uncooked rotini pasta cooks to about 1½ cups.

Each serving equals:

HE: 2 Protein • 1½ Vegetable • ½ Bread • ¼ Slider •
10 Optional Calories

195 Calories • 3 gm Fat • 19 gm Protein •
23 gm Carbohydrate • 353 mg Sodium •
28 mg Calcium • 2 gm Fiber

DIABETIC: 2 Meat • 1 Vegetable •
1 Starch/Carbohydrate

Scalloped Turkey with Broccoli and Potatoes

If there was ever a complete meal-in-one, this recipe would be at the top of the list! You're getting plenty of healthy protein, plus lots of veggies and tummy-filling carbs. Why, I bet you could run a marathon after dining on this dish—but only if you *really* wanted to! ☻ Serves 6 (1 cup)

> 6 cups shredded loose-packed frozen potatoes
> 1½ cups frozen chopped broccoli, thawed
> 1 cup chopped onion
> 2 full cups (12 ounces) diced cooked turkey breast
> 1 (10¾-ounce) can Healthy Request Cream of Chicken
>   Soup
> 1 cup + 2 tablespoons shredded Kraft reduced-fat
>   Cheddar cheese
> ½ cup (one 2.5-ounce jar) sliced mushrooms,
>   drained
> ¼ cup (one 2-ounce jar) chopped pimiento, drained
> ⅛ teaspoon black pepper

Spray a slow cooker container with butter-flavored cooking spray. In prepared container, combine potatoes, broccoli, and onion. Stir in turkey. Add chicken soup, Cheddar cheese, mushrooms, pimiento, and black pepper. Mix well to combine. Cover and cook on LOW for 6 to 8 hours. Mix well before serving.

HINTS: 1. Mr. Dell's frozen shredded potatoes are a good choice, or raw shredded potatoes may be used in place of frozen potatoes.
2. Thaw broccoli by placing in a colander and rinsing under hot water for one minute.
3. If you don't have leftovers, purchase a chunk of cooked turkey breast from your local deli.

Each serving equals:

HE: 3 Protein • 1 Vegetable • ⅔ Bread • ¼ Slider • 10 Optional Calories

274 Calories • 6 gm Fat • 27 gm Protein • 28 gm Carbohydrate • 240 mg Sodium • 202 mg Calcium • 4 gm Fiber

DIABETIC: 2½ Meat • 1½ Starch/Carbohydrate • 1 Vegetable

Creamed Turkey Pot Pie
Sauce over Noodles

Another reason (among many) to love your slow cooker is that it doesn't heat up the kitchen the way your oven does. That way, it's perfect for all year round cooking. You're saving energy (good for you *and* the environment), and you're still getting to enjoy a cozy-warm meal without a fuss.   ☻   Serves 6

> 1 (10¾-ounce) can Healthy Request Cream of Chicken
>   Soup
> ¼ cup Land O Lakes Fat Free Half & Half
> 2 full cups (12 ounces) diced cooked turkey breast
> 1 cup (one 4-ounce can) sliced mushrooms, drained
> ¼ cup (one 2-ounce jar) chopped pimiento, drained
> 2 cups (one 16-ounce can) diced carrots, rinsed and
>   drained
> 1 cup (one 8-ounce can) peas, rinsed and drained
> 1 tablespoon dried onion flakes
> 1½ teaspoons dried parsley flakes
> 3 cups hot cooked noodles, rinsed and drained

Spray a slow cooker container with butter-flavored cooking spray. In prepared container, combine chicken soup, half & half, and turkey. Add mushrooms, pimiento, carrots, and peas. Mix well to combine. Stir in onion flakes and parsley flakes. Cover and cook on LOW for 3 to 4 hours. For each serving, place ½ cup noodles on a plate and spoon ⅔ cup turkey mixture over top.

HINTS: 1. If you don't have leftovers, purchase a chunk of cooked turkey breast from your local deli.
   2. Usually 2⅔ cups uncooked noodles cooks to about 3 cups.
   3. Also good over mashed potatoes, toast, or any type of pasta.

Each serving equals:

HE: 2 Protein • 1⅓ Bread • 1 Vegetable • ¼ Slider •
16 Optional Calories

263 Calories • 3 gm Fat • 25 gm Protein •
34 gm Carbohydrate • 567 mg Sodium •
55 mg Calcium • 3 gm Fiber

DIABETIC: 2 Meat • 1½ Starch • 1 Vegetable

Creamy Turkey and Noodles

There's a football game on television, you've got presents to wrap, and the wind is blowing cold just outside your window. What a great post-Thanksgiving day, right? Because you cleverly planned to have leftover turkey, you don't need to ask what's for dinner tonight—this smooth and luscious dish will fit the bill.

○ Serves 6 (1 cup)

> 1 (10¾-ounce) can Healthy Request Cream of Chicken Soup
> ½ cup water
> 2 full cups (12 ounces) diced cooked turkey breast
> ½ cup finely chopped onion
> ½ cup (one 2.5-ounce jar) sliced mushrooms, drained
> 1 cup (one 8-ounce can) peas and carrots, rinsed and drained
> 2½ cups cooked noodles, rinsed and drained
> 1 teaspoon dried parsley flakes

Spray a slow cooker container with butter-flavored cooking spray. In prepared container, combine chicken soup and water. Stir in turkey, onion, mushrooms, and peas and carrots. Add noodles and parsley flakes. Mix well to combine. Cover and cook on HIGH for 3 to 4 hours. Mix well before serving.

HINTS: 1. If you don't have leftovers, purchase a chunk of cooked turkey breast from your local deli.
2. Usually 2¼ cups uncooked noodles cooks to about 2½ cups.

Each serving equals:

HE: 2 Protein • 1 Bread • ½ Vegetable • ¼ Slider • 10 Optional Calories

210 Calories • 2 gm Fat • 22 gm Protein • 26 gm Carbohydrate • 288 mg Sodium • 29 mg Calcium • 2 gm Fiber

DIABETIC: 2 Meat • 1½ Starch • ½ Vegetable

Turkey Stuffing Divan

Cole Porter wrote a song that called a particular evening "delightful, delicious, and de-lovely." He could have been describing this delectable dish that combines the marvelous cheesy tastes of a traditional "divan" dish with the tummy-soothing magic that only stuffing can provide. Your family will surely sing your praises after a bite of this!

● Serves 6 (1 cup)

2 cups (one 16-ounce can) Healthy Request Chicken Broth
1 (10¾-ounce) can Healthy Request Cream of Chicken Soup
3 cups purchased herb seasoned stuffing mix
1 teaspoon dried onion flakes
1 teaspoon dried parsley flakes
1½ cups frozen chopped broccoli, thawed
2 cups (10 ounces) diced cooked turkey breast
¾ cup shredded Kraft reduced-fat Cheddar cheese

Spray a slow cooker container with butter-flavored cooking spray. In a large bowl, combine chicken broth and chicken soup. Stir in stuffing mix, onion flakes, and parsley flakes. Add broccoli, turkey, and Cheddar cheese. Mix well to combine. Cover and cook on LOW for 6 to 8 hours. Mix well before serving.

HINTS: 1. Brownberry seasoned toasted bread cubes work great.
2. Thaw broccoli by placing in a colander and rinsing under hot water for one minute.
3. If you don't have leftovers, purchase a chunk of cooked turkey breast from your local deli.

Each serving equals:

HE: 2⅓ Protein • 1 Bread • ½ Vegetable • ¼ Slider • 17 Optional Calories

241 Calories • 5 gm Fat • 24 gm Protein • 25 gm Carbohydrate • 622 mg Sodium • 128 mg Calcium • 2 gm Fiber

DIABETIC: 2 Meat • 1½ Starch • ½ Vegetable

Leftover Turkey Casserole

Hmm, looks like it, smells like it, tastes like it—must be leftover holiday turkey, right? Well, not necessarily! I've seasoned it like the real thing, you've filled the house with the perfectly luscious aroma—but you can fix this flavorful "potful of pleasure" any time of year. Even if you ate out on the holiday this year, you can surprise your fellow diners with the best kind of "leftovers."

○ Serves 6 (1 cup)

2 cups (one 16-ounce can) Healthy Request Chicken Broth
1 (10¾-ounce) can Healthy Request Cream of Chicken Soup
2 full cups (12 ounces) diced cooked turkey breast
1 teaspoon dried sage
½ teaspoon poultry seasoning
⅛ teaspoon black pepper
12 slices day-old reduced-calorie white bread, cut into cubes
1 cup chopped celery
½ cup chopped onion

Spray a slow cooker container with butter-flavored cooking spray. In prepared container, combine chicken broth, chicken soup, and turkey. Stir in sage, poultry seasoning, and black pepper. Add bread cubes, celery, and onion. Mix well to combine. Cover and cook on LOW for 6 to 8 hours. Mix well before serving.

HINT: If you don't have leftovers, purchase a chunk of cooked turkey breast from your local deli.

Each serving equals:

HE: 2 Protein • 1 Bread • ½ Vegetable • ¼ Slider • 17 Optional Calories

210 Calories • 2 gm Fat • 24 gm Protein • 24 gm Carbohydrate • 612 mg Sodium • 54 mg Calcium • 1 gm Fiber

DIABETIC: 2 Meat • 1½ Starch/Carbohydrate • ½ Vegetable

BBQ Loose Meat Burgers

Cooking for a crowd? We all have to do it from time to time, but some of us are always serving six, eight, or even more for supper. I think the slow cooker is the ideal "crowd-cooker's" assistant, since it makes stirring up big pots of food oh-so-simple! Here's a party-pleaser that is sure to satisfy the biggest appetite.

☻ Serves 8

32 ounces extra-lean ground turkey or beef
1 (10¾-ounce) can Healthy Request Tomato Soup
1½ teaspoons Worcestershire sauce
1 teaspoon prepared yellow mustard
1 cup chopped onion
1 cup chopped green bell pepper
1½ teaspoons dried parsley flakes
8 small hamburger buns

In a large skillet sprayed with butter-flavored cooking spray, brown meat. Spray a slow cooker container with butter-flavored cooking spray. In prepared container, combine browned meat, tomato soup, Worcestershire sauce, and mustard. Add onion, green pepper, and parsley flakes. Mix well to combine. Cover and cook on LOW for 6 to 8 hours. For each sandwich, spoon about ½ cup meat mixture between a hamburger bun.

Each serving equals:

HE: 3 Protein • 1 Bread • ½ Vegetable • ¼ Slider • 3 Optional Calories

242 Calories • 6 gm Fat • 25 gm Protein • 22 gm Carbohydrate • 385 mg Sodium • 10 mg Calcium • 2 gm Fiber

DIABETIC: 3 Meat • 1 Starch • ½ Vegetable

Buffet BBQ Beef Sandwiches

Keeping food warm during a festive family meal used to require little cans of Sterno and way too much special attention, but when you enlist your slow cooker to help, life is so much easier. I'd suggest this for a post–carol singing party or a harvest season soirée with your neighbors. ☻ Serves 8

> 32 ounces extra-lean ground turkey or beef
> 1 cup finely chopped onion
> ½ cup finely chopped green bell pepper
> 1 (10¾-ounce) can Healthy Request Tomato Soup
> 1 tablespoon cider vinegar
> 1 tablespoon pourable Splenda or Sugar Twin
> 1 teaspoon chili seasoning
> ⅛ teaspoon black pepper
> 8 small hamburger buns

Spray a slow cooker container with butter-flavored cooking spray. In prepared container, combine uncooked meat, onion, and green pepper. Stir in tomato soup, vinegar, Splenda, chili seasoning, and black pepper. Cover and cook on LOW for 6 to 8 hours. Mix well before serving. For each serving, spoon about ½ cup meat mixture between a bun.

Each serving equals:

HE: 3 Protein • 1 Bread • ½ Vegetable • ¼ Slider •
3 Optional Calories

---

238 Calories • 6 gm Fat • 24 gm Protein •
22 gm Carbohydrate • 370 mg Sodium •
10 mg Calcium • 2 gm Fiber

DIABETIC: 3 Meat • 1½ Starch/Carbohydrate

Family Reunion Meat Loaf

Meat loaf is a mainstay all over America, but especially in the Midwest. Since there is no rule that meat loaf has to be served only in loaf shape, I decided to try this culinary classic "in the round"! My taste testers thought meat loaf "pie" made the meal that much more fun. ☻ Serves 8

> *32 ounces extra-lean ground turkey or beef*
> *20 Ritz Reduced Fat Crackers, made into crumbs*
> *1 cup finely chopped onion*
> *½ cup reduced-sodium ketchup*
> *2 teaspoons dried parsley flakes*
> *⅛ teaspoon black pepper*

Spray a slow cooker container with butter-flavored cooking spray. In prepared container, combine meat, cracker crumbs, onion, ketchup, parsley flakes, and black pepper. Pat mixture into prepared container. Cover and cook on LOW for 8 hours. Cut into 8 wedges. When serving, carefully remove wedges from slow cooker container.

HINT: A self-seal sandwich bag works great for crushing crackers.

Each serving equals:

HE: 3 Protein • ½ Bread • ¼ Vegetable •
15 Optional Calories

190 Calories • 6 gm Fat • 23 gm Protein •
11 gm Carbohydrate • 136 mg Sodium •
16 mg Calcium • 1 gm Fiber

DIABETIC: 3 Meat • ½ Starch • ½ Vegetable

Three Bean Supper Pot

This warm and wonderful three-bean-salad-plus-meat combo is a true team effort, as each ingredient supports the special talents of all the rest. Did you ever think you could feed a family of six on half a pound of meat? Well, with your thrifty slow cooker on board, you'll hear only compliments, not complaints!

● Serves 6 (1 cup)

8 ounces extra-lean ground turkey or beef

1 cup chopped onion

1 cup (one 8-ounce can) Hunt's Tomato Sauce

1 cup (one 8-ounce can) tomatoes, finely chopped and undrained

10 ounces (one 16-ounce can) red kidney beans, rinsed and drained

10 ounces (one 16-ounce can) butter beans, rinsed and drained

2 cups (one 16-ounce can) cut green beans, rinsed and drained

¼ cup pourable Splenda or Sugar Twin

¼ cup Hormel Bacon Bits

1 teaspoon dried parsley flakes

⅛ teaspoon black pepper

In a large skillet sprayed with butter-flavored cooking spray, brown meat and onion. Spray a slow cooker container with butter-flavored cooking spray. In prepared container, combine browned meat mixture, tomato sauce, and undrained tomatoes. Stir in kidney beans, butter beans, and green beans. Add Splenda, bacon bits, parsley flakes, and black pepper. Mix well to combine. Cover and cook on LOW for 6 to 8 hours. Mix well before serving.

Each serving equals:

HE: 2 Vegetable • 1½ Protein • 1 Bread • ¼ Slider • 1 Optional Calorie

187 Calories • 3 gm Fat • 16 gm Protein • 24 gm Carbohydrate • 859 mg Sodium • 54 mg Calcium • 6 gm Fiber

DIABETIC: 2½ Meat • 1½ Vegetable • 1 Starch

Olé Spanish Rice

When I lifted the lid off the pot to serve this dish, my kitchen was instantly filled with the flavors of sunny Spain! The tangy veggies, the hearty meat, the spicy tomato flavors all joined hands to dance up a storm. This main-dish rice recipe is sure to become a regular on your table. ☻ Serves 8 (1 cup)

16 ounces extra-lean ground turkey or beef

1¾ cups (one 14.5-ounce can) diced tomatoes, undrained

1 cup (one 8-ounce can) Hunt's Tomato Sauce

1½ cups reduced-sodium tomato juice

1½ cups chopped onion

1 cup chopped green bell pepper

1 cup uncooked instant rice

1 tablespoon Worcestershire sauce

2 tablespoons pourable Splenda or Sugar Twin

1½ teaspoons chili seasoning

In a large skillet sprayed with butter-flavored cooking spray, brown meat. Spray a slow cooker container with butter-flavored cooking spray. In prepared container, combine browned meat, undrained tomatoes, tomato sauce, and tomato juice. Stir in onion, green pepper, and uncooked rice. Add Worcestershire sauce, Splenda, and chili seasoning. Mix well to combine. Cover and cook on LOW for 6 to 8 hours. Mix well before serving.

Each serving equals:

HE: 2 Vegetable • 1½ Protein • ⅓ Bread • 1 Optional Calorie

159 Calories • 3 gm Fat • 14 gm Protein • 19 gm Carbohydrate • 387 mg Sodium • 28 mg Calcium • 2 gm Fiber

DIABETIC: 2 Meat • 2 Vegetable • 1 Starch

Supper's Ready!

"Is it ready yet?" your children love asking, poking their heads into the kitchen as the afternoon turns to evening and those tummies start to rumble a bit. "Soon," you always used to answer, spending precious minutes pulling a meal together when you are exhausted yourself. Well, now you can return home after work, peek into the kitchen, and ask the same question as the kids. When you use your slow cooker, "Supper's ready!" ❂ Serves 4 (1½ cups)

8 ounces extra-lean ground turkey or beef
1 (10¾-ounce) can Healthy Request Tomato Soup
1 cup (one 8-ounce can) tomatoes, finely chopped and undrained
2 cups diced raw potatoes
⅓ cup uncooked instant rice
½ cup chopped onion
1½ cups shredded carrots
1 cup diced celery
1 teaspoon dried parsley flakes
⅛ teaspoon black pepper

In a large skillet sprayed with butter-flavored cooking spray, brown meat. Spray a slow cooker container with butter-flavored cooking spray. In prepared container, combine browned meat, tomato soup, and undrained tomatoes. Stir in potatoes, uncooked rice, onion, carrots, and celery. Add parsley flakes and black pepper. Mix well to combine. Cover and cook on LOW for 6 to 8 hours. Mix well before serving.

Each serving equals:

HE: 2 Vegetable • 1½ Protein • ¾ Bread • ½ Slider • 5 Optional Calories

---

248 Calories • 4 gm Fat • 15 gm Protein • 38 gm Carbohydrate • 465 mg Sodium • 45 mg Calcium • 4 gm Fiber

---

DIABETIC: 2 Vegetable • 1½ Meat • 1½ Starch

Tommy's Hamburger Milk Gravy Casserole

Hamburger milk gravy is a passion with my son Tommy, who's loved it since he was little. This version incorporates pasta with his favorite beefy-creamy blend, making an "old reliable" new and improved! ☻ Serves 6 (1⅓ cups)

> 16 ounces extra-lean ground turkey or beef
> 1 (10¾-ounce) can Healthy Request Cream of Mushroom Soup
> 1½ cups (one 12-fluid-ounce can) Carnation Evaporated Skim Milk
> ¼ cup Land O Lakes Fat Free Half & Half
> 3 cups cooked rotini pasta, rinsed and drained
> 1½ teaspoons dried parsley flakes
> ⅛ teaspoon black pepper

In a large skillet sprayed with butter-flavored cooking spray, brown meat. Spray a slow cooker container with butter-flavored cooking spray. In prepared container, combine browned meat, mushroom soup, evaporated skim milk, and half & half. Stir in rotini pasta, parsley flakes, and black pepper. Cover and cook on HIGH for 2 hours. Mix well before serving.

HINT: Usually 2½ cups uncooked rotini pasta cooks to about 3 cups.

Each serving equals:

HE: 2 Protein • 1 Bread • ½ Skim Milk • ¼ Slider • 7 Optional Calories

209 Calories • 5 gm Fat • 23 gm Protein • 33 gm Carbohydrate • 335 mg Sodium • 228 mg Calcium • 1 gm Fiber

DIABETIC: 2 Meat • 1½ Starch/Carbohydrate • ½ Skim Milk

Hamburger Rice Casserole

The slow cooker does a great job with inexpensive meals, and here's a perfect example. I simply combined a pound of ground beef with some canned soup and milk, added rice and some veggies, and let it cook until it was a supper worth more than a few hurrays!

◐ Serves 6 (1 cup)

> 16 ounces extra-lean ground turkey or beef
> 1 (10¾-ounce) can Healthy Request Cream of Mushroom Soup
> 1½ cups (one 12-fluid-ounce can) Carnation Evaporated Skim Milk
> ½ cup water
> 1⅓ cups uncooked instant rice
> 2 cups finely chopped celery
> 1 cup chopped onion
> 1½ teaspoons parsley flakes
> ⅛ teaspoon black pepper

In a large skillet sprayed with butter-flavored cooking spray, brown meat. Spray a slow cooker container with butter-flavored cooking spray. In prepared container, combine meat, mushroom soup, evaporated skim milk, and water. Stir in uncooked rice, celery, and onion. Add parsley flakes and black pepper. Mix well to combine. Cover and cook on LOW for 6 to 8 hours. Mix well before serving.

Each serving equals:

HE: 2 Protein • 1 Vegetable • ⅔ Bread •
½ Skim Milk • ¼ Slider • 8 Optional Calories

261 Calories • 5 gm Fat • 22 gm Protein •
32 gm Carbohydrate • 359 mg Sodium •
232 mg Calcium • 2 gm Fiber

DIABETIC: 2 Meat • 1 Starch • 1 Vegetable •
½ Skim Milk

Josh's Easy Spaghetti

Ever since he was a baby, my grandson Josh has been a big fan of his grandma's cooking, and always happy to share his thoughts about the dishes he tried. He's become really good at figuring out the different ingredients I stir into each dish. This time, though, he said, "Let's make a really easy dish just for me," and so we did.

⏺ Serves 6 (1 cup)

> 16 ounces extra-lean ground turkey or beef
> 1 (26-ounce) jar Old World Style Ragu Traditional Spaghetti
>   Sauce
> ½ cup water
> 3 cups cooked spaghetti, rinsed and drained

In a large skillet sprayed with olive oil–flavored cooking spray, brown meat. Spray a slow cooker container with olive oil–flavored cooking spray. In prepared container, combine browned meat, spaghetti sauce, and water. Stir in spaghetti. Cover and cook on LOW for 8 hours. Mix well before serving.

HINT: Usually 2½ cups broken uncooked spaghetti cooks to about 3 cups.

Each serving equals:

HE: 2 Protein • 2 Vegetable • 1 Bread

244 Calories • 4 gm Fat • 20 gm Protein •
32 gm Carbohydrate • 512 mg Sodium •
43 mg Calcium • 3 gm Fiber

DIABETIC: 2 Meat • 2 Vegetable • 1 Starch

Slow Cooker Bubble Pizza

Sounds like an impossible task, doesn't it, making pizza in a slow cooker? Well, I enjoy taking on the impossible and figuring out how to make it not only possible, but easy, tasty, and healthy all at once! With the help of some handy-dandy ready-made biscuits and my favorite shredded cheese, I found a way. Never say never, whether it's about reinventing a recipe in a healthy way, losing weight, or choosing to live healthy from now on.

● Serves 6 (1 full cup)

> 16 ounces extra-lean ground turkey or beef
> 1 cup (one 8-ounce can) Hunt's Tomato Sauce
> 1 cup (one 8-ounce can) tomatoes, finely chopped
>   and undrained
> 1 (10¾-ounce) can Healthy Request Tomato Soup
> ½ cup (one 2.5-ounce jar) sliced mushrooms,
>   drained
> 1 cup chopped onion
> 1 cup + 2 tablespoons shredded Kraft reduced-fat
>   Cheddar cheese ☆
> 1½ teaspoons pizza or Italian seasoning
> 1 (7.5-ounce) can Pillsbury refrigerated biscuits

In a large skillet sprayed with olive oil–flavored cooking spray, brown meat. Spray a slow cooker container with olive oil–flavored cooking spray. In prepared container, combine meat, tomato sauce, undrained tomatoes, and tomato soup. Add mushrooms, onion, 1 cup Cheddar cheese, and pizza seasoning. Separate biscuits and cut each into 3 pieces. Gently fold biscuit pieces into meat mixture. Evenly sprinkle remaining 2 tablespoons Cheddar cheese over top. Cover and cook on HIGH for 2 to 3 hours. Mix gently before serving.

Each serving equals:

HE: 3 Protein • 1½ Vegetable • 1¼ Bread •
¼ Slider • 10 Optional Calories

---

297 Calories • 9 gm Fat • 24 gm Protein •
30 gm Carbohydrate • 828 mg Sodium •
181 mg Calcium • 2 gm Fiber

DIABETIC: 3 Meat • 1½ Starch/Carbohydrate •
1½ Vegetable

Cliff's Chili Mac Supper

I should own stock in a chili seasoning company, we go through so much of Cliff's favorite spice! He's a man who likes his food spicy and his days full of interesting challenges to solve. In this recipe, my challenge was how to make a tasty supper using familiar ingredients in a fresh and fun way. The reward: Cliff's smile—and his clean plate!   ◐   Serves 6 (1 full cup)

> 16 ounces extra-lean ground turkey or beef
> 1 (10¾-ounce) can Healthy Request Tomato Soup
> 1 cup (one 8-ounce can) tomatoes, finely chopped and undrained
> ½ cup water
> 1½ cups chopped onion
> ½ cup chopped green bell pepper
> 2 cups uncooked elbow macaroni
> 1½ teaspoons chili seasoning

In a large skillet sprayed with butter-flavored cooking spray, brown meat. Spray a slow cooker container with butter-flavored cooking spray. In prepared container, combine browned meat, tomato soup, undrained tomatoes, and water. Stir in onion and green pepper. Add uncooked macaroni and chili seasoning. Mix well to combine. Cover and cook on HIGH for 3 to 4 hours. Mix well before serving.

Each serving equals:

> HE: 2 Protein • 1 Bread • 1 Vegetable • ¼ Slider •
> 10 Optional Calories
> _____
> 277 Calories • 5 gm Fat • 20 gm Protein •
> 38 gm Carbohydrate • 313 mg Sodium •
> 22 mg Calcium • 3 gm Fiber
> _____
> DIABETIC: 2 Meat • 1½ Starch • 1 Vegetable

Tex-Mex Stuffed Peppers

I wonder who first decided to hollow out some gorgeous green peppers and fill them with a mix of meat and rice. Some thrifty, clever housewife and mom, I bet! The classic version is plenty good, but I decided that I could make good even more irresistible with the addition of some corn, onion, and spices. Now I've got a dish sure to be a hit, even "deep in the heart" of Texas!

◗ Serves 4

4 (medium-sized) green bell
    peppers
8 ounces extra-lean ground
    turkey or beef
⅓ cup uncooked instant rice
½ cup frozen whole-kernel
    corn, thawed

½ cup finely chopped onion
1 cup (one 8-ounce can) Hunt's
    Tomato Sauce
2 teaspoons pourable Splenda
    or Sugar Twin
½ teaspoon chili seasoning
2 tablespoons water

Spray a slow cooker container with butter-flavored cooking spray. Cut a thin slice from stem end of each green pepper. Remove seeds and membrane. Rinse peppers. In a large bowl, combine meat, uncooked rice, corn, onion, tomato sauce, Splenda, and chili seasoning. Evenly stuff about ½ cup rice mixture into each pepper. Pour water into prepared container. Arrange stuffed peppers in container. Cover and cook on LOW for 6 to 8 hours.

HINT: Thaw corn by placing in a colander and rinsing under hot water for one minute.

Each serving equals:

HE: 2¼ Vegetable • 1½ Protein • ½ Bread •
1 Optional Calorie

179 Calories • 3 gm Fat • 14 gm Protein •
24 gm Carbohydrate • 382 mg Sodium •
26 mg Calcium • 4 gm Fiber

DIABETIC: 2 Vegetable • 1½ Meat • 1 Starch

Simmered Meatballs and Rice

Sweet and sour meatballs are a beloved tradition in many culinary traditions, from Scandinavia to Eastern Europe. In this country, they're often picked as perfect party food because they reheat beautifully and don't lose any of their attraction while sitting for a while on a buffet table. We had such fun testing these, trying to find just the right mix of sweet and tangy flavor. To quote Professor Higgins in *My Fair Lady,* "I think she's got it!"   ☻   Serves 6 (4 each)

16 ounces extra-lean ground turkey or beef
6 tablespoons dried fine bread crumbs
1½ teaspoons dried parsley flakes
2 teaspoons dried onion flakes
1¾ cups (one 15-ounce can) Hunt's Tomato Sauce ☆
¼ cup grape spreadable fruit
½ teaspoon prepared yellow mustard
3 cups hot cooked rice

Spray a slow cooker container with butter-flavored cooking spray. In a large bowl, combine meat, bread crumbs, parsley flakes, onion flakes, and ¼ cup tomato sauce. Mix well to combine. Form into 24 (1-inch) meatballs. Carefully arrange meatballs in prepared container. In a medium bowl, combine remaining tomato sauce, spreadable fruit, and mustard. Evenly spoon sauce over meatballs. Cover and cook on LOW for 6 to 8 hours. For each serving, place ½ cup hot rice on a plate, arrange 4 meatballs over rice, and spoon about 2 tablespoons sauce over top.

HINT: Usually 2 cups uncooked instant rice cooks to about 3 cups.

Each serving equals:

HE: 2 Protein • 1⅓ Bread • 1 Vegetable • ⅔ Fruit

---

244 Calories • 4 gm Fat • 18 gm Protein •
34 gm Carbohydrate • 539 mg Sodium •
35 mg Calcium • 2 gm Fiber

DIABETIC: 2 Meat • 1½ Starch • 1 Vegetable • ½ Fruit

Swiss Steak Gravy over Noodles

Some meat lovers feel that lean steak can't possibly be flavorful enough because it's the fat content that gives meat its great taste. My answer to that is recipes like this one! A rich and creamy gravy can persuade any piece of steak that it's a star worthy of applause.

● Serves 6

> 6 tablespoons all-purpose flour
> 16 ounces lean round steak, cut into 32 pieces
> 1 (10¾-ounce) can Healthy Request Cream of Mushroom Soup
> 1¾ cups (one 14.5-ounce can) diced tomatoes, undrained
> 1 cup chopped onion
> 1 teaspoon dried parsley flakes
> ⅛ teaspoon black pepper
> 3 cups hot cooked noodles, rinsed and drained

Spray a slow cooker container with butter-flavored cooking spray. Place flour in a shallow saucer. Coat steak pieces in flour. Evenly arrange coated steak pieces in prepared container. In a medium bowl, combine mushroom soup, undrained tomatoes, onion, parsley flakes, black pepper, and any remaining flour. Evenly spoon soup mixture over meat. Cover and cook on LOW for 8 hours. When serving, place ½ cup noodles on a plate and spoon about 1 cup swiss steak gravy over top.

HINT: Usually 2⅔ cups uncooked noodles cooks to about 3 cups.

Each serving equals:

HE: 2 Protein • 1⅓ Bread • 1¼ Vegetable • ¼ Slider • 8 Optional Calories

---

269 Calories • 5 gm Fat • 22 gm Protein • 34 gm Carbohydrate • 322 mg Sodium • 72 mg Calcium • 2 gm Fiber

---

DIABETIC: 2 Meat • 2 Starch • 1 Vegetable

James's Pot Roast

When James and Pam and the kids come for dinner at Timber Ridge Farm, I like to make something a little special. Not every time, maybe, but often. James has always loved pot roast, so I created this slow cooker version with him in mind. Cooking the meat in the same pot as the veggies and potatoes and enveloping all of them in a creamy gravy is a winning combination. ☻ Serves 8

4 cups diced raw potatoes
3 cups sliced carrots
2 cups chopped celery
1 cup chopped onion
1 (32-ounce) lean boneless beef rump roast
1 (12-ounce) jar Heinz Fat Free Beef Gravy
1 (10¾-ounce) can Healthy Request Cream of Mushroom Soup
½ teaspoon dried minced garlic
1½ teaspoons dried parsley flakes
⅛ teaspoon black pepper

Spray a slow cooker container with butter-flavored cooking spray. In prepared container, evenly layer potatoes, carrots, celery, and onion. Place beef roast on top of vegetables. In a medium bowl, combine beef gravy, mushroom soup, garlic, parsley flakes, and black pepper. Evenly spoon gravy mixture over top. Cover and cook on LOW for 8 to 10 hours. Cut roast into 8 pieces. For each serving, place 1 piece of meat on a plate and spoon about 1 cup vegetable mixture next to it.

HINT: A 5-quart slow cooker is recommended for this recipe.

Each serving equals:

HE: 3 Protein • 1½ Vegetable • ½ Bread • ½ Slider

280 Calories • 8 gm Fat • 27 gm Protein •
25 gm Carbohydrate • 500 mg Sodium •
71 mg Calcium • 3 gm Fiber

DIABETIC: 3 Meat • 1 Vegetable • 1 Starch

Asian Pot Roast and Veggies

You don't find sliced meat very often in Asian restaurants, since their tradition tends to shred meats instead. But I thought, why not combine our two traditions? After all, that's the American way, to blend our culinary styles into something uniquely our own. So I created a gravy as savory as my favorite Asian sauces and joined it with some tasty lean beef. I think the result is, truly, "hands across the sea."   ☻   Serves 4

16 ounces lean round steak, cut into 4 pieces
2 cups chopped carrots
2 cups chopped celery
1 cup chopped onion
1 (12-ounce) jar Heinz Fat-Free Beef Gravy
1/4 cup reduced-sodium soy sauce
1/2 teaspoon dried minced garlic

In a large skillet sprayed with butter-flavored cooking spray, brown meat for 3 to 4 minutes on each side. Spray a slow cooker container with butter-flavored cooking spray. In prepared container, layer carrots, celery, and onion. Evenly arrange steak pieces over vegetables. In a medium bowl, combine beef gravy, soy sauce, and garlic. Spoon mixture evenly over steak. Cover and cook on LOW for 8 hours. For each serving, place 1 piece of meat on a plate and spoon about 1 cup vegetable mixture next to it.

Each serving equals:

HE: 3 Protein • 2½ Vegetable • ¼ Slider •
17 Optional Calories

224 Calories • 4 gm Fat • 28 gm Protein •
19 gm Carbohydrate • 989 mg Sodium •
54 mg Calcium • 4 gm Fiber

DIABETIC: 3 Meat • 1½ Vegetable •
½ Starch/Carbohydrate

Rising Sun Beef and Pepper Pot

The image of the rising sun is one of the dawn of a new day, and that's what I hope all these great healthy recipes will offer you—a brand-new approach to eating that provides delicious food made simple and good for you. The Japanese are famous for the quality of their beef, so here is my modest effort to honor that tradition!

● Serves 6

1½ cups coarsely chopped green bell pepper
1 cup chopped onion
½ cup (one 2.5-ounce jar) sliced mushrooms, drained
1 (10¾-ounce) can Healthy Request Tomato Soup

¼ cup water
1 tablespoon reduced-sodium soy sauce
1 teaspoon dried parsley flakes
16 ounces lean round steak, cut into 36 pieces
3 cups hot cooked rice

Spray a slow cooker container with butter-flavored cooking spray. In prepared container, combine green pepper, onion, and mushrooms. Stir in tomato soup, water, soy sauce, and parsley flakes. Add steak pieces. Cover and cook on LOW for 6 to 8 hours. When serving, place ½ cup hot rice on a plate and spoon about 1 cup meat mixture over top.

HINT: Usually 2 cups uncooked instant rice cooks to about 3 cups.

Each serving equals:

HE: 2 Protein • 1 Bread • 1 Vegetable • ¼ Slider • 10 Optional Calories

236 Calories • 4 gm Fat • 20 gm Protein • 30 gm Carbohydrate • 363 mg Sodium • 20 mg Calcium • 2 gm Fiber

DIABETIC: 2 Meat • 1½ Starch/Carbohydrate • 1 Vegetable

Grandma's Beef Hash

I grew up loving all kinds of "hash" dishes. Back then, I didn't think about them as a smart cook's solution to cooking up leftovers that didn't taste like leftovers. I just enjoyed them on their own merits. Now you don't need leftovers to make this tasty blend of meat and potatoes, but if you've got 'em, use 'em! (Otherwise, pick up a chunk of meat at the deli on your way home and make this tomorrow.)

Serves 6 (1 cup)

3 full cups (18 ounces)
    diced cooked lean roast
    beef
6 cups shredded loose-packed
    frozen potatoes
1½ cups finely chopped onion

1 (12-ounce) jar Heinz Fat
    Free Beef Gravy
1 teaspoon Worcestershire
    sauce
1 teaspoon dried parsley flakes
⅛ teaspoon black pepper

Spray a slow cooker container with butter-flavored cooking spray. In prepared container, combine roast beef, potatoes, and onion. Add gravy, Worcestershire sauce, parsley flakes, and black pepper. Mix well to combine. Cover and cook on LOW for 6 to 8 hours. Mix well before serving.

HINTS: 1. If you don't have leftovers, purchase a chunk of lean cooked roast beef from your local deli.
       2. Mr. Dell's frozen shredded potatoes are a good choice, or raw shredded potatoes, rinsed and patted dry, may be used in place of frozen potatoes.

Each serving equals:

HE: 3 Protein • ½ Bread • ½ Vegetable • ¼ Slider •
5 Optional Calories

---

295 Calories • 7 gm Fat • 29 gm Protein •
29 gm Carbohydrate • 398 mg Sodium •
28 mg Calcium • 4 gm Fiber

DIABETIC: 3 Meat • 1½ Starch • ½ Vegetable

Fall Festival Pork

I think pork and apples go together like love and marriage, especially in the fall! This is a simple dish, perfect for a celebration dinner—did your son kick the winning point or did your daughter ace her SATs? Or you can simply celebrate that you're together and healthy. Nothing's more precious or worthy of cheering than that.

● Serves 6 (1 cup)

3 cups unpeeled and chopped raw potatoes
1½ cups chopped carrots
1½ cups chopped celery
1½ cups chopped onion
1 cup (2 small) cored, peeled, and chopped cooking apples
16 ounces lean pork loin, cut into 36 pieces
½ cup unsweetened apple juice
1 teaspoon prepared yellow mustard
1½ teaspoons dried parsley flakes
⅛ teaspoon black pepper

Spray a slow cooker container with butter-flavored cooking spray. In prepared container, combine potatoes, carrots, celery, onion, and apples. Arrange pork pieces over vegetable mixture. In a small bowl, combine apple juice, mustard, parsley flakes, and black pepper. Pour juice mixture evenly over top. Cover and cook on LOW for 6 to 8 hours. Mix well before serving.

Each serving equals:

HE: 2 Protein • 1½ Vegetable • ½ Bread • ½ Fruit

203 Calories • 3 gm Fat • 18 gm Protein •
26 gm Carbohydrate • 83 mg Sodium •
44 mg Calcium • 2 gm Fiber

DIABETIC: 2 Meat • 1½ Vegetable • 1 Starch •
½ Fruit

Italian Pork and Pasta

Do you find that too many "healthy" or "good-for-you" recipes are dry and dull? Most meats taste so much better swathed in a luscious, creamy sauce like the one in this piquant supper dish. Do take the time to chop the tomatoes and onions finely, as bigger pieces might tend to overwhelm the delicate flavors.

● Serves 6 (1 cup)

> 1 (10¾-ounce) can Healthy Request Cream of Mushroom Soup
> 1 cup (one 8-ounce can) Hunt's Tomato Sauce
> 1 cup (one 8-ounce can) tomatoes, finely chopped and undrained
> 16 ounces lean pork tenderloins or cutlets, cut into 36 pieces
> ½ cup finely chopped onion
> 1 cup (one 4-ounce can) sliced mushrooms, drained
> 3 cups cooked rotini pasta, rinsed and drained
> 1 teaspoon Italian seasoning

Spray a slow cooker container with olive oil–flavored cooking spray. In prepared container, combine mushroom soup, tomato sauce, and undrained tomatoes. Stir in pork pieces, onion, and mushrooms. Add rotini pasta and Italian seasoning. Mix well to combine. Cover and cook on HIGH for 4 hours. Mix well before serving.

HINT: Usually 2½ cups uncooked rotini pasta cooks to about 3 cups.

Each serving equals:

HE: 2 Protein • 1½ Vegetable • 1 Bread • ¼ Slider • 8 Optional Calories

---

249 Calories • 5 gm Fat • 21 gm Protein • 30 gm Carbohydrate • 640 mg Sodium • 71 mg Calcium • 2 gm Fiber

---

DIABETIC: 2 Meat • 1½ Starch • 1 Vegetable

Cheesy Broccoli, Ham, and Noodle Bake

I'm not sure why broccoli and cheddar are so splendid together, but when you "couple" that couple with ham and noodles, you discover even more tasty talents that seem to emerge only when they are served holding hands. You can use chopped broccoli or broccoli spears in this recipe, but I recommend cutting the big pieces a bit.

☘ Serves 6 (1 cup)

> 1 (10¾-ounce) can Healthy Request Cream of
>   Mushroom Soup
> 1½ cups shredded Kraft reduced-fat
>   Cheddar cheese
> 3 cups frozen cut broccoli, thawed
> 1 cup chopped onion
> ½ cup (one 2.5-ounce jar) sliced mushrooms,
>   drained
> 1½ cups (9 ounces) diced Dubuque 97% fat-free ham
>   or any extra-lean ham
> 3 cups cooked noodles, rinsed and drained
> ⅛ teaspoon black pepper

Spray a slow cooker container with butter-flavored cooking spray. In prepared container, combine mushroom soup and Cheddar cheese. Add broccoli, onion, mushrooms, and ham. Mix well to combine. Stir in noodles and black pepper. Cover and cook on HIGH for 3 to 4 hours. Mix well before serving.

HINTS: 1. Thaw broccoli by placing in a colander and rinsing under hot water for one minute.
2. Usually 2⅔ cups uncooked noodles cooks to about 3 cups.

Each serving equals:

HE: 2 Protein • 1½ Vegetable • 1 Bread • ¼ Slider •
8 Optional Calories

293 Calories • 9 gm Fat • 21 gm Protein •
32 gm Carbohydrate • 611 mg Sodium •
301 mg Calcium • 4 gm Fiber

DIABETIC: 2 Meat • 1½ Vegetable • 1½ Starch

Ham and Macaroni Deluxe Pot

What makes a hotel room deluxe, you may wonder? Luxury, attention to detail, and nothing but the best. Now translate that notion to a recipe, and you find a similar focus: a creamy, cheesy sauce that tastes like luxury feels; little details (like chopped pimiento and parsley) that have a real impact; and the best healthy ingredients I can find on the shelves. Living well is within everyone's reach!

Serves 6 (1 cup)

> 1 (10¾-ounce) can Healthy Request Cream of
>   Mushroom Soup
> 1 cup + 2 tablespoons shredded Kraft reduced-fat
>   Cheddar cheese
> ¼ cup (one 2-ounce jar) chopped pimiento,
>   undrained
> 2 cups cooked elbow macaroni, rinsed and
>   drained
> 1 cup frozen whole-kernel corn, thawed
> 1½ cups diced Dubuque 97% fat-free ham or any
>   extra-lean ham
> ¾ cup finely chopped onion
> 1½ teaspoons dried parsley flakes
> ⅛ teaspoon black pepper

Spray a slow cooker container with butter-flavored cooking spray. In prepared container, combine mushroom soup, Cheddar cheese, and undrained pimiento. Stir in macaroni, corn, ham, and onion. Add parsley flakes and black pepper. Mix well to combine. Cover and cook on HIGH for 3 to 4 hours. Mix well before serving.

HINTS: 1. Usually 1⅓ cups uncooked elbow macaroni cooks to
           about 2 cups.
        2. Thaw corn by placing in a colander and rinsing under
           hot water for one minute.

Each serving equals:

HE: 2 Protein • 1 Bread • ¼ Vegetable • ¼ Slider •
8 Optional Calories

235 Calories • 7 gm Fat • 16 gm Protein •
27 gm Carbohydrate • 534 mg Sodium •
201 mg Calcium • 2 gm Fiber

DIABETIC: 2 Meat • 1½ Starch/Carbohydrate

Baked Pork with Cherry Glaze

Here's another wonderful way to combine pork with fruit, and I think you'll be astonished at how downright delicious it is! Sometimes, we find just the right ingredients for a recipe in an unexpected place. In this case, cherry pie filling works some culinary magic on a main dish delight. ☻ Serves 4

4 (4-ounce) lean tenderized pork tenderloins or cutlets
1½ teaspoons dried onion flakes
1 (20-ounce) can Lucky Leaf No Sugar Added Cherry Pie Filling
4 teaspoons chopped fresh parsley

In a large skillet sprayed with butter-flavored cooking spray, brown pork for 3 to 4 minutes on each side. Spray a slow cooker container with butter-flavored cooking spray. Evenly arrange meat in prepared container. Stir onion flakes into cherry pie filling. Pour pie filling evenly over browned meat. Cover and cook on LOW for 4 hours. When serving, place 1 piece of meat on a plate, spoon about ½ cup cherry mixture over meat, and garnish with 1 teaspoon fresh parsley.

Each serving equals:

HE: 3 Protein • 1 Fruit

180 Calories • 4 gm Fat • 22 gm Protein •
14 gm Carbohydrate • 62 mg Sodium •
7 mg Calcium • 2 gm Fiber

DIABETIC: 3 Meat • 1 Fruit

Bean and Ham Cassoulet

If you haven't spent as much time reading cookbooks as I have, you might be unfamiliar with the term "cassoulet." This beloved hearty bean dish is a French peasant pleaser that cooks for hours over a low fire. Now you can enjoy a version of that *magnifique* kitchen creation that is *tres facile* (very easy) to prepare!

○ Serves 6 (1⅓ cups)

> *20 ounces (two 16-ounce cans) butter beans, rinsed and drained*
> *2 cups (one 16-ounce can) cut green beans, rinsed and drained*
> *1 cup (one 8-ounce can) sliced carrots, rinsed and drained*
> *1¼ cups chopped onion*
> *1¾ cups (one 14.5-ounce can) diced tomatoes, undrained*
> *¼ cup reduced-sodium ketchup*
> *1½ cups (9 ounces) diced Dubuque 97% fat-free ham or any*
> *extra-lean ham*

Spray a slow cooker container with butter-flavored cooking spray. In prepared container, combine butter beans, green beans, carrots, and onion. Stir in undrained tomatoes and ketchup. Add ham. Mix well to combine. Cover and cook on LOW for 6 to 8 hours. Mix well before serving.

Each serving equals:

HE: 2 Vegetable • 1½ Protein • 1 Bread •
10 Optional Calories

---

182 Calories • 2 gm Fat • 13 gm Protein •
28 gm Carbohydrate • 779 mg Sodium •
74 mg Calcium • 6 gm Fiber

DIABETIC: 2½ Meat • 1½ Starch • 1 Vegetable

Bean and Ham Veggie Pot

Beans are a terrific staple to have on hand, in all their colorful variety. When you've got a stack of cans in your pantry, you've got the makings of many delectably, healthy meals. This is a rich vegetable-based stew made even more savory with the addition of ham.

● Serves 6 (1 cup)

> 30 ounces (three 16-ounce cans) great northern beans, rinsed and
>   drained
> 1 full cup (6 ounces) diced Dubuque 97% fat-free ham or any
>   extra-lean ham
> 1 cup chopped onion
> 2 cups shredded cabbage
> 1 cup (one 8-ounce can) tomatoes, chopped and undrained
> 1 tablespoon pourable Splenda or Sugar Twin
> 1 teaspoon dried parsley flakes
> ⅛ teaspoon black pepper

Spray a slow cooker container with butter-flavored cooking spray. In prepared container, combine great northern beans, ham, onion, and cabbage. Add undrained tomatoes, Splenda, parsley flakes, and black pepper. Mix well to combine. Cover and cook on LOW for 6 to 8 hours. Mix well before serving.

Each serving equals:

HE: 2 Protein • 1 Bread • 1 Vegetable •
1 Optional Calorie

218 Calories • 2 gm Fat • 16 gm Protein •
34 gm Carbohydrate • 303 mg Sodium •
101 mg Calcium • 8 gm Fiber

DIABETIC: 2 Meat • 1½ Starch • 1 Vegetable

Old-Fashioned Green Beans and Ham

Here's a simple Sunday night supper that I can promise you is a husband pleaser—at least, as long as the man loves green beans as much as Cliff does! The ham lends its smoky flavor to all those potatoes, delivering a filling and flavorful meal with very little kitchen time. Add a loaf of crusty bread and a good-looking, good-tasting dessert, and you're done. ☻ Serves 6 (1⅓ cups)

5 cups frozen cut green beans, thawed
3 cups peeled and chopped raw potatoes
1 cup chopped onion
2 full cups (12 ounces) diced Dubuque 97% fat-free ham or any extra-lean ham
¾ cup water
1 teaspoon dried parsley flakes
⅛ teaspoon black pepper

Spray a slow cooker container with butter-flavored cooking spray. In prepared container, combine green beans, potatoes, and onion. Stir in ham. Add water, parsley flakes, and black pepper. Mix well to combine. Cover and cook on LOW for 6 to 8 hours. Mix well before serving.

HINT: Thaw green beans by placing in a colander and rinsing under hot water for one minute.

Each serving equals:

HE: 2 Protein • 2 Vegetable • ½ Bread

170 Calories • 2 gm Fat • 13 gm Protein •
25 gm Carbohydrate • 454 mg Sodium •
55 mg Calcium • 4 gm Fiber

DIABETIC: 2 Vegetable • 1½ Meat • 1 Starch

Angie's Scalloped Potatoes and Ham

Not all daughters-in-law may appreciate having a mom-in-law who's known for her cooking, but Angie has enjoyed my recipes since she and Tommy first met. She's a real fan of creamy dishes like this one, and she's busy enough to value the time-saving pluses of preparing meals in her slow cooker.   ☽   Serves 8 (1 cup)

> 1 (10¾-ounce) can Healthy Request Cream of Mushroom Soup
> 1½ cups (one 12-fluid-ounce can) Carnation Evaporated Skim Milk
> 1 teaspoon prepared yellow mustard
> 2 full cups (12 ounces) diced Dubuque 97% fat-free ham or any extra-lean ham
> 6 cups shredded loose-packed frozen potatoes
> 1 cup frozen peas, thawed
> 1 cup finely chopped onion
> 1½ teaspoons dried parsley flakes
> 1½ cups shredded Kraft reduced-fat Cheddar cheese
> ⅛ teaspoon black pepper

Spray a slow cooker container with butter-flavored cooking spray. In prepared container, combine mushroom soup, evaporated skim milk, and mustard. Stir in ham. Add potatoes, peas, onion, parsley flakes, Cheddar cheese, and black pepper. Mix well to combine. Cover and cook on LOW for 6 to 8 hours. Mix well before serving.

HINTS: 1. Mr. Dell's frozen shredded potatoes are a good choice, or raw shredded potatoes, rinsed and patted dry, may be used in place of frozen potatoes.
2. Thaw peas by placing in a colander and rinsing under hot water for one minute.

Each serving equals:

HE: 2 Protein • ¾ Bread • ⅓ Skim Milk •
¼ Vegetable • ¼ Slider • 1 Optional Calorie

242 Calories • 6 gm Fat • 19 gm Protein •
28 gm Carbohydrate • 569 mg Sodium •
316 mg Calcium • 3 gm Fiber

DIABETIC: 2 Meat • 1 Starch • ½ Skim Milk

Momma's Scalloped Potatoes and Ham

When I began layering the ingredients for this recipe in the cooker container, I could imagine my mother's approval of what I was doing. She taught me so much about cooking well without spending a lot of time or money, and this hearty dish would please her for its thrift, its tastiness, and its time-saving ease.

○ Serves 8 (1 cup)

> 3 cups (18 ounces) diced Dubuque 97% fat-free ham or any
>   extra-lean ham ☆
> 7 cups peeled and thinly sliced raw potatoes ☆
> 1½ cups diced onion ☆
> 1½ cups shredded Kraft reduced-fat Cheddar cheese ☆
> 1 (10¾-ounce) can Healthy Request Cream of Mushroom Soup
> ½ cup (one 2.5-ounce jar) sliced mushrooms, undrained
> 2 teaspoons dried parsley flakes

Spray a slow cooker container with butter-flavored cooking spray. In prepared container, layer half of ham, half of potatoes, half of onion, and half of Cheddar cheese. Repeat layers. In a medium bowl, combine mushroom soup, undrained mushrooms, and parsley flakes. Evenly spoon soup mixture over top. Cover and cook on LOW for 8 hours. Mix well before serving.

Each serving equals:

> HE: 2½ Protein • ¾ Bread • ½ Vegetable •
> ¼ Slider • 1 Optional Calorie
> _____
> 267 Calories • 7 gm Fat • 19 gm Protein •
> 32 gm Carbohydrate • 699 mg Sodium •
> 198 mg Calcium • 3 gm Fiber
> _____
> DIABETIC: 2½ Meat • 1½ Starch/Carbohydrate •
> ½ Vegetable

South Seas Sweet Potatoes and Ham

The warmth of the sun is an invisible ingredient in this somewhat exotic recipe, but you'll taste it in every bite! When it's gray and cold outside, why not bring back a little summer heat by serving a sweetly savory combination that is like a little vacation on a plate?

● Serves 6 (1 cup)

> *3 full cups peeled and thinly sliced raw sweet potatoes*
> *3 full cups (18 ounces) diced Dubuque 97% fat-free ham or any*
> *extra-lean ham*
> *1 cup (one 8-ounce can) pineapple chunks, packed in fruit juice,*
> *drained, and ¼ cup liquid reserved*
> *¾ cup finely chopped onion*
> *¼ cup water*
> *1 teaspoon prepared yellow mustard*
> *2 tablespoons pourable Splenda or Sugar Twin*
> *1½ teaspoons dried parsley flakes*

Spray a slow cooker container with butter-flavored cooking spray. In prepared container, combine sweet potatoes, ham, pineapple chunks, and onion. In a small bowl, combine reserved pineapple juice, water, mustard, Splenda, and parsley flakes. Drizzle liquid mixture evenly over ham mixture. Cover and cook on LOW for 6 to 8 hours. Mix gently before serving.

Each serving equals:

HE: 2 Protein • ⅔ Bread • ⅓ Fruit • ¼ Vegetable • 2 Optional Calories

171 Calories • 3 gm Fat • 15 gm Protein •
21 gm Carbohydrate • 686 mg Sodium •
20 mg Calcium • 2 gm Fiber

DIABETIC: 2 Meat • 1½ Starch/Carbohydrate

Frankfurter Beans Deluxe

Instead of the same old, same old franks-and-beans supper, here's a fast, fun, and flavorful version that adds a lot by doing just a few things differently. Slow cooking is the perfect cooking method for any baked bean–style dish, as you'll discover after just one bite.

● Serves 6 (1 cup)

> 20 ounces (two 16-ounce cans) great northern beans, rinsed and drained
> 2 cups (one 16-ounce can) cut green beans, rinsed and drained
> 1 cup (one 8-ounce can) Hunt's Tomato Sauce
> 1 cup (one 8-ounce can) tomatoes, finely chopped and undrained
> 1 cup chopped onion
> 1/4 cup pourable Splenda or Sugar Twin
> 2 teaspoons prepared yellow mustard
> 1/8 teaspoon black pepper
> 8 ounces Oscar Mayer or Healthy Choice reduced-fat frankfurters, cut into 1/4-inch pieces

Spray a slow cooker container with butter-flavored cooking spray. In prepared container, combine great northern beans, green beans, tomato sauce, and undrained tomatoes. Add onion, Splenda, mustard, and black pepper. Mix well to combine. Stir in frankfurters. Cover and cook on LOW for 6 to 8 hours. Mix well before serving.

Each serving equals:

HE: 2 Vegetable • 1½ Protein • 1 Bread • 1 Optional Calorie

---

211 Calories • 3 gm Fat • 14 gm Protein • 32 gm Carbohydrate • 830 mg Sodium • 82 mg Calcium • 6 gm Fiber

---

DIABETIC: 2 Vegetable • 1½ Meat • 1 Starch

German Frankfurter Supper

I've taken the pure essence of apple, pressed into juice, and coupled it with chunks of fresh apple, in order to transform some potatoes, cabbage, and franks into a festive excursion into the beautiful Black Forest of Germany, where eating off the bounty of the land is a long-held tradition.   ☻   Serves 6 (1 full cup)

1 cup unsweetened apple juice
¼ cup pourable Splenda or Sugar Twin
4 cups shredded cabbage
3 cups diced raw potatoes
1 cup chopped onion
2 cups (4 small) cored, peeled, and diced cooking apples
1 (16-ounce) package Oscar Mayer or Healthy Choice reduced-fat
    frankfurters, cut into 1-inch pieces
1 teaspoon dried parsley flakes

Spray a slow cooker container with butter-flavored cooking spray. In prepared container, combine apple juice and Splenda. Stir in cabbage, potatoes, and onion. Add apples, frankfurters, and parsley flakes. Mix well to combine. Cover and cook on LOW for 6 to 8 hours. Mix well before serving.

Each serving equals:

HE: 2 Protein • 1 Fruit • 1 Vegetable • ½ Bread •
4 Optional Calories

203 Calories • 3 gm Fat • 12 gm Protein •
32 gm Carbohydrate • 783 mg Sodium •
39 mg Calcium • 3 gm Fiber

DIABETIC: 1½ Meat • 1 Fruit • 1 Vegetable • 1 Starch

Spencer's Macaroni and Cheese with Hot Dogs

Not all grandmas enjoy cooking for their grandkids as much as I do—but if you cook for anyone who's as pleased by your cooking as my little Spencer is, you know the feeling of having a fan club! This dish is a real kid pleaser, and because the franks are diced, it's a good choice for little ones as well as big ones.

◑ Serves 6 (¾ cup)

1½ cups (one 12-fluid-ounce can) Carnation Evaporated Skim
    Milk
1½ cups diced Velveeta Light processed cheese
3 cups cooked elbow macaroni, rinsed and drained
8 ounces Oscar Mayer or Healthy Choice reduced-fat
    frankfurters, diced
2 teaspoons dried onion flakes
1 teaspoon dried parsley flakes

Spray a slow cooker container with butter-flavored cooking spray. In prepared container, combine evaporated skim milk and Velveeta cheese. Stir in macaroni, frankfurters, onion flakes, and parsley flakes. Cover and cook on LOW for 3 to 4 hours. Mix well before serving.

HINT: Usually 2 cups uncooked elbow macaroni cooks to about
    3 cups.

Each serving equals:

HE: 2 Protein • 1 Bread • ½ Skim Milk

---

249 Calories • 5 gm Fat • 18 gm Protein •
33 gm Carbohydrate • 913 mg Sodium •
329 mg Calcium • 1 gm Fiber

DIABETIC: 2 Meat • 1½ Starch/Carbohydrate •
½ Skim Milk

Bavarian Kraut and Kielbasa Supper

You'll be amazed to discover how much hearty flavor is still packed into lean sausage like this kielbasa. In the hours those sausage chunks sit side by side with the veggies and potatoes, their flavors mingle like crazy, and the end result is nothing short of spectacular. If a Germany holiday isn't in the cards for this year, travel by taste buds!   ☺   Serves 6 (1 cup)

3 cups chopped unpeeled raw potatoes

2 cups frozen cut carrots, thawed

1 cup chopped onion

1¾ cups (one 14½-ounce can) Frank's Bavarian Style sauerkraut, drained

¼ cup water

1 (16-ounce) package Healthy Choice 97% lean kielbasa sausage, cut into ½-inch pieces

Spray a slow cooker container with butter-flavored cooking spray. In prepared container, combine potatoes, carrots, and onion. Stir in sauerkraut and water. Add kielbasa sausage. Mix well to combine. Cover and cook on LOW for 8 hours. Mix well before serving.

HINTS: 1. Thaw carrots by placing in a colander and rinsing under hot water for one minute.
2. If you can't find Frank's Bavarian sauerkraut, use regular sauerkraut, ½ teaspoon caraway seeds, and 1 teaspoon Brown Sugar Twin.

Each serving equals:

HE: 2 Protein • 1½ Vegetable • ½ Bread

179 Calories • 3 gm Fat • 11 gm Protein •
27 gm Carbohydrate • 675 mg Sodium •
51 mg Calcium • 3 gm Fiber

DIABETIC: 2 Meat • 1½ Vegetable • 1 Starch

Creamy Corned Beef and Cabbage

March 17 comes but once a year, but this yummy Irish-themed dish deserves more than an annual appearance on your table, don't you think? The ingredients are easy to obtain, there's almost no preparation, and the flavor as you lift the lid is enough to start you singing!

○ Serves 6 (1½ cups)

1 (10¾-ounce) can Healthy Request Cream of Mushroom Soup
1 cup water
6 cups coarsely chopped cabbage
3 cups diced raw potatoes
3 cups thinly sliced carrots
1½ cups chopped onion
6 (2.5-ounce) packages Carl Buddig Lean Corned Beef, shredded

Spray a slow cooker container with butter-flavored cooking spray. In prepared container, combine mushroom soup and water. Stir in cabbage, potatoes, carrots, and onion. Add shredded corned beef. Mix well to combine. Cover and cook on LOW for 6 to 8 hours. Mix well before serving.

Each serving equals:

HE: 2½ Vegetable • 2 Protein • ½ Bread • ¼ Slider • 8 Optional Calories

258 Calories • 6 gm Fat • 18 gm Protein • 33 gm Carbohydrate • 991 mg Sodium • 125 mg Calcium • 5 gm Fiber

DIABETIC: 2½ Meat • 2 Vegetable • 1 Starch

Reuben Rice Casserole

One of my favorite recipe "starters" is to think of something delicious in one format, like a sandwich, and translate that taste sensation into another form. Here, I've rethought the classic deli sandwich and turned it into a savory casserole so rich with cheesy goodness you'll cheer! ☻ Serves 6 (1 cup)

½ cup Kraft Fat Free Thousand Island Dressing

1 cup water

2 cups (one 16-ounce can) sauerkraut, well drained

2 (2.5-ounce) packages Carl Buddig Lean Corned Beef, shredded

1 cup uncooked instant rice

4 (¾-ounce) slices Kraft reduced-fat Swiss cheese, shredded

Spray a slow cooker container with butter-flavored cooking spray. In prepared container, combine Thousand Island dressing and water. Stir in sauerkraut, shredded corned beef, and uncooked rice. Add Swiss cheese. Mix well to combine. Cover and cook on LOW for 6 to 8 hours. Mix well before serving.

Each serving equals:

HE: 1½ Protein • ½ Bread • ½ Vegetable •
¼ Slider • 6 Optional Calories

---

165 Calories • 5 gm Fat • 10 gm Protein •
20 gm Carbohydrate • 801 mg Sodium •
148 mg Calcium • 2 gm Fiber

DIABETIC: 1½ Meat • 1 Starch/Carbohydrate •
½ Vegetable

Delectable
Desserts, Drinks,
Dips, and Other
Delights

No matter the time of day, your slow cooker is amazingly versatile, able to turn out brilliant breakfasts, perfect party food, and downright delightful desserts. This astonishingly talented appliance works wonderfully for parties, keeping food warm on your buffet table; it's also a dynamic do-er, ideal for creating the kinds of hot dips you find on favorite restaurant menus but have rarely tried to prepare at home.

This is a section full of fun food, the kinds of recipes that make life more festive and interesting. If you're planning a company brunch, you can choose from a scrumptious pleaser like **Breakfast Cheese Soufflé** or **Egg-Mushroom Scramble**. Delectable dips and super sauces abound, from **Chili Cheese Dip** to **Potluck Spaghetti Meat Sauce**. You now have all kinds of bountiful beverages to serve to family and friends, like **Comforting Citrus Cider** and **Spiced Holiday Punch**. And none of my books would be complete without dazzling desserts, from **Maple Apple Crumble** to **Cheyanne's Cherry Cobbler**, from a dramatic **Pears Helene Bread Pudding** to a supremely satisfying **Brownie Walnut Pudding Cake**.

Hot Spiced Cherry Cider

Oh, I know you may think that Kool-Aid is just for kids, but when you fiddle with it just a bit and spice it up, you've got a steamy hot beverage that is equally appealing to adults.

🌑 Serves 8 (1 cup)

> 4 cups unsweetened apple juice
> 4 cups Diet Mountain Dew
> 1 (0.13-ounce) package sugar-free cherry Kool-Aid
> ½ teaspoon ground cinnamon

In a slow cooker container, combine apple juice and Diet Mountain Dew. Add dry Kool-Aid and cinnamon. Mix well to combine. Cover and cook on HIGH for 2 to 3 hours. Mix well before serving.

Each serving equals:

HE: 1 Fruit

60 Calories • 0 gm Fat • 0 gm Protein •
15 gm Carbohydrate • 15 mg Sodium •
10 mg Calcium • 0 gm Fiber

DIABETIC: 1 Fruit

Comforting Citrus Cider

On those cloudy days when the daylight looks like dusk all day long, you need some sunshine in a cup, and this cozy-warm blend is just right! Resist the urge to lift the lid on your cooker while this is brewing, but once it's time to serve it, a houseful of people will quickly beat a path to your kitchen just because it smells sooooo good! ☾ Serves 12 (1 full cup)

> 7 cups unsweetened apple juice
> 1 cup unsweetened orange juice
> 4 cups Diet Mountain Dew
> 1/2 cup pourable Splenda or Sugar Twin
> 1 1/2 teaspoons apple pie spice

In a slow cooker container, combine apple juice, orange juice, and Diet Mountain Dew. Stir in Splenda and apple pie spice. Cover and cook on LOW for 2 to 3 hours. Mix well before serving.

Each serving equals:

HE: 1 1/3 Fruit • 4 Optional Calories

80 Calories • 0 gm Fat • 0 gm Protein •
20 gm Carbohydrate • 12 mg Sodium •
13 mg Calcium • 0 gm Fiber

DIABETIC: 1 Fruit

Spiced Holiday Punch

This rosy-colored, homey-spiced drink is a great way to get some healthy fruit into your diet during those festive days and weeks when you're busy from dawn to bedtime. It has a delicious aroma, which makes it ideal to serve at caroling parties or a family potluck.

🌙 Serves 12 (¾ cup)

> 5 cups unsweetened apple juice
> 2 cups Ocean Spray reduced-calorie cranberry juice cocktail
> 2 cups Diet Mountain Dew
> 2 tablespoons pourable Splenda or Sugar Twin
> 1½ teaspoons apple pie spice
> 12 cinnamon sticks, optional

In a slow cooker container, combine apple juice, cranberry juice cocktail, and Diet Mountain Dew. Stir in Splenda and apple pie spice. Cover and cook on LOW for 3 to 4 hours. When serving, pour into mugs and garnish with a cinnamon stick, if desired.

Each serving equals:

HE: 1 Fruit • 1 Optional Calorie

56 Calories • 0 gm Fat • 0 gm Protein •
14 gm Carbohydrate • 8 mg Sodium •
12 mg Calcium • 0 gm Fiber

DIABETIC: 1 Fruit

Rise and Shine Oatmeal

Family members who insist they don't have time for a hot breakfast will stop in their tracks when you ladle out bowls of this fruited hot cereal! The dried fruits bloom in the warmth and moisture of the cooker, and the nuts provide a little pleasing crunch in every bite.

⏺ Serves 4 (½ cup)

> 1 cup quick oats
> ½ cup chopped dried apricots
> 2 tablespoons seedless raisins
> ¼ cup chopped walnuts
> ¼ cup pourable Splenda or Sugar Twin
> ¼ teaspoon apple pie spice
> 2 cups water

Spray a slow cooker container with butter-flavored cooking spray. In prepared container, combine oats, apricots, raisins, walnuts, Splenda, and apple pie spice. Add water. Mix well to combine. Cover and cook on LOW for 6 to 8 hours.

HINT: Start cooking just before going to bed, and it will be ready in the morning.

Each serving equals:

HE: 1 Bread • 1 Fruit • ½ Fat • ¼ Protein •
6 Optional Calories

198 Calories • 6 gm Fat • 5 gm Protein •
31 gm Carbohydrate • 2 mg Sodium •
30 mg Calcium • 3 gm Fiber

DIABETIC: 1 Starch • 1 Fruit • 1 Fat

Egg-Mushroom Scramble

When you have a bunch for brunch, don't chain yourself to the skillet turning out omelets endlessly and miss out on all that visiting you really want to do! Instead, hire yourself a guest chef by using your slow cooker to prepare creamy, delicious scrambled eggs for a crowd. ☻ Serves 6 (1 cup)

> 9 eggs, beaten, or equivalent in egg substitute
> 1 (10¾-ounce) can Healthy Request Cream of Mushroom Soup
> 1 cup (one 4-ounce can) sliced mushrooms, drained
> ½ cup finely chopped onion
> 1 teaspoon lemon pepper

Spray a slow cooker container with butter-flavored cooking spray. In a large bowl, combine eggs and mushroom soup. Add mushrooms, onion, and lemon pepper. Mix well to combine. Pour mixture into prepared slow cooker container. Lightly spray top with butter-flavored cooking spray. Cover and cook on LOW for 4 hours. Mix well before serving.

Each serving equals:

HE: 1½ Protein • ½ Vegetable • ¼ Slider •
8 Optional Calories

---

140 Calories • 8 gm Fat • 10 gm Protein •
7 gm Carbohydrate • 448 mg Sodium •
83 mg Calcium • 1 gm Fiber

DIABETIC: 1½ Meat • ½ Starch/Carbohydrate

Breakfast Cheese Soufflé

Here's a beautiful way to feed your family and friends without a fuss. This layered egg dish is festive and oh-so-flavorful with its bits of ham and rich cheesy sauce. Best of all, you're free to enjoy your guests or simply sit and read the Sunday paper.

☻ Serves 6 (1 cup)

> 8 slices reduced-calorie white bread, torn into small pieces ☆
> 1 full cup diced Dubuque 97% fat-free ham or any extra-lean ham ☆
> 1½ cups shredded Kraft reduced-fat Cheddar cheese ☆
> 4 eggs, beaten, or equivalent in egg substitute
> 1½ cups (one 12-fluid-ounce can) Carnation Evaporated Skim Milk
> ¼ cup Land O Lakes Fat Free Half & Half
> 1½ teaspoons dried parsley flakes
> ½ teaspoon lemon pepper
> ⅛ teaspoon paprika

Spray a slow cooker container with butter-flavored cooking spray. In prepared container, layer half of bread, half of ham, and half of Cheddar cheese. Repeat layers. In a large bowl, combine eggs, evaporated skim milk, half & half, parsley flakes, and lemon pepper. Carefully pour egg mixture into slow cooker container. Sprinkle paprika evenly over top. Cover and cook on HIGH for 2 hours.

Each serving equals:

HE: 2 Protein • ⅔ Bread • ½ Skim Milk • 6 Optional Calories

265 Calories • 9 gm Fat • 23 gm Protein • 23 gm Carbohydrate • 537 mg Sodium • 401 mg Calcium • 0 gm Fiber

DIABETIC: 2 Meat • 1 Starch • ½ Skim Milk

Brunch Casserole

Whoever invented the lovely custom of combining breakfast and lunch on a leisurely weekend must have hoped for a main dish that filled you up without filling you out! Instead of the ham or bacon that so many brunch dishes contain, your family will be pleased to see something a little different in the chunks of kielbasa stirred into the eggs. ☻ Serves 6 (1 cup)

> 4 eggs, beaten, or equivalent in egg substitute
> 1½ cups (one 12-fluid-ounce can) Carnation Evaporated Skim Milk
> ½ teaspoon prepared yellow mustard
> 1 teaspoon dried parsley flakes
> 4½ cups shredded loose-packed frozen potatoes
> 8 ounces Healthy Choice 97% lean kielbasa sausage, cut into ¼-inch pieces
> ¾ cup shredded Kraft reduced-fat Cheddar cheese

Spray a slow cooker container with butter-flavored cooking spray. In a large bowl, combine eggs, evaporated skim milk, mustard, and parsley flakes. Pour mixture into prepared container. Stir in potatoes and kielbasa sausage. Add Cheddar cheese. Mix well to combine. Cover and cook on LOW for 3 to 4 hours. Mix well before serving.

HINT: Mr. Dell's frozen shredded potatoes are a good choice, or raw shredded potatoes, rinsed and patted dry, may be used in place of frozen potatoes.

Each serving equals:

HE: 2½ Protein • ½ Skim Milk • ½ Bread

---

231 Calories • 7 gm Fat • 18 gm Protein •
24 gm Carbohydrate • 451 mg Sodium •
297 mg Calcium • 1 gm Fiber

DIABETIC: 2 Meat • 1 Starch • ½ Skim Milk

"Refried" Bean Dip

Healthy party food isn't impossible, but it takes a little ingenuity—and a lot of taste testing to get it just right. Refried beans have always been a no-no for health-conscious eaters, because they are usually made with oil or lard. But you'll hear nothing but joyful applause when you serve this bubbling bean and cheese dip to your guests. Olé!

   ○   Serves 8 (⅓ cup)

20 ounces (two 16-ounce cans) pinto beans, rinsed and drained
¼ cup bottled taco sauce
1 cup finely chopped onion
1 cup + 2 tablespoons shredded Kraft reduced-fat Cheddar cheese

In a large bowl, mash pinto beans with a potato masher. Stir in taco sauce. Spray a slow cooker container with butter-flavored cooking spray. In prepared container, combine bean mixture, onion, and Cheddar cheese. Cover and cook on LOW for 2 hours. Mix well before serving.

Each serving equals:

HE: 1 Bread • ½ Protein • ½ Vegetable

116 Calories • 4 gm Fat • 7 gm Protein •
13 gm Carbohydrate • 251 mg Sodium •
147 mg Calcium • 3 gm Fiber

DIABETIC: 1 Starch • ½ Meat • ½ Vegetable

Chili Cheese Dip

Low heat is perfect for blending up this luscious spicy cheese dip that's as yummy as the nachos served at your favorite Mexican restaurant. You can serve it with a favorite brand of baked chips or with cut-up veggies, whatever you prefer. I caught Cliff pouring half a jar of green chilies into the pot and knew I wouldn't be eating another bite of that batch. Lucky for me, I had another potful nearby!   ☻   Serves 8 (⅓ cup)

> 8 ounces extra-lean ground turkey or beef
> 1 cup (one 8-ounce can) Hunt's Tomato Sauce
> ¼ cup chunky salsa (mild, medium, or hot)
> 1 tablespoon Worcestershire sauce
> ½ teaspoon chili seasoning
> 3 cups (12 ounces) cubed Velveeta Light processed cheese

In a large skillet sprayed with butter-flavored cooking spray, brown meat. Spray a slow cooker container with butter-flavored cooking spray. In prepared container, combine tomato sauce, salsa, Worcestershire sauce, and chili seasoning. Stir in browned meat. Add Velveeta cheese. Mix well to combine. Cover and cook on LOW for 1 hour. Mix well before serving.

HINT: For those who want "hotter dip," add as many chopped green chilies as you choose.

Each serving equals:

> HE: 1½ Protein • ½ Vegetable
> _____
> 142 Calories • 6 gm Fat • 14 gm Protein •
> 8 gm Carbohydrate • 939 mg Sodium •
> 251 mg Calcium • 1 gm Fiber
> _____
> DIABETIC: 2 Meat • ½ Vegetable

Simmered Marinara Sauce

Commercial pasta sauces are popular, easy, and inexpensive, so why spend time making your own? There are several good reasons—one, if you've got tomato sauce and tomatoes on hand but no jars or cans of spaghetti sauce; two, you like the idea of a sauce with only the ingredients you add and no preservatives; and three, it can be fun to simmer a sauce from scratch. Whatever your reason, enjoy!

○ Serves 8 (½ cup)

> 1¾ cups (one 15-ounce can) Hunt's Tomato Sauce
> 3½ cups (two 14.5-ounce cans) diced tomatoes, undrained
> ¼ cup water
> 1 teaspoon olive oil
> ¼ cup pourable Splenda or Sugar Twin
> 1½ teaspoons Italian seasoning
> 1 cup finely chopped onion
> ¼ cup sliced ripe olives

Spray a slow cooker container with olive oil–flavored cooking spray. In prepared container, combine tomato sauce, undrained tomatoes, water, and olive oil. Stir in Splenda and Italian seasoning. Add onion and olives. Mix well to combine. Cover and simmer on LOW for 6 to 8 hours. Mix well before serving.

Each serving equals:

HE: 2 Vegetable • ¼ Fat • 4 Optional Calories

49 Calories • 1 gm Fat • 1 gm Protein •
9 gm Carbohydrate • 478 mg Sodium •
25 mg Calcium • 2 gm Fiber

DIABETIC: 2 Vegetable

Potluck Spaghetti Meat Sauce

Once you start making your own pasta sauce, you may find that you like experimenting with the recipe enough to keep adding different items to it. (Maybe it's the tasting that is so hard to resist?) Here's a sauce I created after stirring in a little of this and a little of that. Just as a potluck provides surprises when you don't know exactly what your guests are bringing, this kind of cooking produces taste surprises for the cook!

❂ Serves 8 (scant 1 cup)

16 ounces extra-lean ground turkey or beef

1¾ cups (one 15-ounce can) Hunt's Tomato Sauce

1¾ cups (one 14.5-ounce can) diced tomatoes, undrained

¾ cup reduced-sodium tomato juice

1½ cups chopped onion

½ cup chopped green bell pepper

2 tablespoons pourable Splenda or Sugar Twin

2 teaspoons Italian seasoning

In a large skillet sprayed with olive oil–flavored cooking spray, brown meat. Spray a slow cooker container with olive oil–flavored cooking spray. In prepared container, combine browned meat, tomato sauce, undrained tomatoes, and tomato juice. Stir in onion and green pepper. Add Splenda and Italian seasoning. Mix well to combine. Cover and cook on LOW for 6 to 8 hours. Mix well before serving.

Each serving equals:

HE: 2 Vegetable • 1½ Protein • 2 Optional Calories

115 Calories • 3 gm Fat • 12 gm Protein •
10 gm Carbohydrate • 460 mg Sodium •
23 mg Calcium • 2 gm Fiber

DIABETIC: 2 Vegetable • 1½ Meat

Baked Sliced Apples

If your family enjoys visiting "pick your own" apple orchards but then can't figure out what to do with all those bushels of fruit, here's a splendid way to prepare a dessert so old-fashioned-good, you may have to put a lock on your slow cooker so little elves don't gobble it all down when you turn your back!   ◐   Serves 6 (⅓ cup)

3½ cups cored, peeled, and thickly sliced cooking apples
¼ cup seedless raisins
¼ cup pourable Splenda or Sugar Twin
1½ teaspoons apple pie spice
2 tablespoons unsweetened apple juice
1 tablespoon reduced-calorie margarine

Spray a slow cooker container with butter-flavored cooking spray. In prepared container, combine apples and raisins. Add Splenda, apple pie spice, and apple juice. Mix well to combine. Dot top with margarine. Cover and cook on LOW for 6 to 8 hours.

HINT: Also good as side dish with pork.

Each serving equals:

HE: 1½ Fruit • ¼ Fat • 7 Optional Calories

73 Calories • 1 gm Fat • 0 gm Protein •
16 gm Carbohydrate • 24 mg Sodium •
11 mg Calcium • 2 gm Fiber

DIABETIC: 1½ Fruit

Blushing Apple Tapioca

Here's a dish so eye-catching you're bound to be complimented for it by everyone at your table. All those sweet words may make you turn a lovely shade of pink, but that's not the real reason I used "blushing" in the recipe title. It's the tapioca itself, which is truly "pretty in pink"! ☺ Serves 6 (½ cup)

> 6 cups cored, peeled, and sliced Granny Smith apples
> ½ cup pourable Splenda or Sugar Twin
> ⅓ cup Quick Cooking Minute Tapioca
> ½ teaspoon ground cinnamon
> ¾ cup water
> 5 to 6 drops red food coloring

Spray a slow cooker container with butter-flavored cooking spray. In prepared container, evenly arrange apple slices. In a medium bowl, combine Splenda, tapioca, and cinnamon. Add water and red food coloring. Mix well to combine. Pour mixture evenly over apples. Cover and cook on HIGH for 3 to 4 hours. Mix well before serving. Good warm or cold.

Each serving equals:

HE: 2 Fruit • ½ Slider • 1 Optional Calorie

108 Calories • 0 gm Fat • 0 gm Protein • 27 gm Carbohydrate • 1 mg Sodium • 9 mg Calcium • 3 gm Fiber

DIABETIC: 1 Fruit • ½ Starch

Ellie's Spiced Applesauce

Making applesauce at home may seem like too much work when you first consider it. But if someone presented you with one of those clever apple peelers I saw on QVC recently, you've just got to give it a workout—and what better recipe than this one? There's something sort of soothing about applesauce, and this won the heart of my granddaughter Ellie, who knows what she likes!

○ Serves 12 (½ cup)

> 1 cup unsweetened apple juice
> ½ cup pourable Splenda or Sugar Twin
> ½ teaspoon ground cinnamon
> 11 cups cored, peeled, and thinly sliced cooking apples

Spray a slow cooker container with butter-flavored cooking spray. In prepared container, combine apple juice, Splenda, and cinnamon. Stir in apples. Cover and cook on LOW for 6 to 8 hours. Mix well before serving. Good warm or cold.

Each serving equals:

HE: 1½ Fruit • 4 Optional Calories

72 Calories • 0 gm Fat • 0 gm Protein •
18 gm Carbohydrate • 1 mg Sodium •
9 mg Calcium • 3 gm Fiber

DIABETIC: 1 Fruit

Golden Fruit Compote

Some people turn their noses up at canned fruit, but most of us grew to love sweet, soft canned fruits in childhood, and we are never too old to enjoy them. But those delectable canned peaches and pears are transformed by slo-o-o-w cooking and a few additions into a truly marvelous mélange of flavors.

◒ Serves 6 (⅔ cup)

> 2 cups (one 16-ounce can) sliced peaches, packed in fruit juice, undrained
> 1 cup (one 8-ounce can) pear halves, packed in fruit juice, sliced and undrained
> ½ cup unsweetened orange juice
> ½ cup dried apricots
> ¼ cup seedless raisins
> 2 tablespoons pourable Splenda or Sugar Twin
> ¼ teaspoon apple pie spice

Spray a slow cooker container with butter-flavored cooking spray. In prepared container, combine undrained peaches, undrained pears, and orange juice. Stir in apricots and raisins. Add Splenda and apple pie spice. Mix well to combine. Cover and cook on LOW for 6 to 8 hours. Mix well before serving. Good warm or cold.

Each serving equals:

HE: 2 Fruit • 2 Optional Calories

108 Calories • 0 gm Fat • 1 gm Protein •
26 gm Carbohydrate • 5 mg Sodium •
18 mg Calcium • 2 gm Fiber

DIABETIC: 2 Fruit

Rhubarb Sauce with Orange Dumplings

Here's another beautiful dessert that takes full advantage of the glories of rhubarb, that remarkable creation of nature that is one of my special favorites. Even though this recipe requires a little more effort than many of my slow cooker dishes, the scrumptious result is well worth it! ☻ Serves 6

9 cups diced fresh or frozen rhubarb, thawed
½ cup water
5 to 6 drops red food coloring
¾ cup unsweetened orange juice ☆
2 cups pourable Splenda or Sugar Twin ☆
1 cup + 2 tablespoons Bisquick Reduced Fat Baking Mix
2 tablespoons chopped walnuts

Spray a slow cooker container with butter-flavored cooking spray. In prepared container, combine rhubarb, water, red food coloring, ¼ cup orange juice, and 1½ cups Splenda. Cover and cook on HIGH for 3 to 4 hours. In a medium bowl, combine baking mix, remaining ½ cup Splenda, and walnuts. Add remaining ½ cup orange juice. Mix gently just to combine. Drop batter into hot sauce by the tablespoonful to form 6 dumplings. Re-cover and continue cooking on HIGH for 30 minutes. For each serving, place 1 dumpling in a dessert dish and spoon about ½ cup rhubarb sauce over top.

Each serving equals:

HE: 2 Vegetable • 1 Bread • ¼ Fruit • ¼ Slider • 4 Optional Calories

179 Calories • 3 gm Fat • 4 gm Protein • 34 gm Carbohydrate • 267 mg Sodium • 132 mg Calcium • 3 gm Fiber

DIABETIC: 1 Starch • 1 Fruit

Maple Apple Crumble

If you have difficulty finding this brand of no-sugar pie filling in your grocery store, work with your manager to get it—it's just that good. Sometimes starting with fresh apples doesn't produce the result I want, so I look elsewhere. In this case, I found just what I needed in a couple of cans, and created a special dessert worthy of maple syrup season in Vermont!   ● Serves 6 (1 full cup)

2 (20-ounce) cans Lucky Leaf No Sugar Added Apple Pie Filling
1½ teaspoons apple pie spice
½ cup Log Cabin or Cary's Sugar Free Maple Syrup ☆
¾ cup quick oats
½ cup + 1 tablespoon Bisquick Reduced Fat Baking Mix
¼ cup pourable Splenda or Sugar Twin
¼ cup reduced-calorie margarine

Spray a slow cooker container with butter-flavored cooking spray. In prepared container, combine pie filling, apple pie spice, and ¼ cup maple syrup. In a medium bowl, combine oats, baking mix, and Splenda. Add margarine. Mix well, using a pastry blender or fork, until mixture is crumbly. Evenly sprinkle crumb mixture over apple mixture. Drizzle remaining ¼ cup maple syrup evenly over top. Cover and cook on LOW for 4 to 6 hours.

Each serving equals:

HE: 1⅓ Fruit • 1 Bread • 1 Fat • 15 Optional Calories

189 Calories • 5 gm Fat • 2 gm Protein •
34 gm Carbohydrate • 277 mg Sodium •
21 mg Calcium • 3 gm Fiber

DIABETIC: 1 Fruit • 1 Starch • 1 Fat

Apple Orchard Cobbler

Yes, I confess it. I'm a grandma whose latest apple cobbler recipe isn't made from scratch! But that doesn't mean I love my grandkids any less, just that I want to give them satisfying, sweet, and healthy desserts when they visit me—and that doesn't mean spending all day in the kitchen. The kids said "Yum, yum," so I knew I was doing the right thing. ☻ Serves 6 (1 cup)

2 (20-ounce) cans Lucky Leaf No Sugar Added Apple Pie Filling
1 teaspoon apple pie spice
½ cup + 1 tablespoon Bisquick Reduced Fat Baking Mix
¾ cup quick oats
½ cup pourable Splenda or Sugar Twin
½ cup unsweetened apple juice

Spray a slow cooker container with butter-flavored cooking spray. In prepared container, combine apple pie filling and apple pie spice. In a large bowl, combine baking mix, oats, Splenda, and apple juice. Evenly spoon mixture over apple mixture. Cover and cook on HIGH for 2 hours.

Each serving equals:

HE: 1½ Fruit • ⅔ Bread • 8 Optional Calories

133 Calories • 1 gm Fat • 2 gm Protein •
29 gm Carbohydrate • 110 mg Sodium •
14 mg Calcium • 3 gm Fiber

DIABETIC: 1½ Fruit • ½ Starch

Simmered Apples with Pecan Dumplings

Not one, not two, but three kinds of apple pie flavor make this dish spectacularly good! I call it layering the flavors, and it works beautifully here. Many cooks choose walnuts to go with their apple desserts, but since I've been a pecan lover since childhood, I decided that they'd make my dumplings *dee*-licious!

❂ Serves 6

> 2 (20-ounce) cans Lucky Leaf No Sugar Added Apple Pie Filling
> 2 cups unsweetened apple juice ☆
> ½ cup pourable Splenda or Sugar Twin ☆
> 1½ teaspoons apple pie spice
> 1 cup + 2 tablespoons Bisquick Reduced Fat Baking Mix
> 3 tablespoons chopped pecans

Spray a slow cooker container with butter-flavored cooking spray. In prepared container, combine apple pie filling, 1½ cups apple juice, ¼ cup Splenda, and apple pie spice. Cover and cook on HIGH for 2 hours. In a medium bowl, combine baking mix, remaining ¼ cup Splenda, pecans, and remaining ½ cup apple juice. Mix gently just to combine. Drop batter into hot sauce by the tablespoonful to form 6 dumplings. Recover and continue cooking on HIGH for 30 minutes. For each serving, place 1 dumpling in a dessert dish and spoon about ½ cup apple mixture over top.

Each serving equals:

HE: 1½ Fruit • 1 Bread • ½ Fat • 8 Optional Calories

196 Calories • 4 gm Fat • 2 gm Protein •
38 gm Carbohydrate • 285 mg Sodium •
31 mg Calcium • 3 gm Fiber

DIABETIC: 2 Fruit • 1 Starch • ½ Fat

Cherry Bubble Dessert

The sauce bubbles and simmers as this gorgeous red dessert cooks, and the biscuit bits fluff up prettily into rosy rounds that are a little bubblelike. And when I served this to my grandchildren, they bubbled over with excitement as they gobbled it down. This is a dish to smile over and share with everyone you love.

Serves 6 (1 full cup)

1 (7.5-ounce) can Pillsbury refrigerated buttermilk biscuits
2 (20-ounce) cans Lucky Leaf No Sugar Added Cherry Pie Filling
½ cup unsweetened orange juice
1 teaspoon almond extract
¼ cup slivered almonds

Spray a slow cooker container with butter-flavored cooking spray. Separate biscuits and cut each biscuit into 3 pieces. In prepared slow cooker container, combine pie filling, orange juice, and almond extract. Gently stir in biscuit pieces and almonds. Cover and cook on HIGH for 3 to 4 hours.

Each serving equals:

HE: 1½ Fruit • 1¼ Bread • ⅓ Fat • 10 Optional Calories

195 Calories • 3 gm Fat • 4 gm Protein •
38 gm Carbohydrate • 326 mg Sodium •
16 mg Calcium • 3 gm Fiber

DIABETIC: 1½ Fruit • 1 Starch • ½ Fat

Cheyanne's Cherry Cobbler

Cheyanne loves cherries, and not just because her name and cherries start with the same three letters (though that helps!). She does like the color red, but it's ultimately about the flavor for her—and for most of us. This dessert is best served warm from the slow cooker, and if you're feeling a bit decadent, maybe with a scoop of sugar-free, fat-free ice cream on the side.

○ Serves 6 (⅔ cup)

1 cup + 2 tablespoons Bisquick
    Reduced Fat Baking Mix
¾ cup pourable Splenda or
    Sugar Twin
1 teaspoon baking powder
1 teaspoon ground cinnamon
2 eggs, beaten, or equivalent in
    egg substitute

¼ cup skim milk
2 tablespoons vegetable oil
1 teaspoon vanilla extract
1 (20-ounce) can Lucky Leaf
    No Sugar Added Cherry
    Pie Filling
½ cup hot water

Spray a slow cooker container with butter-flavored cooking spray. In a large bowl, combine baking mix, Splenda, baking powder, and cinnamon. In a small bowl, combine eggs, skim milk, oil, and vanilla extract. Add liquid mixture to dry mixture. Mix well just until combined. Spread batter evenly over bottom of prepared container. Evenly spread cherry pie filling over batter. Pour hot water evenly over top. Cover and cook on HIGH for 2 hours or until a toothpick inserted near center of batter comes out clean.

Each serving equals:

HE: 1 Bread • 1 Fat • ⅔ Fruit • ⅓ Protein •
16 Optional Calories

200 Calories • 8 gm Fat • 4 gm Protein •
28 gm Carbohydrate • 380 mg Sodium •
92 mg Calcium • 1 gm Fiber

DIABETIC: 1 Starch • 1 Fat • 1 Fruit

South Seas Cherry Dessert

It's amazing how much exotic flavor you taste in the tiniest amount of coconut extract, especially when it's heated along with the other ingredients in this recipe. The blend of fruits is not only colorful but fantastically flavorful, too. Even if you're a landlubber with no desire to really sail the seven seas, give this treat a try.

○ Serves 4 (¾ cup)

> 1 (20-ounce) can Lucky Leaf No Sugar Added Cherry Pie Filling
> ½ teaspoon coconut extract
> ¾ cup Bisquick Reduced Fat Baking Mix
> ¼ cup pourable Splenda or Sugar Twin
> 1 cup (one 8-ounce can) crushed pineapple, packed in fruit juice, undrained
> 2 tablespoons chopped pecans
> 2 tablespoons flaked coconut

Spray a slow cooker container with butter-flavored cooking spray. In prepared container, combine cherry pie filling and coconut extract. In a medium bowl, combine baking mix and Splenda. Add undrained pineapple. Mix well to combine. Spread batter evenly over cherry mixture. Evenly sprinkle pecans and coconut over top. Cover and cook on HIGH for 2 hours.

Each serving equals:

HE: 1½ Fruit • 1 Bread • ½ Fat • 14 Optional Calories

197 Calories • 5 gm Fat • 2 gm Protein •
36 gm Carbohydrate • 284 mg Sodium •
34 mg Calcium • 3 gm Fiber

DIABETIC: 1½ Fruit • 1 Starch • 1 Fat

Hawaiian Cherry Rice Pudding

Rice pudding still turns up on the menus of most American diners and country-style restaurants, and I think it's because it reminds people of happy times in childhood when they eat it. I don't need any more reason than the fact that Cliff loves it to create lots of ways to serve this old-fashioned creamy treat. See what you think of this island-inspired one! ☺ Serves 6 (½ cup)

1 (20-ounce) can Lucky Leaf No Sugar Added Cherry Pie Filling
1½ cups cooked rice
1 cup (one 8-ounce can) crushed pineapple, packed in fruit juice, undrained
½ cup water
1 (4-serving) package JELL-O sugar-free vanilla cook-and-serve pudding mix
½ teaspoon coconut extract
2 tablespoons flaked coconut

Spray a slow cooker container with butter-flavored cooking spray. In prepared container, combine cherry pie filling and rice. In a small bowl, combine undrained pineapple, water, dry pudding mix, and coconut extract. Stir pineapple mixture into cherry mixture. Cover and cook on HIGH for 2 hours. Mix well. When serving, top each dish with 1 teaspoon coconut.

HINT: Usually 1 cup uncooked instant rice cooks to about 1½ cups.

Each serving equals:

HE: 1 Fruit • ½ Bread • 18 Optional Calories

113 Calories • 1 gm Fat • 1 gm Protein •
25 gm Carbohydrate • 94 mg Sodium •
9 mg Calcium • 2 gm Fiber

DIABETIC: 1 Fruit • ½ Starch

Pears Helene Bread Pudding

If you asked me to choose my favorite recipe in this book, this would be the one. It's delicious, it's beautiful, and it's a dish I'd be proud to serve at my fanciest dinner party (though to be honest, I don't give them very often!). I'll always choose bread pudding over just about any other dessert, and I'll choose this version now as one I love best. ☻ Serves 8 (1 cup)

12 slices day-old reduced-calorie white bread, torn into large
    pieces ☆
4 cups (two 16-ounce cans) pear halves, coarsely chopped,
    drained, and 1 cup liquid reserved ☆
¼ cup chopped walnuts ☆
¼ cup mini chocolate chips ☆
2 (4-serving) packages JELL-O sugar-free chocolate cook-and-
    serve pudding mix
⅔ cup Carnation Nonfat Dry Milk Powder
2 cups water

Spray a slow cooker container with butter-flavored cooking spray. In prepared container, layer half of bread pieces, half of pears, half of walnuts, and half of chocolate chips. Repeat layers. In a medium bowl, combine dry pudding mixes, dry milk powder, reserved pear liquid, and water. Mix well using a wire whisk. Pour mixture evenly over top. Cover and cook on HIGH for 2 hours. Let set 5 minutes before serving.

Each serving equals:

HE: 1 Fruit • ¾ Bread • ¼ Skim Milk • ¼ Fat •
½ Slider • 11 Optional Calories

201 Calories • 5 gm Fat • 7 gm Protein •
32 gm Carbohydrate • 315 mg Sodium •
109 mg Calcium • 2 gm Fiber

DIABETIC: 1 Fruit • 1 Starch • 1 Fat

Apricot-Raisin Bread Pudding

You can never have too many bread pudding recipes, in my opinion! When you combine apricots and raisins, you're combining perfection.   ☻   Serves 6 (⅔ cup)

> 1 (4-serving) package JELL-O sugar-free vanilla cook-and-serve
>   pudding mix
> 1½ cups (one 12-fluid-ounce can) Carnation Evaporated
>   Skim Milk
> 1 cup water
> ¼ cup apricot spreadable fruit
> ¼ cup pourable Splenda or Sugar Twin
> 1 teaspoon vanilla extract
> 1 teaspoon apple pie spice
> ¼ cup seedless raisins
> 12 slices day-old reduced-calorie white bread, torn into large
>   pieces

Spray a slow cooker container with butter-flavored cooking spray. In prepared container, combine dry pudding mix, evaporated skim milk, and water. Stir in spreadable fruit, Splenda, vanilla extract, and apple pie spice. Add raisins and bread pieces. Mix well to combine. Cover and cook on HIGH for 2 hours.

Each serving equals:

HE: 1 Bread • 1 Fruit • ½ Skim Milk •
17 Optional Calories

197 Calories • 1 gm Fat • 9 gm Protein •
38 gm Carbohydrate • 390 mg Sodium •
200 mg Calcium • 1 gm Fiber

DIABETIC: 1 Starch • 1 Fruit • ½ Skim Milk

English Bread Pudding

The Brits call dishes like this one "nursery food," the kind of soft, sweet, and utterly delicious desserts we first tasted as toddlers and have never stopped adoring. The fruited custard at the heart of this recipe is unusual but one I believe you'll really enjoy.

◑ Serves 8 (¾ cup)

1½ cups (one 12-fluid-ounce can) Carnation Evaporated Skim Milk

1½ cups water

1 (4-serving) package JELL-O sugar-free vanilla cook-and-serve pudding mix

¼ cup pourable Splenda or Sugar Twin

1½ teaspoons apple pie spice

2 tablespoons + 2 teaspoons reduced-calorie margarine, melted

12 slices day-old reduced-calorie white bread, torn into large pieces

1 (7-ounce) package mixed dried fruit, cut into small pieces

½ cup chopped walnuts

Spray a slow cooker container with butter-flavored cooking spray. In prepared container, combine evaporated skim milk, water, dry pudding mix, Splenda, and apple pie spice. Add margarine. Stir in bread, fruit, and walnuts. Mix well to combine. Cover and cook on LOW for 3 to 4 hours. Mix gently before serving.

Each serving equals:

HE: 1 Fruit • 1 Fat • ¾ Bread • ⅓ Skim Milk • 13 Optional Calories

260 Calories • 8 gm Fat • 9 gm Protein • 38 gm Carbohydrate • 335 mg Sodium • 187 mg Calcium • 3 gm Fiber

DIABETIC: 1½ Starch • 1 Fruit • 1 Fat

Becky's Peach Dessert

Oh, why oh why is fresh peach season so short? I guess maybe it's so we truly treasure the sensual sweetness and unforgettable texture of ripe peaches. I've tried this with frozen peach slices, but it's just not the same, so plan to enjoy it often when the summer sun readies those golden fruits for our delight. This is for my daughter, Becky, who relishes peaches more than any fruit there is.

Serves 6 (½ cup)

> 6 tablespoons Bisquick Reduced Fat Baking Mix
> ½ cup quick oats
> ½ cup pourable Splenda or Sugar Twin
> 1 teaspoon ground cinnamon
> 4½ cups (9 medium) peeled and sliced ripe peaches
> ½ cup water

Spray a slow cooker container with butter-flavored cooking spray. In prepared container, combine baking mix, oats, Splenda, and cinnamon. Add peaches and water. Mix well to combine. Cover and cook on LOW for 6 hours.

Each serving equals:

HE: 1½ Fruit • ⅔ Bread • 8 Optional Calories

117 Calories • 1 gm Fat • 2 gm Protein • 25 gm Carbohydrate • 87 mg Sodium • 21 mg Calcium • 3 gm Fiber

DIABETIC: 1½ Fruit • ½ Starch

Pumpkin Pie Dessert

If you're a fan of pumpkin pie, why not try this crustless version that delivers the flavors you love in a slightly different format? It's a quick and tasty treat that only requires a couple of hours in the slow cooker, so it's a good choice when you decide Sunday afternoon that it's just what you want for Sunday supper.

♥ Serves 6 (⅔ cup)

1 (4-serving) package JELL-O sugar-free vanilla cook-and-serve pudding mix

1½ cups (one 12-fluid-ounce can) Carnation Evaporated Skim Milk

¼ cup water

2 cups (one 15-ounce can) pumpkin

1½ teaspoons vanilla extract

½ cup + 1 tablespoon Bisquick Reduced Fat Baking Mix

¼ cup pourable Splenda or Sugar Twin

2 teaspoons pumpkin pie spice

½ cup chopped walnuts

6 tablespoons seedless raisins

Spray a slow cooker container with butter-flavored cooking spray. In a large bowl, combine dry pudding mix, evaporated skim milk, and water. Add pumpkin, vanilla extract, baking mix, Splenda, and pumpkin pie spice. Mix well to combine. Stir in walnuts and raisins. Pour mixture into prepared container. Cover and cook on HIGH for 2 hours. Mix gently to combine. Evenly spoon mixture into 6 dessert dishes. Good warm or cold.

HINT: Good topped with 1 tablespoon Cool Whip Lite, but don't forget to count the few additional calories.

Each serving equals:

HE: ⅔ Fat • ⅔ Vegetable • ½ Skim Milk • ½ Bread • ½ Fruit • ⅓ Protein • 13 Optional Calories

223 Calories • 7 gm Fat • 8 gm Protein • 32 gm Carbohydrate • 292 mg Sodium • 201 mg Calcium • 4 gm Fiber

DIABETIC: 1 Fat • 1 Starch • ½ Skim Milk • ½ Fruit

Brownie Walnut Pudding Cake

Who doesn't love an incredibly moist, chocolatey-rich nutty cake? This deep, dark brownie-style cake is definitely irresistible, so it's a good thing I created a Healthy Exchanges version that everyone can enjoy without guilt.   ◐   Serves 8 (½ cup)

1½ cups all-purpose flour

1½ cups pourable Splenda or Sugar Twin ☆

½ cup unsweetened cocoa ☆

¼ cup chopped walnuts

1½ teaspoons baking powder

1 cup skim milk

2 tablespoons vegetable oil

1 teaspoon vanilla extract

1½ cups boiling water

Spray a slow cooker container with butter-flavored cooking spray. In a large bowl, combine flour, ¾ cup Splenda, ¼ cup cocoa, walnuts, and baking powder. Add skim milk, oil, and vanilla extract. Mix gently just to combine. Spoon mixture into prepared container. In a medium bowl, combine remaining ¼ cup cocoa and remaining ¾ cup Splenda. Gradually add boiling water. Carefully pour hot mixture over batter in slow cooker container. DO NOT stir. Cover and cook on HIGH for 2 hours. Evenly spoon into 8 dessert dishes.

Each serving equals:

HE: 1 Bread • 1 Fat • ¼ Slider • 13 Optional Calories

187 Calories • 7 gm Fat • 5 gm Protein •
26 gm Carbohydrate • 109 mg Sodium •
102 mg Calcium • 2 gm Fiber

DIABETIC: 1½ Starch • 1 Fat

Heavenly Lemon Pudding Cake

Most of the time, I get my lemon flavor from Diet Mountain Dew, but here's one recipe where making a special effort and squeezing in some real lemon juice is worth the trouble! This light and fluffy dessert is luscious with a capital L, perfect for sharing with your favorite little angels!   ☻   Serves 6 (scant ½ cup)

3 eggs, separated
¼ cup lemon juice
3 tablespoons reduced-calorie
    margarine, melted
1½ cups (one 12-fluid-ounce
    can) Carnation
    Evaporated Skim Milk

¼ cup + 1½ teaspoons
    all-purpose flour
¾ cup pourable Splenda or
    Sugar Twin
⅛ teaspoon table salt

Spray a slow cooker container with butter-flavored cooking spray. In a medium bowl, beat egg whites with an electric mixer until stiff peaks form. Set aside. In a large bowl, beat egg yolks. Stir in lemon juice, melted margarine, and evaporated skim milk. Add flour, Splenda, and salt. Mix well, using an electric mixer, until mixture is smooth. Fold in beaten egg whites using a rubber spatula. Spoon batter into prepared slow cooker container. Cover and cook on HIGH for 2 to 3 hours. Good warm or cold.

HINTS: 1. Good topped with 1 tablespoon Cool Whip Lite, but don't forget to count the few additional calories.
2. The texture of cake will be soufflé like—be careful when serving.

Each serving equals:

HE: ¾ Fat • ½ Skim Milk • ½ Protein • ¼ Bread •
12 Optional Calories

125 Calories • 5 gm Fat • 7 gm Protein •
13 gm Carbohydrate • 228 mg Sodium •
175 mg Calcium • 0 gm Fiber

DIABETIC: 1 Fat • ½ Skim Milk • ½ Meat

Cook It Slowly, Enjoy It Longer

Menus

Meal planning can be a challenge when your goal is living healthy and feeding a family, but the slow cooker makes it more of a breeze than usual! Not everyone will choose to stock their kitchens with several slow cookers, but by planning ahead, you can prepare entire meals using this handy appliance.

Cozy Winter Brunch

Breakfast Cheese Soufflé
Creamy Turkey and Noodles
Golden Fruit Compote
Hot Spiced Cherry Cider

Wearing O' the Green Parade Lunch

Slow Roasted Veggies
Green Beans with Onion-Mushroom Sauce
Creamy Corned Beef and Cabbage
Apple Orchard Cobbler

Spring Fling Luncheon

Abram's Turkey Veggie Soup
Cauliflower and Rice Side Dish
Hot Tuna Salad Casserole
Rhubarb Sauce with Orange Dumplings

Love in Bloom Anniversary Dinner

Grande Vegetable Platter
Provençal Chicken
Make-Ahead Mashed Potatoes
Pears Helene Bread Pudding

A Festive Fiesta Party

"Refried" Bean Dip
Cheesy Rice and Tomatoes
Tex-Mex BBQ Chicken over Pasta
Brownie Walnut Pudding Cake

Hearty Holiday Supper

Comforting Citrus Cider
Potato Corn Chowder
Bean and Ham Cassoulet
Pumpkin Pie Dessert

Making Healthy Exchanges Work for You

You're ready now to begin a wonderful journey to better health. In the preceding pages, you've discovered the remarkable variety of good food available to you when you begin eating the Healthy Exchanges way. You've stocked your pantry and learned many of my food preparation "secrets" that will point you on the way to delicious success.

But before I let you go, I'd like to share a few tips that I've learned while traveling toward healthier eating habits. It took me a long time to learn how to eat *smarter*. In fact, I'm still working on it. But I am getting better. For years, I could *inhale* a five-course meal in five minutes flat—and still make room for a second helping of dessert!

Now I follow certain signposts on the road that help me stay on the right path. I hope these ideas will help point you in the right direction as well.

1. **Eat slowly** so your brain has time to catch up with your tummy. Cut and chew each bite slowly. Try putting your fork down between bites. Stop eating as soon as you feel full. Crumple your napkin and throw it on top of your plate so you don't continue to eat when you are no longer hungry.

2. **Smaller plates** may help you feel more satisfied by your food portions *and* limit the amount you can put on the plate.

3. **Watch portion size.** If you are *truly* hungry, you can always add more food to your plate once you've finished your initial serving. But remember to count the additional food accordingly.

4. **Always eat at your dining room or kitchen table.** You deserve better than nibbling from an open refrigerator or over the sink. Make an attractive place setting, even if you're eating alone. Feed your eyes as well as your stomach. By always eating at a table, you will become much more aware of your true food intake. For some reason, many of us conveniently "forget" the food we swallow while standing over the stove or munching in the car or on the run.

5. **Avoid doing anything else while you are eating.** If you read the paper or watch television while you eat, it's easy to consume too much food without realizing it, because you are concentrating on something else besides what you're eating. Then, when you look down at your plate and see that it's empty, you wonder where all the food went and why you still feel hungry.

Day by day, as you travel the path to good health, it will become easier to make the right choices, to eat *smarter*. But don't ever fool yourself into thinking that you'll be able to put your eating habits on cruise control and forget about them. Making a commitment to eat good, healthy food and sticking to it takes some effort. But with all the good-tasting recipes in this Healthy Exchanges cookbook, just think how well you're going to eat—and enjoy it—from now on!

Healthy Lean Bon Appetit!

Index

I want to hear from you . . .

Besides my family, the love of my life is creating "common folk" healthy recipes and solving everyday cooking questions in *The Healthy Exchanges Way*. Everyone who uses my recipes is considered part of the Healthy Exchanges Family, so please write to me if you have any questions, comments, or suggestions. I will do my best to answer. With your support, I'll continue to stir up even more recipes and cooking tips for the Family in the years to come.

Write to: JoAnna M. Lund
c/o Healthy Exchanges, Inc.
P.O. Box 80
DeWitt, IA 52742-0080

If you prefer, you can fax me at 1-563-659-2126 or contact me via e-mail by writing to HealthyJo@aol.com. Or visit my Healthy Exchanges Internet website at: http://www.healthyexchanges.com.

Now That You've Seen
Another Potful of Recipes, Why Not Order *The Healthy Exchanges Food Newsletter?*

If you enjoyed the recipes in this cookbook and would like to cook up even more of these "common folk" healthy dishes, you may want to subscribe to *The Healthy Exchanges Food Newsletter.*

This monthly 12-page newsletter contains 30-plus new recipes *every month,* in such columns as:

- Reader Exchange
- Reader Requests
- Recipe Makeover
- Micro Corner
- Dinner for Two

- Crock Pot Luck
- Meatless Main Dishes
- Rise & Shine
- Our Small World

- Brown Bagging It
- Snack Attack
- Side Dishes
- Main Dishes
- Desserts

In addition to all the recipes, other regular features include:

- The Editor's Motivational Corner
- Dining Out Question & Answer
- Cooking Question & Answer
- New Product Alert
- Success Profiles of Winners in the Losing Game
- Exercise Advice from a Cardiac Rehab Specialist
- Nutrition Advice from a Registered Dietitian
- Positive Thought for the Month

The cost for a one-year (12-issue) subscription is $25. To order, call our toll-free number and pay with your VISA or MasterCard.

1-800-766-8961 for customer orders
1-563-659-8234 for customer service

Thank you for your order, and for choosing to become a part of the Healthy Exchanges Family!

About the Author

JoAnna M. Lund, a graduate of the University of Western Illinois, worked as a commercial insurance underwriter for eighteen years before starting her own business, Healthy Exchanges, Inc., which publishes cookbooks, a monthly newsletter, motivational booklets, and inspirational audiotapes. Healthy Exchanges Cookbooks have more than 1 million copies in print. A popular speaker with hospitals, support groups for heart patients and diabetics, and service and volunteer organizations, she has appeared on QVC, on hundreds of regional television and radio shows, and has been featured in newspapers and magazines across the country.

The recipient of numerous business awards, JoAnna was an Iowa delegate to the national White House Conference on Small Business. She is a member of the International Association of Culinary Professionals, the Society for Nutritional Education, and other professional publishing and marketing associations. She lives with her husband, Clifford, in DeWitt, Iowa.